W9-CHT-724

CHARMING SMALL HOTEL GUIDES

Italy

CHARMING SMALL HOTEL GUIDES

Italy

Series editor: Andrew Duncan

DUNCAN PETERSEN

HUNTER
PUBLISHING

Copyright © Duncan Petersen Publishing Ltd 1999
Reprinted 2000

All rights reserved. No reproduction, copy or transmission of this
publication may be made without written permission. No
paragraph of this publication may be reproduced, copied or
transmitted save with written permission or in accordance with
the provisions of the Copyright Act 1956 (as amended). Any
person who does any unauthorized act in relation to this
publication may be liable to criminal prosecution and civil claims
for damages.

Conceived, designed and produced by
Duncan Petersen Publishing Ltd

Editorial Director	Andrew Duncan
Production Editor	Nicola Davies
Art Director	Mel Petersen
Maps	Christopher Foley

We acknowledge with thanks the work of two guest contributors
to this edition, Roger Bevan and Fred Mawer

This edition published in the UK and Commonwealth 1999 by
Duncan Petersen Publishing Ltd,
31 Ceylon Road, London W14 OPY

Sales representation and distribution in the U.K. and Ireland by
Portfolio Books Limited
Unit 1C West Ealing Business Centre
Alexandria Road
London W13 0NJ
Tel: 0181 579 7748

ISBN 1 872576 80 X

A CIP catalogue record for this book is available
from the British Library

AND

Published in the USA 1999 by
Hunter Publishing Inc.,
130 Campus Drive, Edison, N.J. 08818.
Tel (732) 225 1900 Fax (732) 417 1744
For details on hundreds of other travel guides and language
courses, visit Hunter's Web site at hunterpublishing.com

ISBN 1-55650-867-0

Typeset by Duncan Petersen Publishing Ltd
Printed by G. Canale & Co SpA, Turin

Contents

Readers' Reports

Reports from readers are of enormous interest to us in
keeping up to date with the hotels in this guide – and
others that should be in it. More information on page 11.

Introduction

Welcome to this new edition of *Charming Small Hotel Guide* to Italy, the eighth since it was first published in 1988. The guide has been completely revised, with its coverage of Rome, Sardinia and Sicily much increased. It joins 14 other titles (for details, see page 239) in an expanding series.

This remains the only independently inspected UK-originated colour accommodation guide to charming and interesting places to stay in Italy. No hotel pays for inclusion. Beware of imitators who do not admit on the cover that they accept payment for inclusion, but only do so in small print on the inside pages. They say they are selective, but a quick comparison with this guide will prove that this is a hollow claim. And if money has changed hands, it is impossible to write the whole truth about a hotel.

Charming and small

There really are relatively few *genuine* charming small hotels. Unlike other guides, we are particularly fussy about size. In Italy, even family-run hotels seem to grow inevitably, and the ten-room hotel is a rarity, but most of our recommendations have fewer than 30 rooms. If a hotel has more than that, it needs to have the feel of a much smaller place to be in this guide.

We attach more importance to size than other guides because we think that unless a hotel is small, it cannot give a genuinely personal welcome, or make you feel like an individual, rather than just a guest. For what we mean by a personal welcome, see below.

Unlike other guides, we often rule out places that have great qualitites, but are nonetheless no more nor less than – hotels. Our hotels are all special in some way.

We think that we have a much clearer idea than other guides of what is special and what is not; and we think we apply these criteria more consistently than other guides because we are a small and personally managed company rather than a bureaucracy. We have a small team of like-minded inspectors, chosen by the editor and thoroughly rehearsed in recognizing what we want. While we very much appreciate readers' reports - see below - they are not our main source of information.

Last but by no means least, we're independent – there's no payment for inclusion.

So what exactly do we look for?
• An attractive, preferably peaceful setting.
• A building that is either handsome or interesting or historic, or at least with a distinct character.
• Ideally, we look for adequate space, but on a human scale: we don't go for places that rely on grandeur, or that have pretensions that could intimidate.

been for some time now – thanks predominantly to the weakness of the country's currency. With an exchange rate of more than 2,500 lire to £1, prices in Italy compare favourably even with those in Britain, and very favourably with prices in some of Italy's neighbours on the Continent.

This is not to say that Italy is actually cheap, in the way that Eastern European countries and some more exotic destinations are. But we know from our own travels that the pleasant surprises outnumber the unpleasant ones.

We have always included some undeniably expensive hotels in these pages, on the grounds that they offer truly memorable experiences that discerning travellers may be willing to pay heavily for, even if they do not possess infinitely elastic plastic. But we remain very sensitive to value for money, and the majority of hotels recommended here are, we believe, affordable by most international travellers.

As we have noted above, Italy is not predisposed to smallness in its hotels; there seems to be a tendency for any hotelier worth his salt to demonstrate his success by growing to 40-50 rooms. But there are plenty of exceptions and, we are happy to report, they seem to be growing in number.

In the tourist heartland of Tuscany, in particular, there is an ever-growing number of personal, informal, country hotels. Some are part of the *agriturismo* initiative that seeks to encourage the development of tourist accommodation in rural areas – usually bed-and-breakfast places on working estates. Others are more polished and hotel-like, with restaurants and other trappings. Whenever we go back to Italy, we find new and exciting establishments to add to these pages.

As usual, accommodating those entries has meant losing others. Some have had seriously poor reports from readers; some have been forced out by superior competitiors, but are still worth bearing in mind. This is one sort of hotel that we cover in our ten area introduction pages; it's worth glancing at these pages for supplements to our main recommendations. Reports on all the hotels appearing in the guide are received gratefully – see page 11.

How to find an entry
In this guide, the entries are arranged in geographical groups. First, the whole country is divided into three major sections; we start with Northern Italy and proceed to Central and finally Southern Italy. Within these sections, the entries are grouped into regions; some of these correspond to the administrative regions of the country (Tuscany and Emilia-Romagna, for example); some are combinations of these regions (Lazio and Abruzzi, for

example): and some are broader (the North-West, for example).

Each regional section follows a set sequence:

- First comes an Area introduction – an overview of the hotel scene in that region, incorporating brief notes on hotels which have not justified a longer entry (hotels in cities which, would otherwise not feature here at all, for example).

- Then come the main, full-page entries for that region, arranged in alphabetical order by town. These are generally the hotels that we judge most attractive.

- Finally come the shorter quarter-page entries for that state, similarly arranged alphabetically by town. These are generally not as special as the hotels given a full-page entry; but don't disregard them – they are still hotels we would happily stay at, and many are clear candidates for 'promotion' in later editions.

- To find a hotel in a particular area, simply browse through the headings at the top of the pages until you find that area – or use the maps following this intro-duction to locate the appropriate pages. The maps show not only the place, name under which each hotel appears, but also the page number of the entry.

To locate a specific hotel or a hotel in a specific place, use the indexes at the back which list the entries alphabetically, first by name and then by place-name.

How to read an entry
At the top of each entry is a coloured bar highlighting the name of the town or village where the establishment is located, along with a categorization which gives some clue to its character. These categories are as far as possible self-explanatory. The term 'villa' needs, perhaps, some qualification: it is reserved for places with gardens which have something of the air of a country house, even if they are in a town or at the seaside.

Fact boxes
The fact box given for each hotel follows a standard pattern, with more detail given in long entries than in short ones.

Under **Tel** we give the telephone number starting with the area code used within Italy. The zero at the beginning of the number must now be included. We also give a **Fax**

Introduction

number; in some cases, to save space, we omit the area code.

E-mail and **Website** addresses are also listed, where applicable.

Under **Location** we give information on the setting of the hotel and on its parking arrangements, as well as pointers to help you find it.

Under **Food & drink** we list the meals available.

The basic **Prices** in this volume – unlike our volume on Britain and Ireland – are **per room**.
  We use price bands rather than figures:

L	up to L80,000
LL	L80,000-160,000
LLL	L160,000-300,000
LLLL	over L300,000

Normally, a range of prices is given representing the smallest and largest amounts you might pay in different circumstances – typically, the minimum is the cost of the cheapest single room in low season, while the maximum is the cost of the dearest double in high season. If breakfast is included we say so; if not, where possible we give a price for breakfast, per person.
  After the room price, we give either the price for dinner, bed and breakfast (DB&B), or full board (FB – that is, all meals included) or, instead, an indication of the cost of individual meals.
  All of these meal-inclusive prices are **per person**.

The price bands for meals are different to those for accommodation:

L	up to L50,000
LL	L50,000-100,000
LLL	over L100,000

After all this basic information comes, where space allows, a summary of reductions available for long stays or for children. Sometimes we note the price for breakfast or for parking where these will be a significant extra. Always check the actual room price before making a booking.

Under **Rooms** we summarize the number and style of bedrooms available. Our lists of facilites in bedrooms cover only mechanical gadgets and not ornaments such as

Introduction

flowers or consumables such as toiletries or free drinks.

Under **Facilities** we list public rooms and then outdoor and sporting facilities which are either part of the hotel or immediately on hand; facilities in the vicinity of the hotel but not directly connected with it (for example a nearby golf-course) are not listed, though they sometimes feature at the end of the main description in the **Nearby** section, which presents a selection of interesting things to see or do in the locality.

We use the following abbreviations for **Credit cards**:

AE   American Express
DC   Diners Club
MC   MasterCard (Access/Eurocard)
V   Visa (Barclaycard/Bank Americard/Carte Blue etc)

The final entry in a fact box is normally the name of the proprietor(s); but where the hotel is run by a manager we give his or her name instead.

Reporting to the guide

Please write and tell us about your experiences of small hotels, guest-houses and inns, whether good or bad, whether listed in this edition or not. As well as hotels in Italy, we are interested in hotels in Britain and Ireland, France, Italy, Spain, Austria, Germany, Switzerland, and New England. We assume that reporters have no objections to our publishing their views unpaid, either verbatim or in edited form.

Readers whose reports prove particularly helpful may be invited to join our Reporters' Register. Register members who report regularly and reliably may be invited to join our Travellers' Panel. Members give us notice of their own travel plans; we suggest hotels that they might inspect, and contribute to the cost of accommodation.

The address to write to is:

Editor, *Charming Small Hotel Guides,*
Duncan Petersen Publishing Limited
31 Ceylon Road
London W14 0PY

Checklist
Please use a separate sheet of paper for each report; include your name and address on each report.

Your reports will be received with particular pleasure if they are typed, and if they are organized under the following headings:

Name of establishment
Town or village it is in, or nearest
Full address, including post code
Date and duration of visit
The building and setting
The public rooms
The bedrooms and bathrooms
Comfort (chairs, beds, heat, light, hot water)
Standards of maintenance and housekeeping
Atmosphere, welcome and service
Food
Value for money

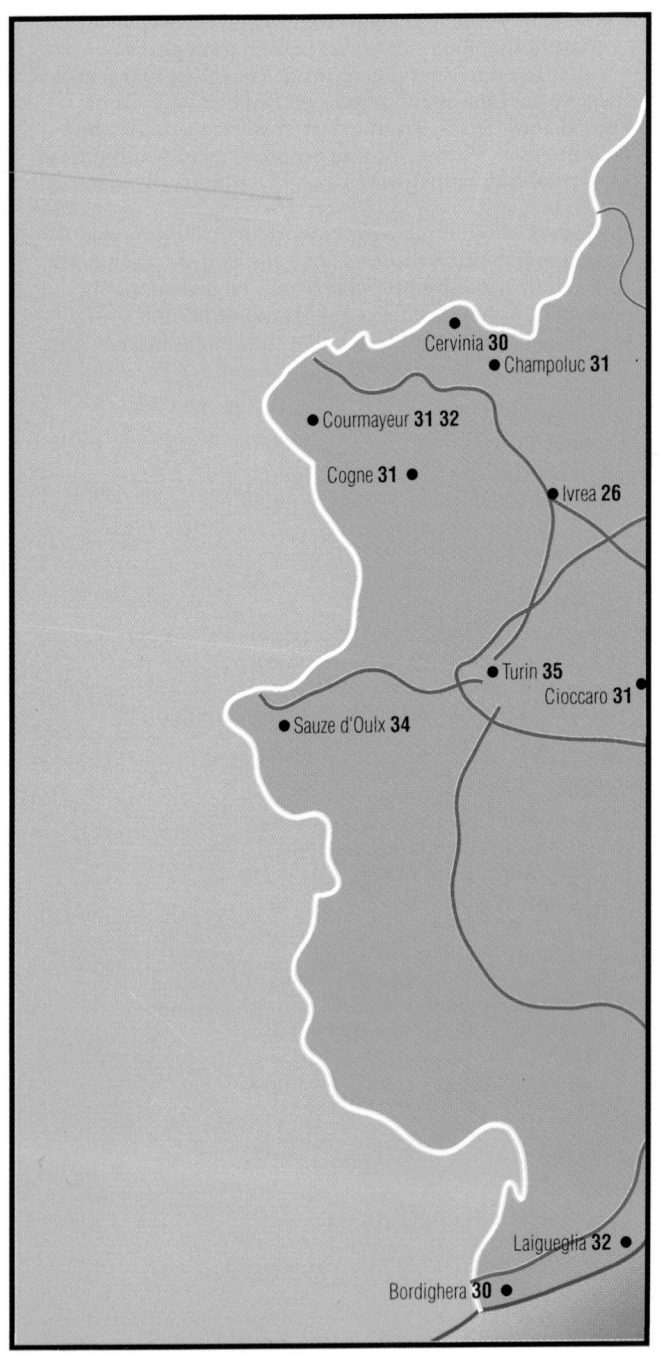

Cervinia **30**
Champoluc **31**
Courmayeur **31 32**
Cogne **31**
Ivrea **26**
Turin **35**
Cioccaro **31**
Sauze d'Oulx **34**
Laigueglia **32**
Bordighera **30**

Hotel location maps

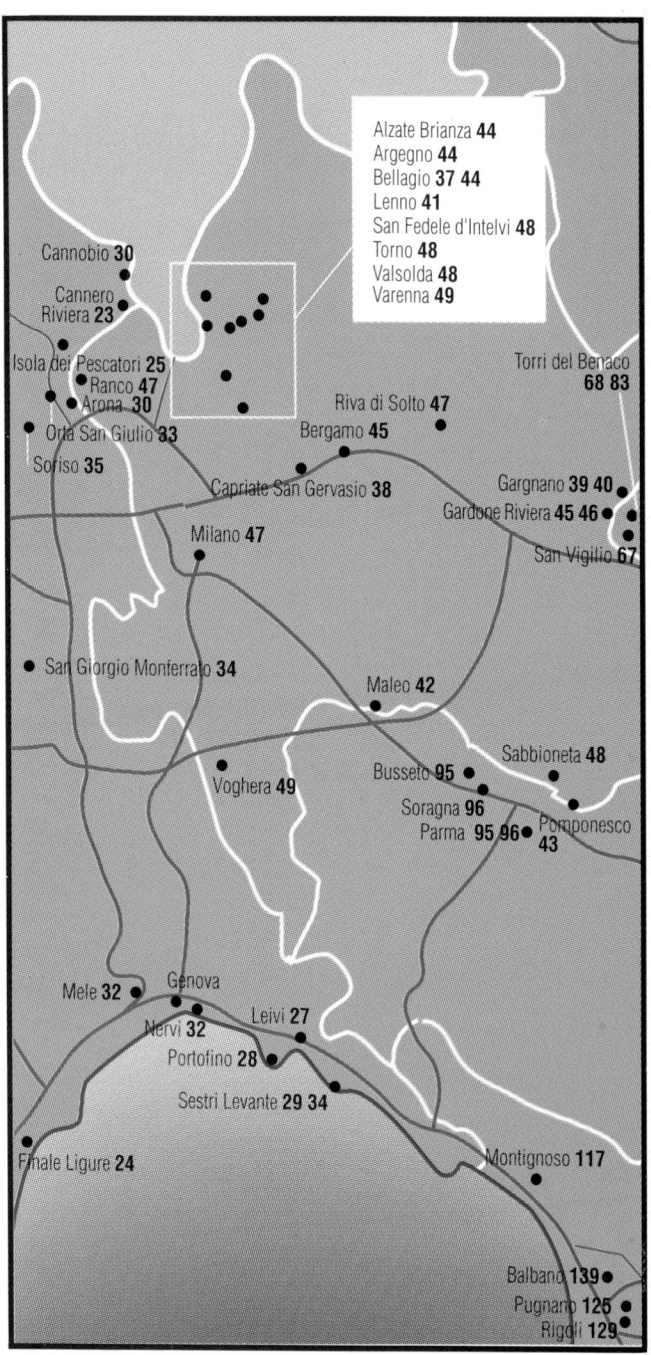

Alzate Brianza **44**
Argegno **44**
Bellagio **37 44**
Lenno **41**
San Fedele d'Intelvi **48**
Torno **48**
Valsolda **48**
Varenna **49**

Cannobio **30**

Cannero Riviera **23**

Isola dei Pescatori **25**
Ranco **47**
Arona **30**
Orta San Giulio **33**
Soriso **35**

Torri del Benaco **68 83**

Riva di Solto **47**

Bergamo **45**

Capriate San Gervasio **38**

Milano **47**

Gargnano **39 40**
Gardone Riviera **45 46**
San Vigilio **67**

San Giorgio Monferrato **34**

Maleo **42**

Sabbioneta **48**

Busseto **95**

Voghera **49**

Soragna **96**
Parma **95 96**
Pomponesco **43**

Mele **32**
Genova
Nervi **32**
Leivi **27**
Portofino **28**
Sestri Levante **29 34**

Finale Ligure **24**

Montignoso **117**

Balbano **139**
Pugnano **125**
Rigoli **129**

13

Hotel location maps

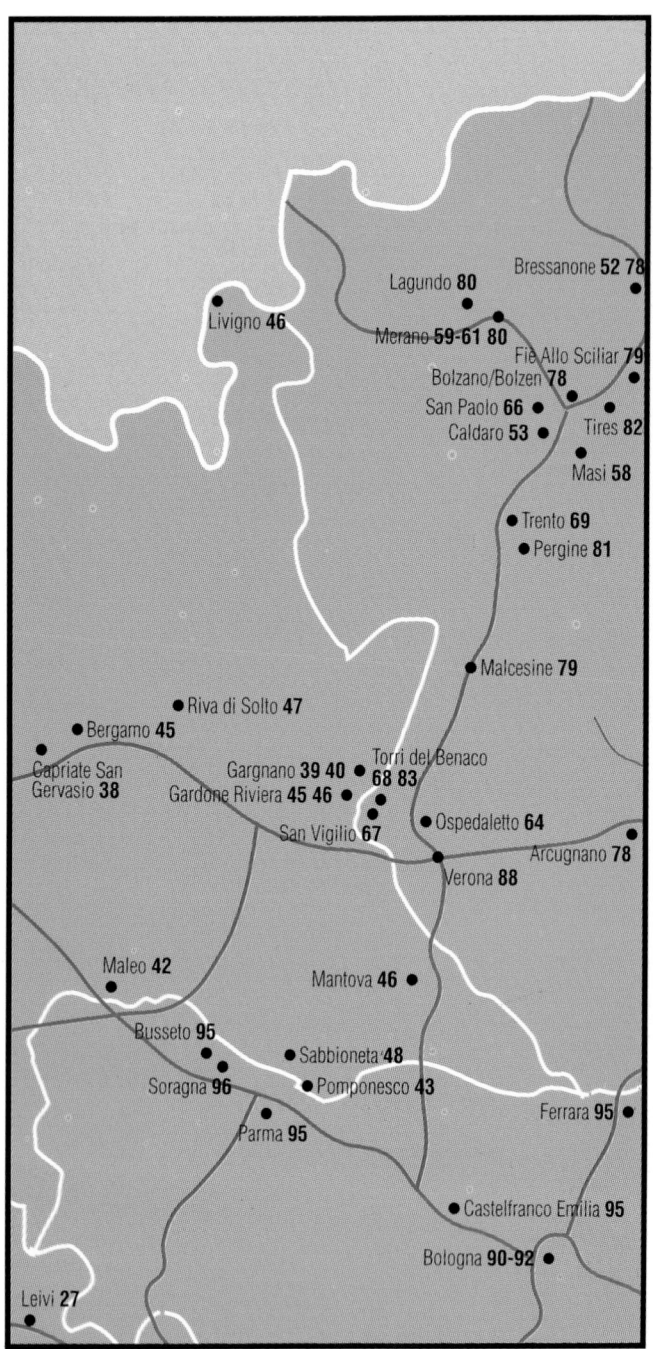

Bressanone **52 78**

Lagundo **80**

Livigno **46**

Merano **59-61 80**

Fiè Allo Sciliar **79**

Bolzano/Bolzen **78**

San Paolo **66**

Caldaro **53**

Tires **82**

Masi **58**

Trento **69**

Pergine **81**

Malcesine **79**

Riva di Solto **47**

Bergamo **45**

Capriate San
Gervasio **38**

Torri del Benaco
68 83

Gargnano **39 40**

Gardone Riviera **45 46**

San Vigilio **67**

Ospedaletto **64**

Arcugnano **78**

Verona **88**

Maleo **42**

Mantova **46**

Busseto **95**

Sabbioneta **48**

Soragna **96**

Pomponesco **43**

Parma **95**

Ferrara **95**

Castelfranco Emilia **95**

Bologna **90-92**

Leivi **27**

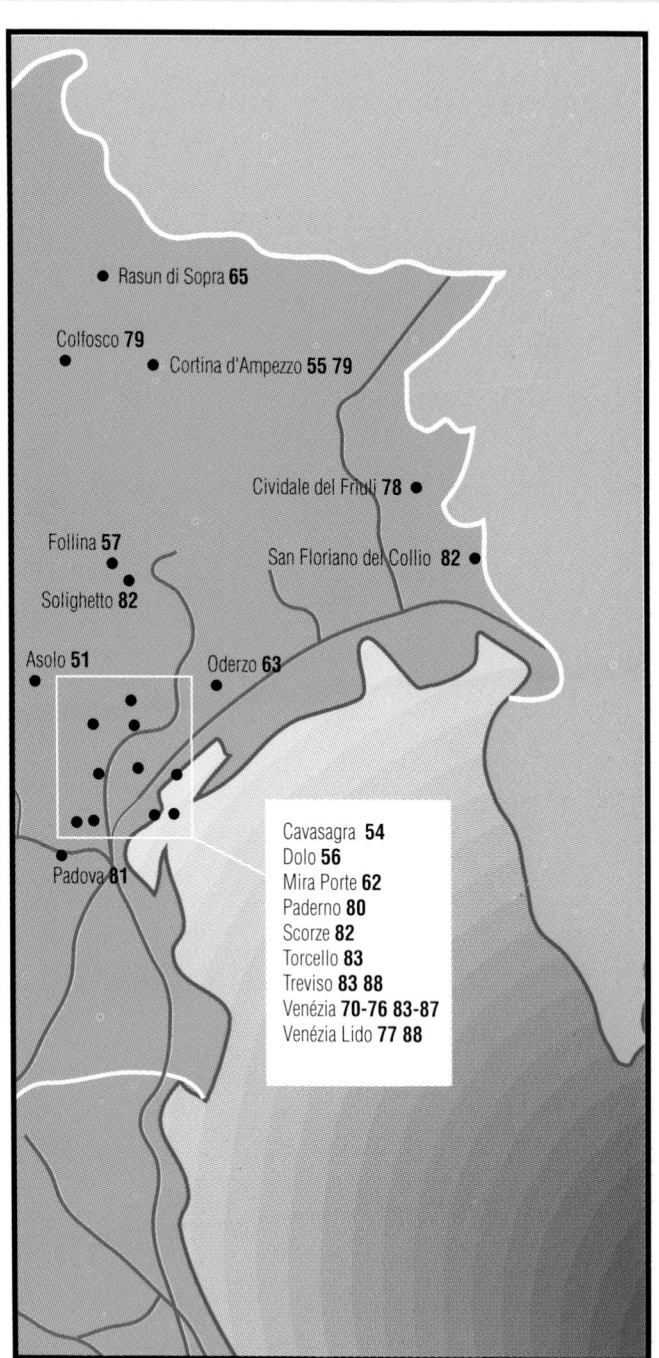

Rasun di Sopra **65**

Colfosco **79**

Cortina d'Ampezzo **55 79**

Cividale del Friuli **78** ●

Follina **57**

San Floriano del Collio **82** ●

Solighetto **82**

Asolo **51**

Oderzo **63**

Cavasagra **54**
Dolo **56**
Mira Porte **62**
Paderno **80**
Scorze **82**
Torcello **83**
Treviso **83 88**
Venézia **70-76 83-87**
Venézia Lido **77 88**

Padova **81**

Hotel location maps

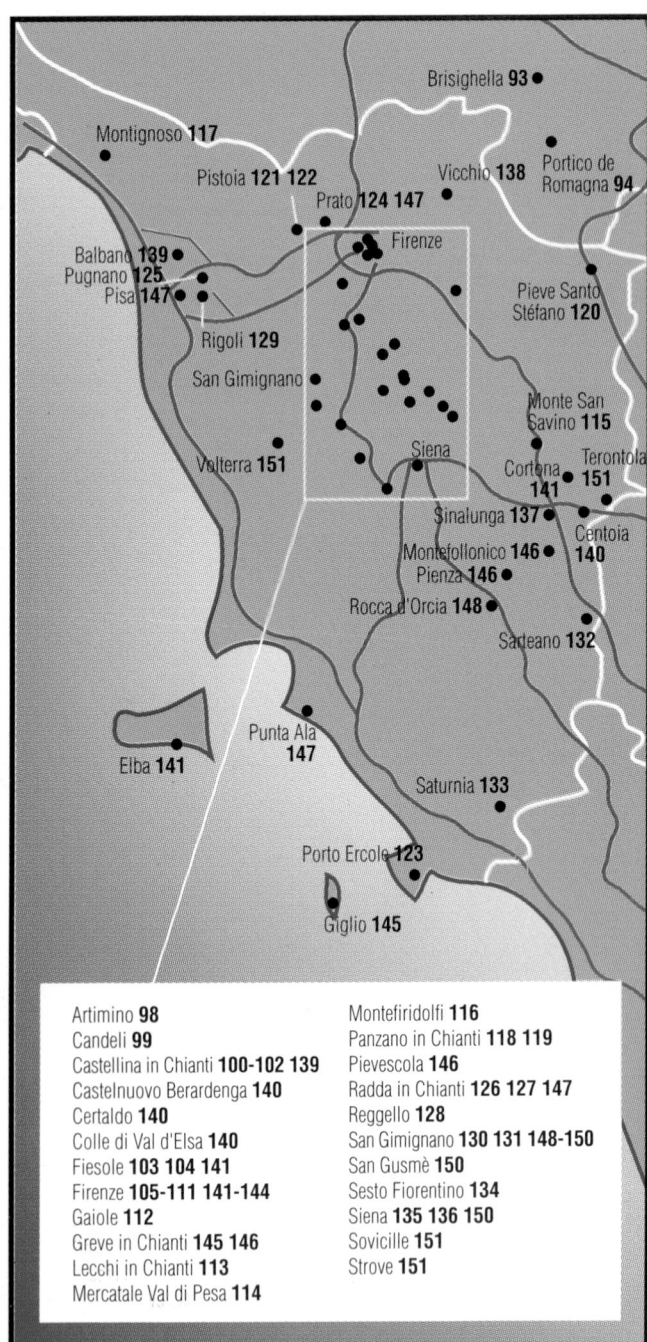

Brisighella **93**

Montignoso **117**

Pistoia **121 122**

Vicchio **138**

Portico de Romagna **94**

Prato **124 147**

Firenze

Balbano **139**
Pugnano **125**
Pisa **147**

Pieve Santo Stéfano **120**

Rigoli **129**

San Gimignano

Monte San Savino **115**

Volterra **151**

Siena

Cortona **141**

Terontola **151**

Sinalunga **137**

Centoia **140**

Montefollonico **146**

Pienza **146**

Rocca d'Orcia **148**

Sardeano **132**

Punta Ala **147**

Elba **141**

Saturnia **133**

Porto Ercole **123**

Giglio **145**

Hotel location maps

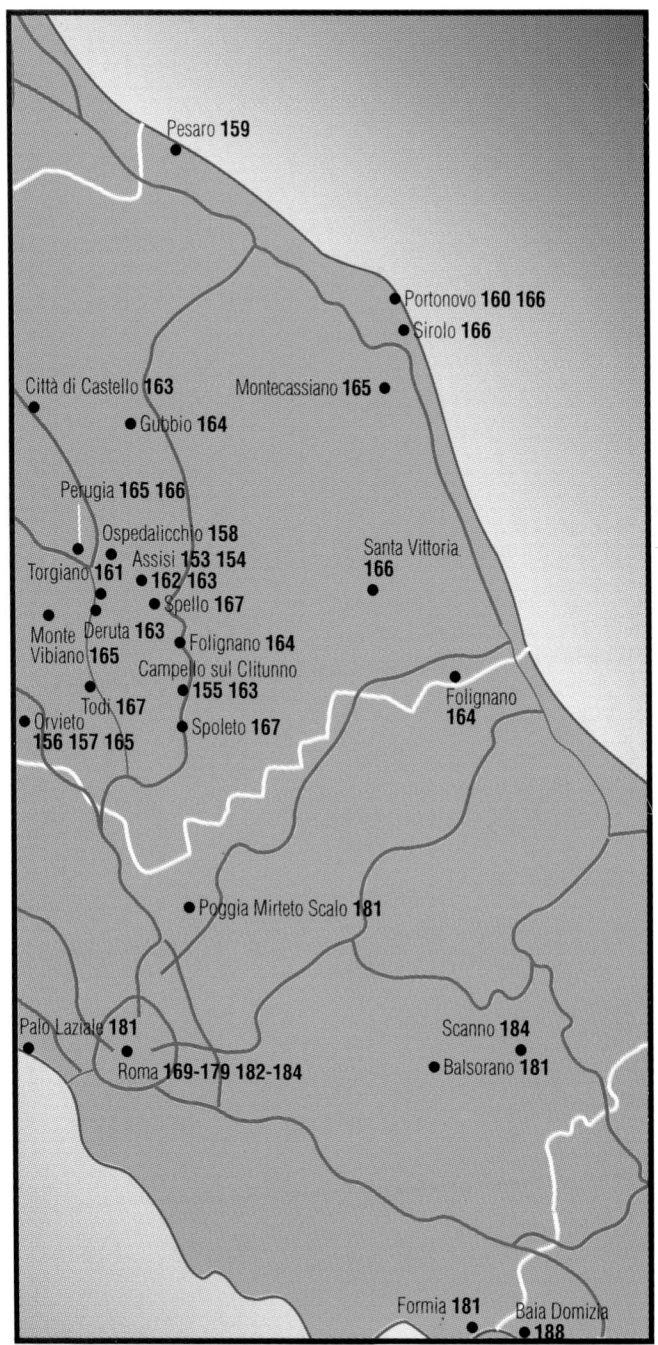

Pesaro **159**

Portonovo **160 166**
Sirolo **166**

Città di Castello **163**   Montecassiano **165**

Gubbio **164**

Perugia **165 166**

Ospedalicchio **158**   Santa Vittoria **166**
Assisi **153 154**
Torgiano **161**   **162 163**
Spello **167**
Monte Deruta **163**
Vibiano **165**   Folignano **164**
Campello sul Clitunno
155 163
Todi **167**   Folignano **164**
Orvieto   Spoleto **167**
156 157 165

Poggia Mirteto Scalo **181**

Palo Laziale **181**   Scanno **184**
Roma **169-179 182-184**   Balsorano **181**

Formia **181**   Baia Domizia **188**

17

Hotel location maps

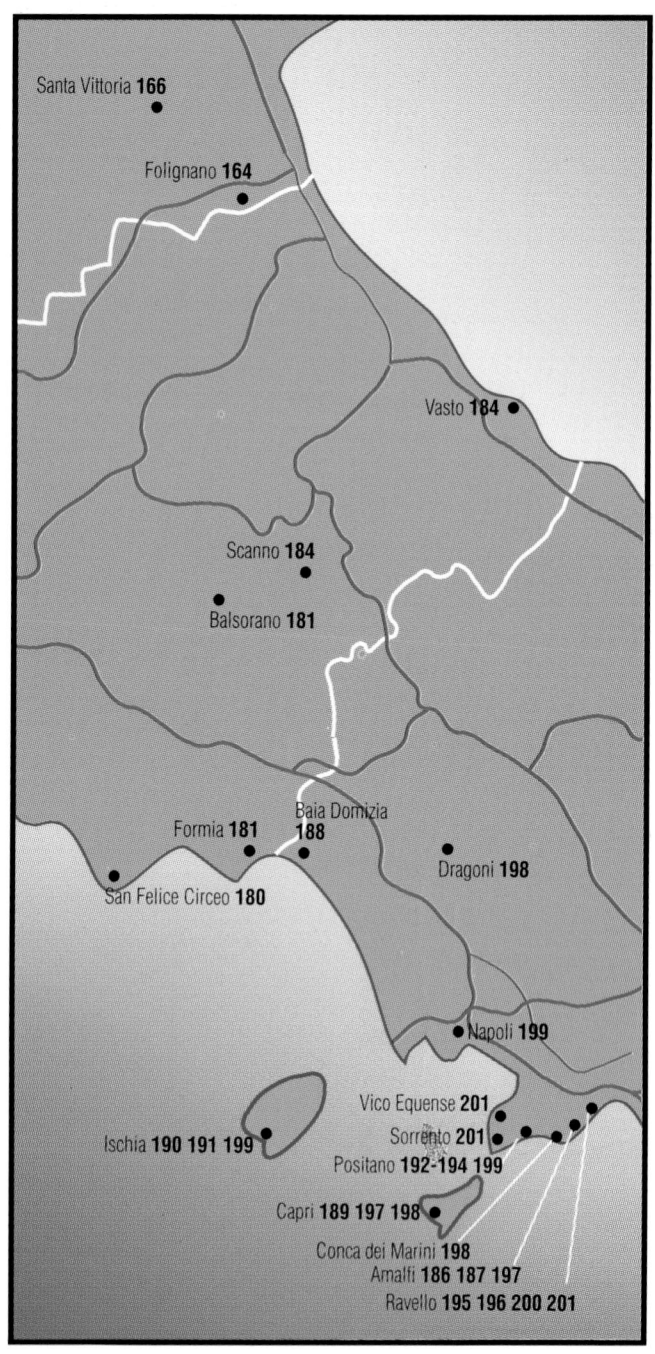

Santa Vittoria **166**

Folignano **164**

Vasto **184**

Scanno **184**

Balsorano **181**

Baia Domizia **188**

Formia **181**

Dragoni **198**

San Felice Circeo **180**

Napoli **199**

Vico Equense **201**

Sorrento **201**

Positano **192-194 199**

Ischia **190 191 199**

Capri **189 197 198**

Conca dei Marini **198**

Amalfi **186 187 197**

Ravello **195 196 200 201**

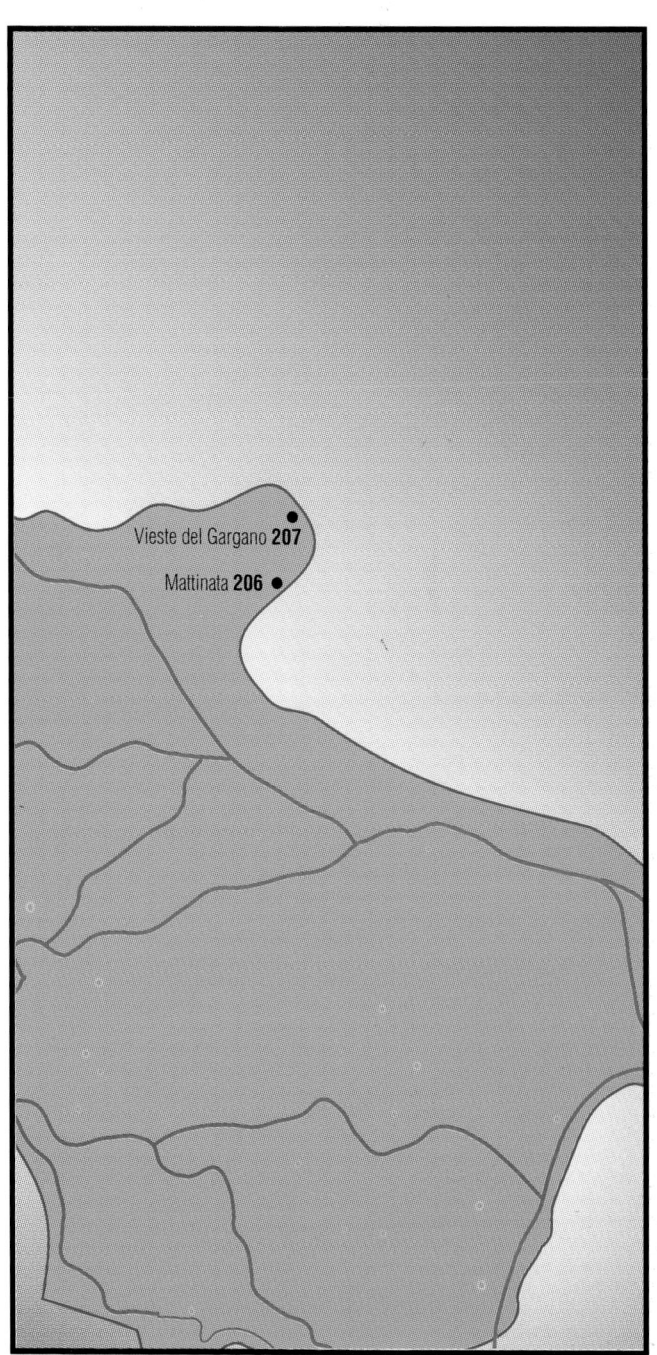

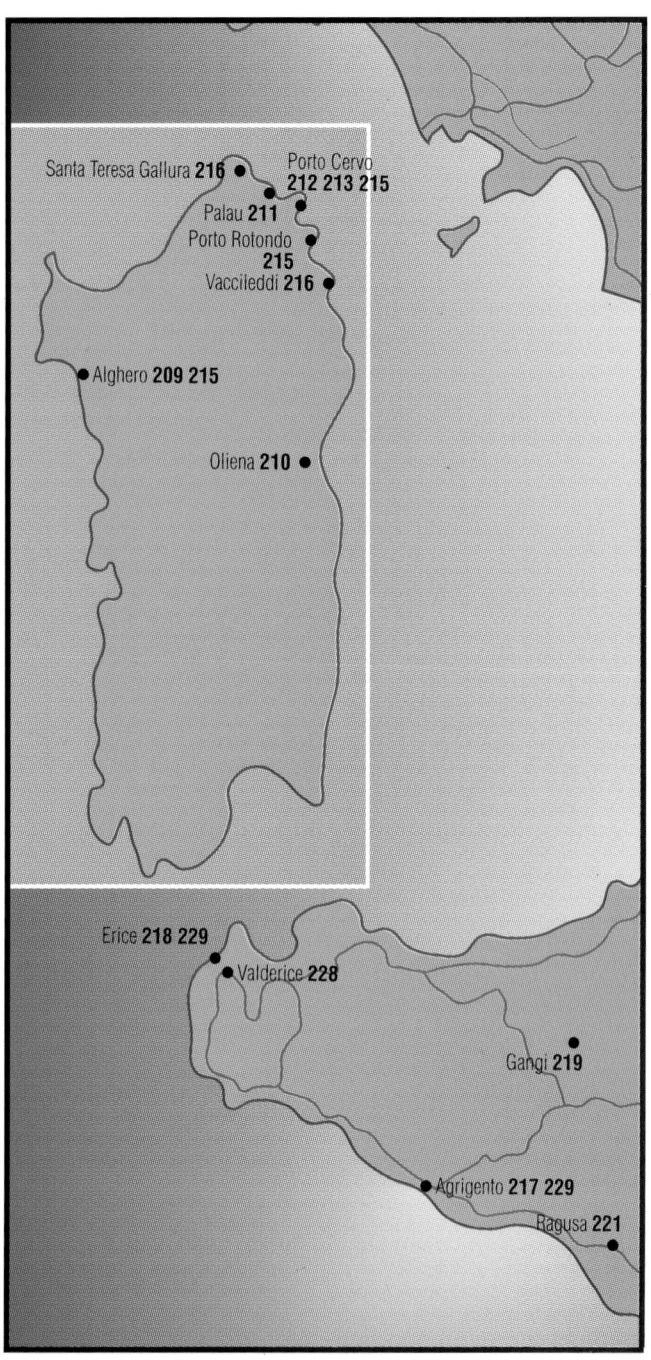

Santa Teresa Gallura **216**
Porto Cervo
212 213 215
Palau **211**
Porto Rotondo
215
Vaccileddi **216**
Alghero **209 215**
Oliena **210**
Erice **218 229**
Valderice **228**
Gangi **219**
Agrigento **217 229**
Ragusa **221**

Hotel location maps

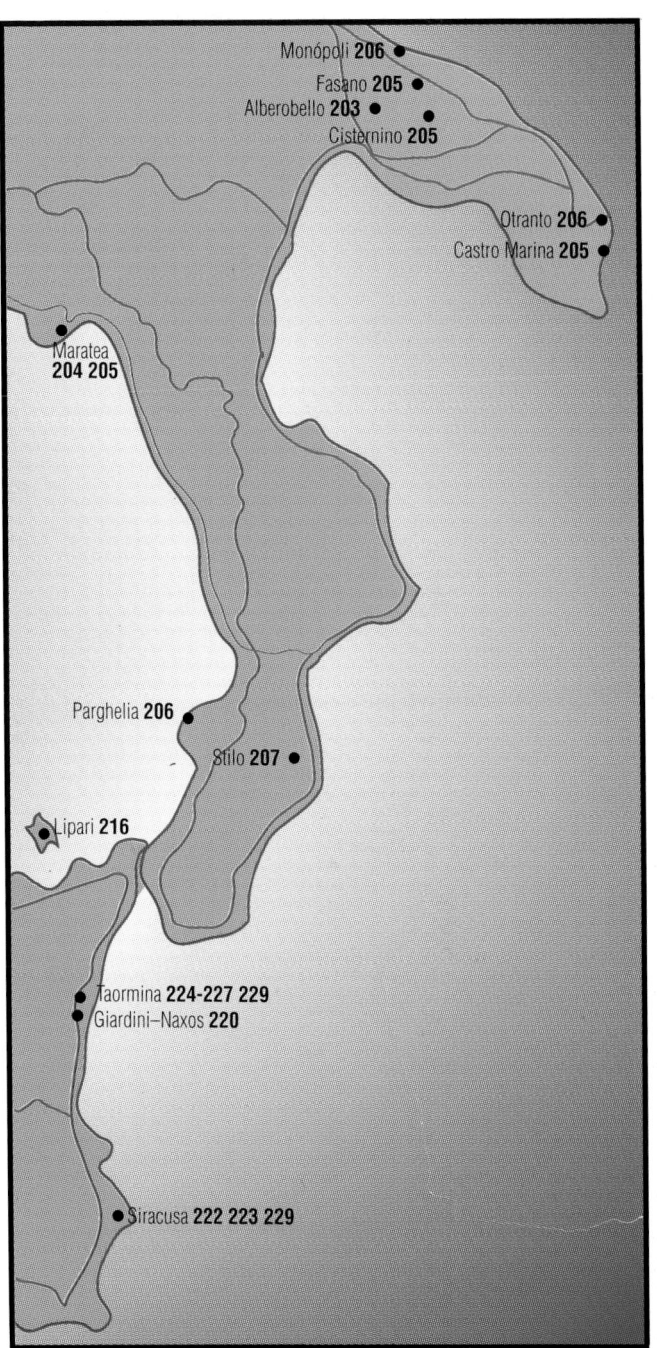

Monópoli **206**
Fasano **205**
Alberobello **203**
Cisternino **205**

Otranto **206**
Castro Marina **205**

Maratea
204 205

Parghelia **206**
Stilo **207**

Lipari **216**

Taormina **224-227 229**
Giardini–Naxos **220**

Siracusa **222 223 229**

The north-west

Hotels in the north-west

North-west Italy offers three contrasting regions: the land 'at the foot of the mountains', Piedmont; the mountainous Valle d'Aosta; and the coastal Liguria.

Piedmont does, no doubt, have its attractions, but they do not impress themselves on many foreign visitors, who tend to hurry across this large region on their way to the recognized glories of Italy to the east and south.

To the traveller, as to the resident, the region is dominated by the city lying at its heart – Turin. We have not found hotels in the middle of the city which deserve to be picked out in these pages but this does not mean that the city lacks comfortable hotels: there is certainly no shortage of swish, large impersonal places right in the heart of things. Of these, the most attractive (and not quite the most expensive) is the Jolly Hotel Ligure (Tel (011) 55641, fax 535438). Of the more modest places, the Genio (Tel (011) 650 5771, fax 8264) and the stylish Victoria (Tel (011) 561 1909, fax 1806) are smartly modern, of moderate size and central the former particularly handy for the station. Only a little further away from the middle is the cheaper Piedmontese (Tel (011) 669 8101, fax 0571) – ideal for travellers on a tight budget who do not wish to be confined to the suburbs. Within easy reach of Turin, we can recommend the Salzea (Tel (011) 649 7809, fax 0366) at Trofarello and the Panoramica (Tel (0125) 8549, fax 669969) at Loranze.

To the north of Turin is the mainly French-speaking Valle d'Aosta, a steep-sided valley surrounded by the highest peaks in the Alps, and best known for its mountain scenery and winter sports facilities. Courmayeur, at the foot of Mont Blanc, and close to the road tunnel, is a popular ski-resort in winter but worth visiting in summer too. For a comfortable stay, try the Del Viale (Tel (0165) 846712, fax 844513), the Bouton d'Or (Tel (0165) 846729, fax 842152), both in Courmayeur, or La Brenva (Tel (0165) 89285, fax 89301, 14 rooms) at Entrèves, the entry (or exit) point of the Mont Blanc Tunnel. At Gressoney-La-Trinité, Lo Scoiattolo (Tel (0125) 366313, fax 366220) is a chalet-style hotel worth trying, as is Les Neiges d'Antan (Tel (0166) 948775, fax 948852) in Cervinia.

The third region is Liguria, a thin strip of mountainous coastline dominated by the Italian Riviera, for which we offer several full recommendations and add the following possibilities here: La Meridiana at Garlenda (Tel (0182) 580271, fax 580150); the Claudio at Bergeggi, near Savona (Tel and fax (019) 859750); and on the Gulf of Spezia, the Porto Roca at Monterosso (Tel (0187) 817502, fax 817692) and the Nido near Lerici (Tel (0187) 967286, fax 964225). If you want to visit Genoa, you would do best to do so from a base on the Riviera itself.

This page acts as an introduction to the features and hotels of North-west Italy, and gives brief recommendations of reasonable hotels that for one reason or another have not made a full entry. The long entries for this region – covering the hotels we are most enthusiastic about – start on the next page. But do not neglect the shorter entries starting on page 30: these are all hotels that we would happily stay at.

The north-west

Lakeside hotel, Cannero Riviera

Cannero

Cannero is one of the quietest resorts on Lake Maggiore and its most desirable hotels lie right on the shore. Only the ferry landing-stage and a dead-end road separate the Cannero from the waters of Maggiore.

The building was once a monastery, though only an old stone column, a couple of vaulted passageways, a quiet courtyard and a beautifully preserved 17thC well suggest it is anything other than a modern hotel. The emphasis is on comfort and relaxation and the atmosphere is very friendly, thanks largely to the attention of Signora Gallinotto and her family. Downstairs, big windows and terraces make the most of the setting. The restaurant focuses on the lake, with an outdoor terrace running alongside. Choose the *à la carte* menu, advises a reader. Bedrooms are light and well cared for with adequate bathrooms. There are gorgeous views of lake and mountains from front rooms, all with balconies, though many guests are happy overlooking the pool at the back – which, if anything, is quieter. By day this provides a delightful spot to take a dip or lounge under yellow parasols.

Nearby Borromean Islands – daily connections by boat; Ascona (21 km), Locarno (25 km) and other resorts of Lake Maggiore.

Lungo Lago 2, Cannero Riviera 28051 Verbania
Tel (0323) 788046
Fax (0323) 788048
Location in resort, overlooking lake; garden and 2 car parks
Food & drink breakfast, lunch, poolside snacks, dinner
Prices rooms LLL with buffet breakfast; meals LL
Rooms 37 double, 3 single, all with bath or shower; all rooms have central heating, phone; also 5 self-catering apartments

nearby **Facilities** sitting-room, piano bar, dining-room, library; 2 lakeside terraces; tennis, pool, solarium, bicycles
Credit cards AE, DC, MC, V
Children welcome; separate dining-room for children; baby-sitter on request
Disabled 10 rooms accessible; lift/elevator **Pets** accepted if well behaved (not in main sitting-room) **Closed** Nov to mid-Mar **Proprietors** Sga Gallinotto and sons

The north-west

Punta Est

The Italian Riviera west of Genoa is for the most part disappointing: most of its resorts are dreary, and most of its hotels mediocre. Happily, both the Punta Est and Finale Ligure are exceptions. The hotel is converted from a splendid 18thC villa which stands high and proudly pink above the buzz of the main coastal road, overlooking the sea. Signor Podesta, who used to be a sculptor, has acted as resident architect since the hotel was first created in the late 1960s, and with great success. By preserving the original features of the house and adding to it in a sympath-etic style, he has managed to preserve the atmosphere of a private villa. The interior is cool and elegant – all dark-wood antiques, fine stone arches, fireplaces and tiled floors. But with such an impressive setting, for most months of the year the focus is on the outdoor terraces, pool and gardens, with their pines, potted plants and lovely views.

Breakfast is taken (off Staffordshire china) in a sort of canopied greenhouse – a lovely sunny spot, surrounded by greenery. Other meals are served in a dining-room in the annexe, where stone arches and beams create a vaguely medieval setting. You can choose between international and Ligurian dishes, including bass cooked with strong aromatic local herbs. The beach is only a couple of minutes' walk down the hillside.

Nearby Finale Borgo (3 km), Alassio (26 km).

Via Aurelia l, Finale Ligure 17024 Savona
Tel (019) 600612
Fax (019) 600611
Location E of the historic town, in private gardens; private car parking
Food & drink breakfast, lunch, dinner
Prices rooms LLL-LLLL; meals L-LL
Rooms 30 double, 4 single, 5 suites; all with bath and shower; all rooms have central heating, phone; minibar, TV in 25 rooms
Facilities sitting-room, bar, TV room, conference room, piano bar; swimming-pool, solarium
Credit cards AE, V
Children accepted, provided they are under control
Disabled access difficult
Pets not accepted
Closed Oct to Easter
Proprietors Podesta family

The north-west

Verbano

The Isola dei Pescatori may not have the *palazzo* or gardens of neighbouring Isola Bella (unlike the other islands, it has never belonged to the wealthy Borromeo family), but it is just as charming in its own way. The cafés and the slightly shabby, painted fishermens' houses along the front are, perhaps, reminiscent of a Greek island – though not an undiscovered one.

The Verbano is a large russet-coloured villa occupying one end of the island, its garden and terraces looking across the lake to Isola Bella. It does not pretend to be a hotel of great luxury, but it can offer lots of character and local colour, and the Zacchera family are friendly hosts. There are beautiful views from the bedrooms, and 11 of the 12 have balconies. Each room is named after a flower; most are prettily and appropriately furnished in old-fashioned style, with painted furniture; those which were a little tired-looking have apparently been refurbished.

But the emphasis is really on the restaurant, with home-made pastas a speciality. If weather prevents eating on the terrace you can still enjoy the views through the big windows of the dining-room. 'Excellent food, friendly staff,' says a visitor.

Nearby Isola Bella (5 minutes by boat); Stresa, Pallanza, Baveno.

Via Ugo Ara 2, Isola dei Pescatori, Stresa 28049 Novara
Tel (0323) 30408/32534
Fax (0323) 33129
E-mail hotelverbano@gse.it
Location on tiny island with waterside terraces; regular boats from Stresa, where there is ample car parking space
Food & drink breakfast, lunch, dinner
Prices rooms LLL with breakfast; DB&B LL; FB LLL
Rooms 12 double, 8 with bath, 4 with shower; all rooms have central heating
Facilities dining-room, sitting-room, bar, terrace
Credit cards AE, DC, MC, V
Children accepted
Disabled no special facilities
Pets accepted
Closed never
Proprietors Zacchera family

The north-west

Castello San Giuseppe

This *castello* was originally a monastery for Carmelite monks before Napoleon took it over as a fort and although it is high on an isolated hill commanding views over the surrounding lakes, inside the walled grounds the atmosphere remains far more reflective than military. There is lots to explore. The hotel is centred around a peaceful inner garden, with ornamental pond, ancient cedars, monkey trees, magnolias, Sicilian figs and olive trees. The open reception has a sitting-area with comfortable chairs.

Upstairs, the bedrooms are rustically stylish, in the best Italian tradition – wrought-iron beds, red-tiled floors, flowing curtains wafting in the breeze from the hills beyond. The grandest rooms have frescoed ceilings. The dining-room, with its frescoed, vaulted ceiling, high-backed chairs and candles, leaves the single diner crying out for a hand to hold. Fortunately the cuisine is more than sufficiently diverting, incorporating some interesting regional dishes, and there is a good choice of wines. Breakfast is served in a more informal room upstairs. A recent visitor appreciated the peace there and wants to go back 'just to eat dinner'.
Nearby Lake Sirio (2 km); Ivrea (3 km); local castles.

Chiaverano d'Ivrea
10010 Torino
Tel (0125) 424370
Fax (0125) 641278
Location 3 km NE of Ivrea, near Chiaverano; in grounds, with ample car parking
Food & drink breakfast, dinner
Prices rooms LL-LLL with breakfast; meals L-LL
Rooms 9 double, 4 with bath, 5 with shower; 7 single, 2 with bath, 5 with shower; all rooms have central heating, phone, TV, hairdrier, safe
Facilities dining-room, breakfast-room, bar, TV room, banqueting hall
Credit cards AE, DC, MC, V
Children welcome
Disabled no special facilities
Pets allowed if small and quiet
Closed never
Proprietor Pasquale and Renata Naghiero

The north-west

Ca' Peo

This rambling farmhouse in the hills east of Portofino has been in the Solari family for four generations. Franco and Melly Solari opened their attractive, bay-windowed dining-room, with its magnificent views over the bay and hills, to guests in 1973. Melly produces the generous seasonal menus, while Franco provides the wine chosen from the 350 different vintages in his cellar. Both now enjoy a high reputation, and booking for the restaurant is essential.

In addition to its home-like atmosphere, the house has many delightful features, including black slate fixtures of varying antiquity (a local speciality – slate is mined in the hills around here). Accommodation is in apartments with a kitchen and dining area, all modern, in an annexe set into olive terraces below the main building; they are comfortable and airy, with new pine furniture and bright sofas.

This makes a quiet, attractive base for exploring the Gulf de Tigullio, between Portofino and Sestri Levante – provided you don't mind negotiating the winding access road.

Nearby walks in chestnut woods; Portofino (22 km); Cinque Terre within reach.

Via dei Caduti 80,
Leivi 16040 Genova
Tel (0185) 319696
Fax (0185) 319671
Location 6 km N of Chiavari, in hills; with garden and car parking
Food & drink breakfast, lunch, dinner
Prices rooms LLL
Rooms 5 apartments; all have phone, TV, kitchen facilities
Facilities dining-room, sitting-room, bar, wine cellar

Credit cards AE, DC, MC, V
Children accepted
Disabled access difficult
Pets in bedrooms only
Closed November; restaurant, Mon, Tue lunch
Proprietors Franco and Melly Solari

The north-west

Town hotel, Portofino

Eden

Such is the popularity of Portofino – a chic and enchanting little port – that even out of season you are likely to have to wait to get into the town, and in season the wait for a parking space can last for hours. Naturally, the charms of the place are affected by the crowds. But stay the night and you can see a different Portofino; you can dine on the waterfront in relative peace, and watch the fishermen coming and going before the crowds arrive.

Hotel rooms are at a premium. There is the grand (and expensive) Hotel Splendid, and a few much smaller, more modest hotels. The Eden is one of these – a tiny place down a narrow street a couple of minutes from the waterfront. The garden, shaded by a large palm and a mass of greenery, is a quiet enclave in the middle of the resort. Meals are taken here on the terrace when weather permits, or in the trattoria-style dining-room which overlooks the garden. The only other public area is the lobby-cum-bar, with the reception desk tucked under the stairs. Bedrooms are light and fresh, with neat, spotless bathrooms.

We have heard of some double-booking problems recently, so more feedback on the Eden from visitors would be welcome.

Nearby lighthouse; San Fruttuoso (by boat or 2 hr walk).

Portofino 16034 Genoa
Tel (0185) 269091
Fax (0185) 269047
Location in middle of resort, with private garden in front; public car park only (L27,000 per day)
Food & drink breakfast, lunch, dinner
Prices rooms LLL with breakfast; meals LL
Rooms 12 double, all with bath; all have central heating, phone, TV; some have air-conditioning
Facilities dining-room with outdoor terrace, bar
Credit cards AE, DC, MC, V
Children welcome if well behaved
Disabled no special facilities
Pets accepted, but not in restaurant
Closed never
Proprietor Osta Ferruccio

The north-west

Helvetia

The Helvetia's claim that it has 'the quietest and most enchanting position of Sestri Levante' is no exaggeration; it stands at one end of the appropriately named Baia del Silenzio. The hotel is distinguished by its spotless white façade, and the yellow and white canopies that shade its balconies and terrace.

Lorenzo Pernigotti devotes himself wholeheartedly to his guests and provides the sort of extras – including 15 gleaming yellow bikes – that you might expect to find in a four-star hotel; but the Helvetia remains small and personal; one satisfied guest says he 'felt just like part of the family'. Another was delighted by the sophisticated key system which controls the lights and music in the bedrooms. The sitting-room/bar has the air of a private home – antiques, coffee-table books, newspapers, potted plants – and the breakfast room is lovely, with views of the bay. Bedrooms are light and airy, overlooking either the bay or the gardens. The day starts on the terrace, with an unusually liberal help-yourself breakfast. Luxuriant gardens climb up the hillside, with tables in the shade of palm trees. Serious sunbathers can take to sunbeds. And there is a tiny pebble beach just across the road.

Nearby Beauty spots of the eastern Riviera; eg Portofino (28 km).

Via Cappuccini 43, Sestri
Levante 16039 Genova
Tel (0185) 41175
Fax (0185) 457216
Location overlooking small
beach, with private garage
and limited car parking
Food & drink breakfast
Prices rooms LLL with
breakfast; 30% reduction for
children under 6 sharing
parents' room
Rooms 24 double, with bath
or shower; all rooms have
central heating, phone,
hairdrier, radio, colour TV,
video, minibar
Facilities sitting-room, TV/
video room, dining-room,
bar, terrace; solarium, ping-
pong, free bicycles
Credit cards MC, V
Children welcome; small beds
provided **Disabled** no special
facilities **Pets** dogs accepted
but not in dining-room
Closed Nov to Feb
Proprietor Lorenzo Pernigotti

The north-west

Lakeside hotel, Arona

Giardino

We get mixed reports on this comfortable lakeside hotel, though no one disputes the attractions of its position, with a large terrace looking across the road to Lake Maggiore, or the friendliness of the staff. The dining-room is undistinguished, but the bedrooms have some individuality, and the hall has recently been updated.

■ Via Repubblica 1, 28041 Arona (Novara) **Tel** (0322) 45994 **Fax** (0322) 249401 **Meals** breakfast, lunch, dinner **Prices** rooms LL; FB LL; breakfast L 14,000; meals L **Rooms** 56, all with bath or shower, central heating, satellite TV, minibar, phone, safe **Credit cards** AE, DC, MC, V **Closed** never

---

Seaside villa, Bordighera

Villa Elisa

An attractive old house set among sub-tropical gardens in the quiet area at the back of this popular family resort. Public rooms are peaceful and civilized, bedrooms spacious and pleasantly old-fashioned. Private parking and swimming-pool.

■ Via Romana 70, 18012 Bordighera (Imperia) **Tel** (0184) 261313 **Fax** (0184) 261942 **E-mail** villaelisa@masterweb.it **Website** http://www.masterweb.it/villaelisa **Meals** breakfast, lunch, dinner **Prices** rooms LL-LLL; meals L-LL **Rooms** 35, all with bath or shower, phone, TV, minibar, safe; 10 with air-conditioning **Credit cards** AE, DC, MC, V **Closed** Nov to mid-Dec

---

Hotel, Cannobio

Pironi

The Pironi is an arcaded medieval building at the heart of the unspoilt lakeside village of Cannobio, and when we last saw it the hotel too seemed perfectly preserved. Reports on any changes would be very welcome.

■ Via Marconi 35, 28822 Cannobio (Verbania) **Tel** (0323) 70624 **Fax** (0323) 72184 **Meals** breakfast **Prices** rooms LLL with breakfast **Rooms** 12, all with bath or shower, central heating, phone, minibar, safe **Credit cards** AE, DC, MC, V **Closed** Nov to Feb

---

Mountain chalet, Cervinia

Hermitage

A civilised Relais & Châteaux retreat in a mountain resort that is something of a blot on the high-altitude landscape. The Hermitage is a low-built chalet with as many suites as bedrooms, and spacious sitting areas combining country-house furnishings with chalet-style woodwork. Indoor pool and beauty centre; heated garage.

■ 11021 Cervinia (Aosta) **Tel** (0166) 948998 **Fax** (0166) 949032 **Meals** breakfast, lunch, dinner **Prices** DB&B LL-LLLL **Rooms** 36, all with bath, phone, satellite TV, minibar **Credit cards** AE, DC, MC, V **Closed** May, Jun, mid-Sep to Nov

The north-west

Mountain chalet, Champoluc

Villa Anna Maria

A chalet-style 1920s villa in a quiet, wooded hillside setting close to the village of Champoluc – main community of a steep-sided valley beneath the Monte Rosa. Wood panelling, simple but cosy furnishings and country decorations.

■ Via Croues 5, 11020 Champoluc (Aosta) **Tel** (0125) 307128 **Fax** (0125) 307984 **E-mail** hotel.annamaria@flashnet.it **Website** www.to2.flashnet.it/anna **Meals** breakfast, lunch, dinner **Prices** rooms L-LL; meals L **Rooms** 20, all with central heating, phone, TV **Credit cards** MC, V **Closed** restaurant only, Oct to Nov; May to late Jun (weather permitting)

Converted monastery, Cioccaro di Penango

Locanda del Sant'Uffizio

The addition of bedrooms over ten years ago turned this well-established restaurant into a very attractive small hotel. Original features have been preserved, and furnishings are a mix of antique and chic modern. Readers approve of the fine food and warm welcome. Attractive swimming-pool.

■ 14030 Cioccaro di Penango (Asti) **Tel** (0141) 916292 **Fax** (0141) 916068 **Meals** breakfast, lunch, dinner **Prices** B&B LLL, DB&B LLL; meals LL **Rooms** 31, all with bath or shower, central heating, minibar, TV **Credit cards** DC, MC, V **Closed** 3 weeks in Jan and Aug

---

Mountain chalet, Cogne

Bellevue

A substantial hotel, in the same family since its construction in the 1920s, in a glorious setting on the flat grassy floor of a valley from which the Gran Paradiso and other Alps rise. Traditional family hotel standards are kept up. Antique furniture, along with displays of local art, lace and alpine flowers. Sauna and pool.

■ Rue Grand Paradis, 11012 Cogne (Aosta) **Tel** (0165) 74825 **Fax** (0165) 749192 **E-mail** hotelbellevuecogne@notvalloo.it **Website** www.hotelbellevuecogne.it **Meals** breakfast, lunch, dinner **Prices** DB&B LLL-LLLL; meals LL **Rooms** 33; 3 chalets, all with bath or shower, central heating, phone, TV, hairdrier, radio, minibar; some with sitting-room and fireplace **Credit cards** DC, MC, V **Closed** Oct to mid-Dec

---

Mountain chalet, Courmayeur

La Grange

This 13thC chalet-style farmhouse, with stone walls, stone roof and wooden trimmings, has made a handsome little hotel. The rustic style is carried through into the welcoming interior, with country antiques dotted around. Bedrooms are plain but comfortable and well equipped.

■ Entreves, 11013 Courmayeur (Aosta) **Tel** (0165) 869733 **Fax** (0165) 869744 **Meals** breakfast, snacks **Prices** rooms L-LLLL; meals L **Rooms** 23, all with bath or shower, central heating, TV, minibar, phone, radio **Credit cards** AE, DC, MC, V **Closed** May to Jun, Oct to Nov

The north-west

Mountain chalet, Courmayeur

Palace Bron

Courmayeur is one of the most captivating of Italian mountain resorts. The Palace Bron is a tall chalet-style hotel set above the town in a grassy garden with great views of Mont Blanc. Inside, no hint of rusticity: comfortable armchairs, oriental rugs and chandeliers.

■ Via Plan Gorret, 41, 11013 Courmayeur (Aosta) **Tel** (0165) 846742 **Fax** (0165) 844015 **Meals** breakfast, lunch, dinner **Prices** DB&B LLL (min 3 nights; reductions for 7 nights) **Rooms** 27, all with bath, phone, TV, radio **Credit cards** AE, DC, MC, V **Closed** May, Jun, Oct, Nov

---

Seaside hotel, Genova-Nervi

Villa Pagoda

An unusual pagoda-shaped villa, built in the 19thC, and set in parkland bordering the seaside promenade of Nervi. Bedrooms are simply furnished; public areas are more elegant, with antiques. Ligurian seafood specialities such as anchovies, seasbass and squid are served in the restaurant. A new entry this year.

■ Via Capolungo 15,16167 Genova-Nervi **Tel** (010) 323200/3726161 **Fax** (010) 321218 **Website** http://www.romantikhotels.com./pages/rhgenov/ **Meals** breakfast, lunch, dinner **Prices** DB&B LLL; meals from L65,000 **Rooms** 14, 4 suites, all with bath or shower, phone, TV, minibar **Credit cards** AE, DC, MC, V **Closed** May, Jun, Oct, Nov

---

Seaside hotel, Laigueglia

Splendid

The well in the dining-room and the vaulted ceilings testify to the monastic origins of this neat hotel in the middle of Laigueglia. Furnishings mix antique and modern happily. A key feature is the small garden, with its inviting pool, where drinks are served.

■ Piazza Badaro 3, 17020 Laigueglia (Savona) **Tel** (0182) 690325 **Fax** (0182) 690894 **Meals** breakfast, lunch, dinner **Prices** rooms LL-LLL with breakfast; DB&B LL-LLL; FB LL; 20% reduction for children under 7 **Rooms** 45, all with bath or shower, central heating, phone, TV **Credit cards** AE, DC, MC, V **Closed** Oct to Mar

---

Country hotel, Mele

Hotel Fado 78

Gianni Canepa and his English wife Christine have made their modest country hotel a welcoming port of call. The 19thC shuttered house has been modernized inside and the plain, comfortable bedrooms are in a modern extension. Lovely little garden, good views; indifferent breakfast, according to a reporter.

■ Via Fado 82, 16010 Mele (Genova) **Tel** (010) 631852/6971060 **Meals** breakfast, lunch, dinner, snacks **Prices** rooms L-LL; meals L **Rooms** 8, all with bath or shower, central heating, phone, TV **Credit cards** not accepted **Closed** never

The north-west

Country hotel, Orta San Giulio

La Bussola

This modern building enjoys splendid views over Lake Orta and its island of San Guilio, and has been built (in traditional villa style) to make the best of them. The dining-room is simple, light and spacious, and there is a small terrace. The large garden includes a fair-sized secluded pool. Friendly place, with good food.

■ 28016 Orta San Giulio (Novara) **Tel** (0322) 911913 **Fax** (0322) 911934 **Meals** breakfast, lunch, dinner **Prices** rooms LL-LLL; DB&B LL (obligatory Jun-Sep); meals LL **Rooms** 16, all with bath or shower, phone, central heating, TV, minibar; 12 rooms have minibar **Credit cards** AE, MC, V **Closed** Nov

---

Seaside hotel, Orta San Giulio

Leon d'Oro

More appealing from outside than in, this hotel is recommended for its marvellous setting on the edge of Lake Orta. The dining-room is large and lacks character, the bedrooms are functional and unimaginative (ask for one with a terrace). Not the place to spend a whole holiday, but good value.

■ 28016 Orta San Giulio (Novara) **Tel** (0322) 911991/90254 **Fax** (0322) 90303 **Meals** breakfast, lunch, dinner **Prices** rooms LL, LL-LLL with breakfast; DB & B LL; FB LLL; meals L **Rooms** 32, all with bath or shower, central heating, phone **Credit cards** AE, MC, V **Closed** Jan

---

Lakeside hotel, Orta San Giulio

Olina

We include the Piccolo Hotel and Restaurant Olina for the first time this year, following an enthusiastic recommendation from a reader who raved about the food there. Comfortable bedrooms in warm tones, some with tiled floors and wooden ceilings are in a separate building.

■ via Olina 40, Orta San Giulio (Novara) **Tel** (0322) 905656 **Fax** (0322) 905645 **Meals** breakfast, lunch, dinner **Prices** rooms LL; DB & B LL; FB LL **Rooms** 8, all with bath or shower, central heating, phone, TV, view of lake **Credit cards** AE, MC, V **Closed** 10 Nov to 20 Mar

---

Seaside hotel, Orta San Giulio

Orta

The endearingly shabby façade of the Orta forms one side of the main piazza of Orta San Giulio, and its café tables spill out on to the square. Around the corner, the restaurant terrace overhanging Lake Orta gives glorious views. The hotel is pleasantly spacious and old-fashioned.

■ 28016 Orta San Giulio (Novara) **Tel** (0322) 90253 **Fax** (0322) 905646 **Meals** breakfast, lunch, dinner **Prices** rooms with breakfast LL; DB & B LL; FB LL **Rooms** 35, all with bath or shower, central heating, phone, TV view of lake **Credit cards** AE, DC, MC, V **Closed** Nov to Mar

The north-west

Restaurant-with-rooms, San Giorgio Monferrato

Castello di San Giorgio

A quite grand little pink-painted mansion, mainly dating from the 16thC, set in extensive parkland. The elegant restaurant, with vaulted ceiling and murals, is the focus, and you must eat here – expensively, if Maurizio Grossi has his way – to stay here. Rooms are relatively plain.

■ Via Cavalli d'Olivola 3, 15020 San Giorgio Monferrato (Alessandria) **Tel** (0142) 806203 **Fax** (0 142) 806505 **Meals** breakfast, lunch, dinner **Prices** rooms LLL; DB&B LLL; meals LL **Rooms** 11, all with bath, central heating, phone, TV, minibar **Credit cards** AE, DC, V **Closed** 10 days Jan, 3 weeks Aug; restaurant only, Mon

---

Mountain chalet, Sauze d'Oulx

Il Capricorno

To the British, Sauze is a downmarket ski resort, but it attracts quite a smart Italian clientele, winter and summer. This chalet is cosily traditional – rough beams, hand-made furniture – and set in an isolated position on the wooded slopes above the village.

■ Case Sparse 21, Le Clotes, 10050 Sauze d'Oulx (Torino) **Tel** (0122) 850273 **Fax** (0122) 850497 **Meals** breakfast, lunch, dinner **Prices** rooms LLL with breakfast; DB&B LLL; meals LL **Rooms** 8, all with shower, central heating, phone, TV **Credit cards** DC, V **Closed** May to mid-June, mid-Sep to Nov

---

Converted castle, Sestri Levante

Grand Hotel dei Castelli

This hotel was included on the strength of its splendid location, high up on Sestri Levante's wooded peninsula. It has undergone extensive renovation in recent years and we welcome reports on the changes.

■ Via Penisola 26, 16039 Sestri Levante (Genova) **Tel** (0185) 487220 **Fax** (0185) 44767 **Meals** breakfast, lunch, dinner **Prices** rooms LLL-LLLL; DB&B LLL; FB LLL; meals LL **Rooms** 30, all with bath, central heating, air-conditioning, phone, TV, minibar, hairdrier **Credit cards** AE, DC, MC, V **Closed** winter

---

Seaside hotel, Sestri Levante

Miramare

One of several pink, shuttered 19thC houses that line the Baia del Silenzio – but inside cool and contemporary. Huge arched windows make the best of the sea views, and the terrace is an idyllic spot for breakfast. Friendly staff, and we hear that food is now a serious venture – reports please. Garage.

■ Via Cappellini 9, 16039 Sestri Levante (Genoa) **Tel** (0185) 480855 **Fax** (0185) 41055 **Meals** breakfast, lunch, dinner **Prices** rooms LL-LLLL; reduction for children **Rooms** 43, all with bath or shower, air-conditioning, phone, TV, minibar **Credit cards** AE, MC, V **Closed** never

The north-west

Restaurant-with-rooms, Soriso

Al Sorriso

One of Italy's few Michelin two-star restaurants, set in an unremarkable village some way from Lake Orta. The dining-room is the picture of elegance, the service professional. Bedrooms are more ordinary (and more affordable) than you might expect.

■ 28018 Soriso (Novara) **Tel** (0322) 983228 **Fax** (0322) 983328 **Meals** breakfast, lunch, dinner **Prices** rooms LLL with breakfast; meals LL **Rooms** 8, all with bath or shower, phone, TV, minibar **Credit cards** MC, V **Closed** Christmas to 20 Jan; restaurant only, Mon and Tue lunch

Town hotel, Turin

Conte Biancamano

'Faded grandeur' may be a cliché, but it is difficult to avoid in the case of this family-run, city-centre hotel (close to Turin's railway station). The sitting-room is palatial in dimensions and style; bedrooms are plainer, but still comfortable.

■ Corso Vittorio Emanuele II 73, 10128 Turin **Tel** (011) 562 3281 **Fax** (011) 562 3789 **E-mail** cbhtl.to@iol.it **Meals** breakfast, snacks **Prices** rooms LL-LLL with breakfast **Rooms** 27, all with bath or shower, central heating, phone, TV, radio, minibar, hairdrier **Credit cards** AE, DC, MC, V **Closed** Aug

Town villa, Turin

Villa Sassi-El Toulà

A noble 17thC villa, unrivalled in Turin. Many original features have been retained: marble floors, ornate doors and 17thC candelabra. But Villa Sassi is not cheap, and reporters have questioned its value for money, finding the welcome indifferent and the food variable.

■ Traforo del Pino 47, 10132 Turin **Tel** (011) 8980556 **Fax** (011) 898 0095 **Meals** breakfast, lunch, dinner **Prices** rooms LLL-LLLL; meals LL-LLL **Rooms** 17, all with phone, TV, minibar **Credit cards** AE, DC, V **Closed** Aug; restaurant only, Sun

Readers' Reports

Reports from readers are of enormous interest to us in keeping up to date with the hotels in this guide - and others that should be in it. More information on p11

Lombardia

Hotels in Lombardia

Lombardy is an enormous region, stretching from the high Alps bordering Switzerland almost as far as the Adriatic and Ligurian seas. It contains Lake Como, with Lakes Maggiore and Garda forming its boundary in the west and east respectively, and has at its heart the economic and industrial centre of Italy: Milan.

Of all big, glossy Italian cities, none is glossier than Milan and only Rome is bigger. Despite its considerable heritage – notably a marvellous cathedral, important art collections and the world's most famous opera house – its role as Italy's economic capital dominates the visitor's view, and most steer clear. The result is that Milan's hotels are business-oriented – and as big and glossy as the city itself.

Surprisingly though, we have been able to find two excellent small hotels in Milan (see page 47). Centrally placed, but too large for full recommendations, are the Manzoni (Tel (02) 760 05700, fax 784212), a calm, comfortable and reasonably priced hotel, and (if you can stand the extravagance) the Grand Hotel Duomo (Tel (02) 8833, fax 86462027) set in a historic building close to the *duomo* itself and to the famous central shopping arcades.

Our main lakeside recommendations concentrate on Lake Como and Lake Garda. Bellagio is the main resort on Lake Como with Menaggio a close second – try the Bellavista (Tel (0344) 32136, fax 31793) in Menaggio itself, or the Loveno (Tel (0344) 32110) in the village of Loveno 2 km away – a 13-room hotel with a shady garden and views of the lakes and mountains. In Como itself, you could try the Loggiato dei Serviti (Tel (031) 264234, fax 263546), a modern, comfortable hotel close to the railway station.

On Lake Garda, the main resort for the southern end is Sirmione, beautifully situated on the lake, and with the massive Castle of the Scaligers, Roman remains and lovely gardens to visit, but also very conveniently placed for the main Milan-Venice motorway and therefore very busy during the day with trippers trying to 'see' Lake Garda, Verona and Venice in a day. The Golf et Suisse (Tel (030) 990 4188, fax 916304), is a peaceful, modern, 30-room hotel, a mile out of town but still on the lake and with its own beach and jetty. A possibility for Gardone Riviera, in addition to our full recommendations, is the Montefiori (Tel (0365) 290235, fax 21488), an elegant and secluded villa on a hillside above Lake Garda – though we have received disappointing reports from readers in the past.

This page acts as an introduction to the features and hotels of Lombardy, and gives brief recommendations of reasonable hotels that for one reason or another have not made a full entry. The long entries for this region – covering the hotels we are most enthusiastic about – start on the next page. But do not neglect the shorter entries starting on page 44: these are all hotels that we would happily stay at.

Lombardia

Lakeside hotel, Bellagio

Florence

Bellagio is the pearl of Lake Como. It stands on a promontory at the point where the lake divides into two branches, and the views from its houses, villas and gardens are superb. The Florence is a handsome 18thC building occupying a prime position at one end of the main piazza, overlooking the lake. A terrace under arcades, where drinks and snacks are served, provides a welcoming entry to the hotel and the interior is no less appealing. Whitewashed walls, high vaulted ceilings and beams create a cool, attractive foyer; to one side, elegant and slightly faded seats cluster round an old stone fireplace.

Bedrooms have the same old-fashioned charm as the public rooms, furnished with cherry-wood antiques and attractive fabrics; the most sought after, naturally, are those with balconies and views over the lake. Meals (including breakfast, with home-made pastries) can be taken on a delightful terrace under shady trees across the street from the hotel, watching the various craft ply across the lake. In the evening there is jazz in the cocktail bar – one of Lake Como's smarter nightspots. The hotel has been in the same family for 150 years, and is now in the hands of brother and sister, Ronald and Roberta Ketzlar; they both speak good English, and have just created a new gourmet restaurant. A recent visitor was thoroughly enchanted.

Nearby Villa Serbelloni; the Madonna del Ghisallo (37 km).

Piazza Mazzini, Bellagio
22021 Como
Tel (031) 950342
Fax (031) 951722
Location on main piazza overlooking lake, with waterside terrace and garage
Food & drink breakfast, lunch, dinner
Prices LLL with breakfast; DB&B LLL; meals L
Rooms 32 double, 23 with bath, 8 with shower; 6 single; all rooms have central heating, satellite TV, phone, hairdrier
Facilities dining-room, bar, reading and TV room, terrace
Credit cards AE, DC, MC, V
Children accepted
Disabled no special facilities
Pets well behaved ones accepted, but not in restaurant
Closed 20 Oct to 15 Apr
Proprietors Ketzlar family

Lombardia

Restaurant with rooms, Capriate San Gervasio

Vigneto

Capriate San Gervasio is a few minutes' drive from the main autostrada from Milan to Venice, convenient for an overnight stop. The Vigneto is a comfortable villa, perched on a river bank, surrounded by a beautifully kept small garden and terrace. The bedrooms are reasonably sized, with modern furniture, decorated in rather sombre beige and tans; those at the front look out over the tree-lined banks of the river. The dining-room is formal, with many pictures on the walls, and looks out over the covered terrace where you can eat in the summer months. The restaurant is popular with the locals.

Nearby Bergamo (17 km); Milan (35 km).

Capriate San Gervasio
24042 Bergamo
Tel (02) 909 9351
Fax (02) 909 0179
Location 12 km SW of
Bergamo, 2 km N of A4, on
banks of river Adda; with
private car parking
Food & drink breakfast,
lunch, dinner
Prices rooms LL-LLL;
breakfast L; meals L-LL
Rooms 12 rooms, all with
shower, phone, TV

Facilities 2 sitting-rooms,
dining-room, conference
facilities
Credit card AE, V
Children accepted
Disabled no special facilities
Pets not accepted
Closed Mon; Aug
Proprietor Casina Rosella

Lombardia

Lakeside hotel, Gargnano

Baia d'Oro

The Baia d'Oro is a distinctive old yellow building, with green shutters, right on the shore, its little pier jutting out into the dark blue waters of Garda and its flowery terrace commanding superb views of the mountains beyond. This outside terrace provides the focal point of the hotel: in the summer months you breakfast and dine outside. If you are lucky enough to arrive by boat you can moor at the pier and step straight into the hotel.

It is a small, friendly establishment run by the Terzi family. Gianbattista is an artist – you can see some of his water-colours of the lakes in the rooms of the hotel. It was his wife who transformed the building from a private home into a delightful hotel which has retained its former intimacy.

The main public room is a light and inviting area with bowls of freshly cut flowers, pretty arches and glass doors opening on to the terrace. Bedrooms are bright and lovingly cared for, several with lakeside balconies.

The Terzis no longer serve dinner here, but are happy to advise on eating places; their son has a restaurant nearby.

Nearby Gardone Riviera, Desenzano, Sirmione, Garda, Malcesine.

Via Gamberera 13, Gargnano 25084 Brescia
Tel (0365) 71171
Fax (0365) 72568
Location in resort, with private car parking (L15,000)
Food & drink breakfast
Prices rooms LLL; DB&B LLL
Rooms 11 double, all with bath and shower;
2 single with shower; all have central heating, phone, minibar

Facilities dining-room, bar, TV room, sitting-room
Credit cards AE, MC, V
Children accepted
Disabled access difficult
Pets dogs accepted
Closed end Oct to Easter
Proprietors Terzi family

Lombardia

Lakeside hotel, Gargnano

Giulia

From a *pensione* with no private bathrooms, the Giulia has been upgraded over the years to a three-star hotel. But happily it retains the atmosphere of a family-run guest-house. It is a beautiful, spacious villa, built over a hundred years ago in Victorian style with Gothic touches. Signora Rina Bombardelli has been here for over 40 years, and has gradually made the Giulia one of the most delightful places to stay on the entire lake.

For a start, it has a wonderful location, with gardens and terraces running practically on the water's edge. Inside, light and airy rooms lead off handsome corridors – a beautiful dining-room with Murano chandeliers, gold walls and elegant seats; a civilized sitting-room with Victorian armchairs; and bedrooms which range from light and modern to large rooms with timbered ceilings, antiques and balconies overlooking the garden and lake. According to a very unhappy solo visitor, the singles are not nearly as attractive. At garden level a second, simpler dining-room opens out on to a terrace with ample space and gorgeous views. At any time of day, it is a lovely spot to linger among the palm trees and watch the boats plying the blue waters of Garda.

Nearby ferry services to villages and towns around Lake Garda.

Gargnano, Lago di Garda
25084 Brescia
Tel (0365) 71022
Fax (0365) 72774
Location 150 m from middle of resort, with garden and terrace down to lake; private car park
Food & drink breakfast, lunch, dinner
Prices rooms LLL-LLLLL with breakfast; DB&B LLL; meals LL
Rooms 19 double, 3 single; all with bath or shower; all rooms have central heating, phone, TV, minibar, safe
Facilities dining-room, veranda taverna, sitting-room, TV room, terrace; beach, swimming-pool, sauna
Credit cards AE, DC, MC, V
Children accepted
Disabled access difficult
Pets accepted (L20,000 per day) **Closed** mid-Oct to mid-Mar **Proprietors** Barbara and Rina Bombardelli

Lombardia

Lakeside hotel, Lenno

San Giorgio

This large white 1920s villa on the shores of Lake Como stands out against a backdrop of wooded hills and immaculate gardens running right down to the shore. A path lined with potted plants leads down through neatly tended lawns to the lakeside terrace and the low-lying stone wall which is all that divides the gardens from the pebble beach and the lake. There are palm trees, arbours and stone urns where geraniums flourish. For a trip on the lake the ferry landing-stage lies close by.

The interior is no disappointment. The public rooms are large and spacious, leading off handsome halls. There are antiques wherever you go, and attractive touches such as pretty ceramic pots and copper pots brimming with flowers. The restaurant is a lovely light room with breathtaking views and the salon is equally inviting, with its ornate mirrors, fireplace and slightly faded antiques. Even the ping-pong room has a number of interesting antique pieces. Bedrooms are large and pleasantly old-fashioned. Antiques and beautiful views are the main features, but there is nothing grand or luxurious about them – hence the reasonable prices. One of our reporters rates this his favourite hotel – 'sensational view, friendly reception, firm bed, great towels'.

Nearby Tremezzo, Cadenabbia, Villa Carlotta (2-4 km); Bellagio (10 min boat crossing from Cadenabbia).

Via Regina 81, Lenno, Tremezzo 22019 Como
Tel (0344) 40415
Location on lakefront in private park, with parking for 30 cars, garage for 6
Food & drink breakfast, lunch, dinner
Prices rooms LLL with breakfast; DB&B LL; meals L
Rooms 26 double, 20 with bath, 6 with shower; 3 single; all rooms have central heating

Facilities dining-room, hall, reading-room, ping-pong room, terrace; tennis
Credit cards MC, V
Children accepted
Disabled access difficult
Pets not accepted
Closed Oct to Apr
Proprietor Margherita Cappelletti

Lombardia

Sole

The exterior of this 15thC coaching inn is marked solely by a gilt wrought-iron sun. Inside, the walls are white-washed, the ceilings timbered and the arched chambers carefully scattered with antique furniture, copper pots and ceramics. There are three dining-areas: the old kitchen, with its long table, open fire and old gas hobs where on occasion dishes are finished in front of the guests; a smaller dining-room, with individual tables; and the stone-arched portico which looks out on to the idyllic garden.

The late Franco Colombani had brought his own distinctive personality to the regional cuisine – dark, tasty stews, roast meats and fish, accompanied by vegetables from the kitchen garden and fine wines from the unfathomable cellars. Now his son and daughter are continuing with the tradition that has helped rate the Sole as among the finest restaurants in Italy.

The bedrooms all have individual high points, and good bathrooms. Those above the dining-room are traditional, while those overlooking the garden have a less impressive mix of old and new furnishings.

Nearby Piacenza; Cremona (22 km).

Via Trabattoni 22,
26847 Maleo
Tel (0377) 58142
Fax (0377) 458058
Location behind church, off main piazza of village, 20 km NE of Piacenza; car parking available
Food & drink breakfast, lunch, dinner
Prices rooms LLL; meals LL
Rooms 8 double, all with bath; all rooms have central heating, phone, TV, minibar

Facilities 2 dining-rooms, sitting-room; garden
Credit cards AE, MC, V
Children welcome
Disabled no special facilities
Pets welcome
Closed hotel Jan and Aug; restaurant Sun eve, Mon
Proprietors Mario and Francesca Colombani

Lombardia

Restaurant with rooms, Pomponesco

Il Leone

Pomponesco was once a flourishing town under the Gonzaga family. Now it is a shadow of its former self, surrounded by unsightly modern suburbs. But the old part still has a certain faded charm, and just off the main piazza lies the Leone – an old peeling building which once belonged to a 16thC nobleman.

This is primarily a place to eat (it calls itself a trattoria). There are only nine bedrooms, and by far the most attractive features are the dining-areas. The *pièce de résistance* is the coffered 16thC ceiling and frieze in the main restaurant. Elsewhere the decoration is suitably elegant: 'old master' paintings, gilt wall lamps, a terrazzo floor and tables immaculately laid. Food here is among the best in the region, with unusual combinations of flavour; local specialities include the traditional dish of braised meat with polenta, which was one of the popular dishes of the Gonzagas.

Beyond the restaurant a flower-filled inner courtyard leads to the bedrooms. These are built around an inviting pool and garden area where a country house atmosphere prevails. In contrast with the elegance of the restaurant, the bedrooms have a stark modernity, but they are comfortable and well maintained.

Nearby Mantua, Modena, Parma all within reach.

Piazza IV Martiri 2,
Pomponesco 46030 Mantova
Tel (0375) 86077/86145
Fax (0375) 86770
Location on small piazza,
next to river Po, with garden
and car parking
Food & drink breakfast,
lunch, dinner
Prices rooms LL; DB&B LL;
meals LL
Rooms 6 double, 3 single; all
with shower; all rooms have
central heating, phone,

minibar; all double rooms
have air-conditioning
Facilities dining-room, bar,
TV room; swimming-pool
Credit cards AE, DC, MC, V
Children accepted
Disabled access difficult
Pets accepted
Closed Jan; restaurant only,
Sun pm and Mon
Proprietor Antonio Mori

Lombardia

Country villa, Alzate Brianza

Villa Odescalchi

A rather formal and plush 17thC villa, popular with business visitors, with lush gardens and grand park behind. Bedrooms are tall and spacious; the dining-room is in a modern conservatory extension.

■ Via Anzani 12, 22040 Alzate Brianza (Como) **Tel** (031) 630822 **Fax** (031) 632079 **Meals** breakfast, lunch, dinner **Prices** rooms LL-LLL with breakfast; DB&B LL-LLL; FB LLL-LLLL **Rooms** 64, all with bath or shower, phone, minibar, TV **Credit cards** AE, DC, MC, V **Closed** never, restaurant Tue

---

Lakeside villa, Argegno

Belvedere

'Inexpensive but wonderful little hotel, marvellously located on shores of Como. Excellent although small rooms, beautiful food – lunch by the lakeside dreamy. Very friendly and co-operative people'. So says one reporter; another confirms our recommendation. The lady of the house is Scots – hence the tartan bar.

■ Via Milano 8, 22010 Argegno (Como) **Tel** (031) 821116 **Fax** (031) 821571 **Meals** breakfast , lunch, dinner **Prices** rooms LL with breakfast; meals L **Rooms** 17 **Credit cards** not accepted **Closed** Nov to Mar

---

Lakeside hotel, Bellagio

Hotel du Lac

One of Bellagio's most popular hotels, with a welcoming atmosphere, a delightful setting on the piazza (and an inviting arcaded terrace), and high standards throughout. Signora Leoni's British origins show in such things as the towels and breakfasts (real marmalade, real orange juice). A recent visitor praised the 'consistent helpfulness of the staff'.

■ Piazza Mazzini 32, 22021 Bellagio (Como) **Tel** (031) 950320 **Fax** (031) 951624 **Meals** breakfast, lunch, dinner **Prices** rooms LL-LLL; meals L; lock-up garage L13,000 **Rooms** 48, all with bath or shower, central heating, phone, air-conditioning, satellite TV, minibar, hairdrier **Credit cards** MC, V **Closed** end-Oct to Apr

---

Lakeside hotel, Bellagio

La Pergola

Unlike most of Bellagio's hotels, this one faces the eastern shore of Como – it is tucked away in the tiny village of Pescallo, just to the south. The view is splendid, the house ancient and rustic, the furnishings simple and old-fashioned, the whole operation a family affair.

■ Pescallo, 22021 Bellagio (Como) **Tel** (031) 950263 **Meals** breakfast, lunch, dinner **Prices** rooms L-LL; meals L **Rooms** 10 **Credit cards** AE, DC, MC, V **Closed** Nov to Mar; restaurant only, Tue

Lombardia

Restaurant-with-rooms, Bergamo

Agnello d'Oro

This picturesque, tall and incredibly narrow building lies at the heart of old Bergamo, on a tiny square with a fountain. The restaurant is cosy and characterful, with red-checked tablecloths, and ceramics and copper pans covering the walls. Bright bedrooms, verging on the basic. 'Welcoming staff, reasonably priced and good food' says a recent report.

■ Via Gombito 22, 24100 Bergamo **Tel** (035) 249883 **Fax** (035) 235612 **Meals** breakfast, lunch, dinner **Prices** rooms LL; breakfast L10,000; dinner LL **Rooms** 20, all with bath or shower, central heating, phone, TV **Credit cards** AE, DC, V, MC **Closed** never

---

Restaurant-with-rooms, Bergamo

Gourmet

For the very best food in this gastronomic city you have to head downtown, but in the charming old *città alta* you can still eat well – at the Gourmet, for example. Shady terrace for summer dining. Spacious, light and smart bedrooms with luxury bathrooms.

■ Via San Vigilio 1, 24100 Bergamo **Tel & fax** (035) 256110 **Meals** breakfast, lunch, dinner **Prices** rooms L-LL; meals LL **Rooms** 10, all with bath or shower, phone, TV, radio , minibar **Credit cards** AE, DC, MC, V **Closed** restaurant only, Tue

---

Restaurant-with-rooms, Bergamo

Il Sole

On the corner of the lovely Piazza Vecchia, the Sole catches a lot of Bergamo's tourist trade. The restaurant does not have quite the cosy charm of the Agnello d'Oro, but does not disappoint – and there is an attractive courtyard for summer meals. Bedrooms refurbished in 1992; modest prices.

■ Via Bartolomeo Colleoni 1, Piazza Vecchia, Citta Alta, 24100 Bergamo **Tel** (035) 218238 **Fax** (035) 240011 **Meals** breakfast, lunch, dinner **Prices** rooms LL **Rooms** 11, all with bath or shower, TV, phone and minibar **Credit cards** AE, DC, MC, V **Closed** never

---

Lakeside villa, Gardone Riviera

Villa Fiordaliso

This tall but small villa on the shores of Lake Garda is one of the most exclusive hotels in northern Italy. The emphasis is on the restaurant, which occupies several elegant rooms – and spills on to the waterside terrace. The few bedrooms, named after exotic flowers, are richly decorated and beautifully furnished.

■ Corso Zanardelli 132, 25083 Gardone Riviera (Brescia) **Tel** (0365) 20158 **Fax** (0365) 290011 **Meals** breakfast, lunch, dinner **Prices** rooms LLLL with breakfast; DB&B LLL; meals LL **Rooms** 7, all with bath, central heating, air-conditioning, minibar, TV, radio, phone **Credit cards** AE, V **Closed** Jan and Feb

Lombardia

Lakeside villa, Gardone Riviera

Villa del Sogno

The 'Dream Villa' earns its name by its position, overlooking Lake Garda and secluded in its own luxuriant park with a swimming-pool and vast terrace. The interior is a mix of traditional and modern, much of it renovated in the past few years.

■ Via Zanardelli 107, Fasano di Gardone Riviera, 25083 Gardone Riviera (Brescia) **Tel** (0365) 290181 **Fax** (0365) 290230 **Meals** breakfast, lunch, dinner **Prices** rooms LLL-LLLL with breakfast; DB&B LLLL; meals LL **Rooms** 34, all with bath or shower, central heating, phone, TV, minibar **Credit cards** AE, DC, MC, V **Closed** mid-Oct to Mar

---

Mountain chalet, Livigno

Camana Veglia

A delightful old wooden chalet, close to ski lifts, at the north end of this high, remote ski resort. It is a popular place to eat, with abundant local colour, but also a welcoming place to stay – provided of course you don't mind a certain simplicity. Garage.

■ via Ostaria, 107, 23030 Livigno (Sondrio) **Tel & Fax** (0342) 996310/996904 **Meals** breakfast, lunch, dinner **Prices** DB&B LL (for 7-day stay) **Rooms** 10 suites; 2 singles, all with bath or shower, 6 with whirlpool bath, phone, TV **Credit cards** AE, DC, V **Closed** May to mid-Jun, Nov

---

Town hotel, Mantua

Broletto

Sandwiched between the arcaded Piazza delle Erbe and the huge Piazza Sordello, the little Broletto has an unbeatable location. It is a new building in an old shell, with the emphasis on clean simplicity. Bedrooms are compact, staff friendly.

■ Via Accademia 1, 46100 Mantua **Tel** (0376) 326784 **Fax** (0376) 221297 **Meals** breakfast **Prices** rooms LL; breakfast L12,000 **Rooms** 16 all with bath or shower, central heating, air-conditioning, minibar, phone, satellite TV, radio **Credit cards** AE, DC, MC, V **Closed** Christmas and New Year

---

Town hotel, Mantua

San Lorenzo

There are fine views of historic Mantua from the terrace of this centrally situated hotel, close to the famous Piazza delle Erbe. Within, the hotel has all the modern comforts (opened in 1967 and recently extensively renovated) but retains an old-fashioned ambience, with ornate furnishings. Bedrooms are tastefully furnished with handsome antiques. Garage.

■ Piazza Concordia 14, 46100 Mantua (Mantova) **Tel** (0376) 220500 **Fax** (0376) 327194 **E-mail** hotel@hotelsanreo.it www.hotelsan lorenzo.it **Meals** breakfast **Prices** rooms LLL with breakfast; suites LLL-LLLL **Rooms** 32, all with bath or shower, central heating, air-conditioning, phone, satellite TV, hairdrier, minibar **Credit cards** AE, DC, MC, V **Closed** never

Lombardia

Town inn, Milan

Antica Locanda Solferino

A surprise in glossy Milan: a simple and modestly priced inn with a rather rustic character. Compact, prettily decorated bedrooms with traditional-style bathrooms. The inn incorporates a separately managed, cosily traditional Paris-style bistro.

Via Castelfidardo 2, 20121 Milan **Tel** (02) 659 2706 **Fax** (02) 657 1361 **Meals** breakfast, brunch **Prices** rooms LL-LLL with breakfast **Rooms** 11, all with bath, central heating, phone **Credit cards** AE, MC, V **Closed** 15 days in Aug

---

Town hotel, Milan

Pierre Milano

A welcome addition to the Milan scene – the old hotel Torino, reborn in 1987 as a hotel of great style and luxury, with a calm atmosphere and personal service. It is set in a relatively quiet area, about 1 km SW of the duomo. Rooms mix occasional antiques in to modern decorative schemes.

■ Via de Amicis 32, 20123 Milan **Tel** (02) 7200 0581 **Fax** (02) 805 2157 **Meals** breakfast, lunch, dinner, snacks **Prices** rooms LLL-LLLL with breakfast; suite LLLL **Rooms** 49, all with bath or shower, central heating, air-conditioning, phone, hairdrier, TV, radio, minibar **Credit cards** AE, DC, MC **Closed** Aug

---

Restaurant-with-rooms, Ranco

Sole

The fifth generation of Brovellis is now in charge here (Carlo), assisted by the sixth (Davide). Carlo's renowned fish specialities are served in friendly but formal style on the lake-view terrace or the refined restaurant. Accommodation is in newly built, swish suites, with terraces and views.

■ Piazza Venezia 5, Lago Maggiore, 21020 Ranco (Varese) **Tel** (0331) 976507 **Fax** (0331) 976620 **Meals** breakfast, lunch, dinner **Prices** rooms LLLL with breakfast; meals LL-LLL **Rooms** 8, and 6 suites, all with bath, central heating, minibar, lake-view terrace, air-conditioning, safe, TV **Credit cards** AE, DC, MC, V **Closed** Jan

---

Country hotel, Riva di Solto

Miranda da Oreste

This modest, modern hotel may be thin on charm, but it is well run and enjoys a splendid position, high up above Lake Iseo, with views shared by the rooms, restaurant, terrace, garden and fair-sized swimming-pool. 'Outstanding food,' says a visitor. And you will find few respectable hotels in Italy offering lower prices.

■ Via Cornello 8, Zorzino, 24060 Riva di Solto (Bergamo) **Tel** (035) 986021 **Fax** (035) 980055 **Meals** breakfast, lunch, dinner **Prices** rooms L-LL with breakfast; DB&B L-LL; FB L-LL **Rooms** 22, all with bath or shower, central heating, phone **Credit cards** AE, MC, V **Closed** Jan

Lombardia

Town hotel, Sabbioneta

Al Duca

Family-run, no-frills but spick-and-span hotel behind a Renaissance façade, close to the central square of a neglected but historic town. The emphasis is on the restaurant – a modest but well-run trattoria. Rooms are modern and bright; 'the welcome is friendly and helpful,' says a satisfied visitor.

■ Via della Stamperia 18, 46018 Sabbioneta (Mantova) **Tel** (0375) 52474 **Fax** (0375) 220021 **Meals** breakfast, lunch, dinner **Prices** rooms L-LL with breakfast; DB&B L (min 3 day stay); lunch and dinner L **Rooms** 10, all with bath or shower, central heating, phone **Credit cards** AE, MC, V **Closed** Jan

Country villa, San Fedele d'Intelvi

Villa Simplicitas

A saffron-coloured 19thC villa in a beautiful country setting high above the lakes. Each room has its own particular interest – a rocking-chair here, a grand old mirror there – and there are breathtaking views to the lakes or mountains. Fresh farm produce in the restaurant. Staff very welcoming and relaxed.

■ Tremezzo, 22010 San Fedele d'Intelvi (Como) **Tel** (031) 831132 **Fax** (02) 66802909 **Meals** breakfast, lunch, dinner **Prices** rooms LL with breakfast; DB&B LL; FB LL **Rooms** 10, all with bath, central heating **Credit cards** not accepted **Closed** Oct to April

Lakeside villa, Torno

Villa Flora

The greatest asset of this unpretentious pinkish-orange villa is its superb lakeside situation. Bedrooms vary from spacious to cramped but all are clean and functional. The sitting-room, with its brocade and ornate ceiling, has more character. A French visitor comments on the welcoming staff. Swimming-pool.

■ Via Torrazza 10, Lago di Como, 22020 Torno (Como) **Tel** (031) 419 222 **Fax** (031) 418318 **Meals** breakfast, lunch, dinner **Prices** rooms LL; breakfast LL; DB&B LL; meals L-LL; **Rooms** 20, all with shower, phone **Credit cards** MC, V **Closed** Jan, Feb; restaurant only, Tue

Lakeside hotel, Valsolda

Stella d'Italia

The shaded, gravelled terrace of this much-extended lakeside villa juts right out into the waters of Lake Lugano, offering marvellous views. The house is spacious, prettily refurbished and pleasantly 'lived-in', with pictures, comfortable furniture and lots of books. The food impresses reporters.

■ Piazza Roma 1, San Mamete, 22010 Valsolda (Como) **Tel** (0344) 68139 **Fax** (0344) 68729 **E-mail** stelladitalia@mclink.it **Meals** breakfast, lunch, dinner **Prices** rooms L-LLL with breakfast; reductions for children **Rooms** 35, all with bath or shower, central heating, balcony, phone, TV, safe **Credit cards** AE, MC, V **Closed** mid-Oct to Apr; rest only, Wed

Lombardia

Lakeside hotel, Varenna

Hotel du Lac

The name could not be more appropriate: this small hotel, down an alley off the central piazza, overhangs the waters of Como – and the position is its main attraction. Dinner on the terrace (excellent food and service) is memorable, with breathtaking views across the lake to the surrounding mountains and villages. Inside, neat modern furnishings dominate; bedrooms are small.

■ Via del Prestino 4, 22050 Varenna (Lecco) **Tel** (0341) 830238 **Fax** (0341) 831081 **Meals** breakfast, lunch, dinner **Prices** rooms LL-LLL with breakfast; DB&B LL-LLL; suite LLL; parking L15,000 **Rooms** 18, all with bath or shower, central heating, phone, TV **Credit cards** AE, DC, MC, V **Closed** mid-Nov to Feb; restaurant mid-Oct to mid-Mar

Converted castle, Voghera

Castello di San Gaudenzio

A convenient stopover for travellers on the A7 and A21 motorways, and an impressive hotel in any case. The 14thC brick-built castle has been immaculately restored and sensitively furnished in mainly modern styles. Immensely spacious, and good value. Reservation for dinner is advisable. A reader points out that there are loud chimes twice an hour from the convent clock bell nearby, though it is mute between midnight and 7 am.

■ Cervesina, 27050 Voghera (Pavia) **Tel** (0383) 3331 **Fax** (0383) 333409 **Meals** breakfast, lunch, dinner **Prices** rooms LL-LLLL; 3 suites LLLL **Rooms** 45, all with bath or shower, central heating, TV, minibar, safe, phone, radio; some with air-conditioning **Credit cards** AE, DC, MC, V **Closed** restaurant only, Tue

Readers' Reports

Reports from readers are of enormous interest to us in keeping up to date with the hotels in this guide - and others that should be in it. More information on p11

The north-east

Hotels in the north-east

The remarkable city of Venice, set on islands in a salt-water lagoon, is the focal point of the area and a 'must' to visit for its beautiful buildings, art treasures and the sheer originality of the place. But whether you stay in the city or travel in from a base outside depends on whether you can stand the high prices and the noise and bustle, even late into the night.

A feast of small hotels in Venice are described on the following pages. Some alternatives, too big for a full recommendation in this guide, are: La Fenice et Des Artistes (Tel (041) 523 2333, fax 520 3721, 65 rooms; the Monaco and Grand Canal (Tel (041) 520 0211, fax 520 0501, 70 rooms) set in an excellent position right on the Grand Canal as its name suggest; and the Gritti Palace (Tel (041) 794611, fax 5200942, 88 rooms), an extraordinarily luxurious hotel set in a beautiful postion, also on the Grand Canal. And we must mention the legendary and extravagant Cipriani (Tel (041) 520 7744, fax 520 7745, e-mail cipriani@gpnet.it, 98 rooms) outside the city of Venice itself and reached by the hotel's private launch. Adjacent, and sharing the Cipriani's facilities, are Palazzo Vendramin and Palazzetto Nani Barbaro, with private butler service.

Staying at the fashionable holiday resort of Venice Lido enables you to combine sightseeing with a beach holiday. The Quattro Fontane (Tel (041) 526 0227, fax 526 0726, 64 rooms) would make an acceptable alternative to the Villa Mabapa (page 77) or Villa Parco (page 88).

The Alto Adige, in the extreme north of Italy, is more like Austria than the rest of Italy and is often known as the South Tirol. It is largely a German-speaking area, so place names, hotel tariffs and brochures are often given in Italian and German. Merano is the biggest resort and a central base for the area – recommendations on pages 59-61. Other major towns are Bolzano – see the Castel Guncina on p78 – and Trento – see the Accademia on p69. A near-miss for a full entry is the Villa Madruzzo (Tel (0461) 986220, fax 986361), an imposing, red-and-yellow building in beautiful gardens on the hillside above Trento.

Cortina d'Ampezzo is the main resort in the Dolomites – a smart ski resort in winter, with many winter sports on offer, but also suitable for a summer visit. The Montana (page 55) and the Menardi (page 79) are our recommendations here, but the 45-room Parc Hotel Victoria (Tel (0436) 3246, fax 4734) is also attractively rustic. Equally well known to skiers is Selva, the main resort of Val Gardena; our favourite is the secluded Sporthotel Granvara (Tel (0471) 795250, fax 794336, e-mail granvara@val-gardena.com). In Corvara, is the equally polished and only slightly larger 50-room La Perla (Tel (0471) 836132, fax 836568).

This page acts as an introduction to the features and hotels of North-east Italy, and gives brief recommendations of reasonable hotels that for one reason or another have not made a full entry. The long entries for this region – covering the hotels we are most enthusiastic about – start on the next page. But do not neglect the shorter entries starting on page 78; these are all hotels that we would happily stay at.

The north-east

Country villa, Asolo

Villa Cipriani

Asolo is a beautiful medieval hilltop village commanding panoramic views. The Villa Cipriani is a mellow ochre-washed house on the fringes of the village, the entrance leading directly from the street into a tiled hall with Oriental-style rugs and a grandfather clock, brass wall lights and an efficient welcome from reception. It belongs to the Sheraton group, but there is no chain-hotel atmosphere – staff are friendly and attentive.

A tall covered terrace furnished in rustic style, and with an unusual pierced minstrel's gallery, leads out through glass doors into the prettiest of gardens, well stocked with flowers and partly laid to grass – a mass of roses, azaleas and mature trees. The restaurant areas dog-leg around the outside of the villa, over-hanging the valley below, with views out through plate-glass windows. For cooler evenings, there is a cosy bar. Most bedrooms have lovely views, and are decorated in old-fashioned style, with prints, fresh flowers and antiques adding interest and colour. Pretty tiles have been used for the bathrooms. The views, the comfort and the peaceful garden combine to make this a most relaxing country hotel. Food is reported to be excellent.

Nearby Treviso (35 km); Padua, Vicenza, Venice within reach.

Via Canova 298, Asolo 31011 Treviso
Tel (0423) 952166
Fax (0423)952095
Location on NW side of village; with small garden and private car parking
Food & drink breakfast, lunch, dinner
Prices rooms LLL-LLLL with breakfast; meals about LLL
Rooms 31 double; all rooms have colour TV, phone, air-conditioning

Facilities dining-room, bar, conference room
Credit cards AE, DC, MC, V
Children accepted
Disabled lift/elevator
Pets accepted
Closed never
Manager Giampaolo Burattin

The north-east

Town hotel, Bressanone

Elefante

Bressanone is a pretty little town at the foot of the Brenner Pass, more Austrian than Italian in character. The same is true of the charming old Elefante, which owes its name to a beast which was led over the Alps for the amusement of Emperor Ferdinand of Austria. The only stable which could house the exhausted creature was that next to the inn, so the innkeeper painted an elephant on the side of his inn and changed its name.

There is an air of solid, old-fashioned comfort throughout. Green-aproned staff lead you through corridors packed with heavily carved and beautifully inlaid pieces of antique furniture. The colours are sumptuous: scarlets, greens, copper, gold; turn a corner, and you may encounter an enormous display of purple iris and tulips in a simple iron pot. The bedrooms are generous and handsomely furnished with graceful antiques and solid old pieces. The breakfast room is panelled entirely in intricately carved wood and the main restaurant is wood-floored, with a moulded ceiling and windows looking out on to a little garden area. Much of the produce served here comes from the large walled garden, and from the adjacent farm belonging to the hotel. The formal sitting-room has been decorated in an elegant 18thC style, with mirrors, chandeliers and plush armchairs.

Nearby cathedral; Novacella monastery (3 km); the Dolomites.

Via Rio Bianco 4, Bressanone
39042 Bolzano
Tel (0472) 832750
Fax (0472) 836579
Location at N end of town, in gardens with car parking and garages
Food & drink breakfast, lunch, dinner
Prices rooms LLL with breakfast; meals LL
Rooms 28 double, all with bath and shower; 16 single, 15 with bath, one with shower; all have central heating, colour TV, phone
Facilities 3 dining-rooms, sitting-room, bar; outdoor swimming-pool, 2 tennis-courts
Credit cards DC, MC, V
Children welcome
Disabled not suitable
Pets accepted by arrangement
Closed Jan to Feb
Managers Elisabeth Heiss and Heinrich Radmüller

The north-east

Leuchtenburg

This solid stone-built 16thC hostel, set in a courtyard and surrounded by vineyards, once housed the peasant servants of Leuchtenburg castle, an arduous hour's trek up the steep wooded mountain behind.

Today, guests in the *pensione* are cosseted, while the castle lies in ruins. The young Sparer family does the cosseting, providing good, solid breakfasts and 3-course dinners of regional cuisine in an unpretentious, home-like atmosphere. The white-painted, low-arched dining-chambers occupy the ground floor; above is the reception, with a large table littered with magazines and surrounded by armchairs.

There is a further sitting-area on the second floor, leading to the bedrooms. These have pretty painted furniture, tiled floors and attractive duvet covers; the rooms on the third floor are plainer. All the rooms are of a reasonable size, and some share the wide views enjoyed from the terrace, across vineyards to the Lago di Caldaro, perhaps better known (at least to wine buffs) as Kalterer See.

Nearby Swimming and fishing in lake.

Campi al Lago 100, Caldaro 39052
Tel & fax (0471) 960093
Location 5 km SE of Caldaro (Kaltern), 15 km SE of Bolzano; adequate car parking
Food & drink breakfast, dinner
Prices rooms LL with breakfast; meals L
Rooms 13 double, 2 with bath, 11 with shower; 3 single with shower; 2 family rooms, one with bath, one with shower; one suite for 2 to 4; all rooms have central heating
Facilities dining-area, sitting-area, bar; private beach
Credit cards none
Children accepted
Disabled no special facilities
Pets accepted
Closed Nov-Easter
Proprietor Markus Sparer

Country villa, Cavasagra

Villa Corner della Regina

Driving through the flat agricultural land west of Treviso, it is something of a surprise to come upon this stately Palladian mansion, set in its vast estate and formal grounds at the end of a gravel drive. Lemon trees in huge terracotta pots and an ancient wisteria decorate your path to the entrance on the ground floor, to the side of a vast, sweeping set of stone steps. Once inside, you are greeted with a magnificent floral display, and it is clear that much of the grandeur of the villa has been preserved.

The grandiose central reception room runs the full width of the villa; intricately carved French windows survey the drive, with floor-to-ceiling drapes trimmed in pink contrasting with the dark panelling and matching the deeply cushioned chairs and sofas. The bedrooms in the main house are huge, light and airy. They offer both character and luxury, with period antiques, decorative painted plaster walls, abundant flowers and prints, and thick pile carpets. Those in the converted outbuildings are relatively anonymous, but still spacious and comfortable.

Hans Weber runs the villa in near faultless fashion. The atmosphere is that of an elegant private home; staff are friendly and helpful; and the food is excellent.

Nearby Palladian villas; Venice (40 km).

Cavasagra, Treviso 31050
Treviso
Tel (0423) 481481
Fax (0423) 451100
Location 15 km W of Treviso,
3 km S of road to Vicenza; in
formal gardens and parkland,
with ample car parking
Food & drink breakfast,
lunch, dinner
Prices rooms LLL-LLLL with
breakfast; dinner LL
Rooms 4 double, 7 suites in
villa and 12 apartments in

annexe, all with bath; all have
TV, telephone, minibar
Facilities dining-rooms,
breakfast room (in old
orangery), sitting-room;
heated outdoor swimming-
pool, sauna, tennis
Credit cards AE, DC, MC, V
Children accepted
Disabled not suitable
Pets dogs accepted in annexe
Closed never
Manager Hans Weber

The north-east

Montana

This small, friendly hotel is situated in a pedestrian precinct in the centre of Cortina d'Ampezzo, 1,224 metres above sea level and surrounded by mountain scenery. It is just a few minutes' walk from the Faloria cable car, which makes it a popular choice with skiiers between December and the end of April, so booking in advance is essential.

The Montana is owned and run with great enthusiasm by Adiano Lorenzi, whose passion for art manifests itself in the numerous original paintings he has collected and which decorate the hotel. The bedrooms are rustic in style, with pine floors and ceilings, some with flower-bedecked balconies overlooking the village and mountains. All have immaculate en suite bathrooms. A buffet breakfast with home-made jam is served in a dining area with pretty, red, flower-print tablecloths, or in the bedrooms at a small extra charge.

Cortina is a popular resort – as well as skiing there is also a bobsleigh run, a ski jump, skating and curling. In summer the mild climate makes it an ideal location for walking, fishing, rock climbing and tennis.

Nearby Faloria lift station; ice stadium; the Dolomites.

Corso Italia 94, Cortina d'Ampezzo 32043
Tel (0436) 862126
Fax (0436) 868211
Location in pedestiran precinct in centre of Cortina d'Ampezzo; private car park
Food & drink breakfast
Prices rooms L-LLL with breakfast
Rooms 15 double, 15 single; all with bath or shower; all rooms have phone, TV, safe
Facilities breakfast room

Credit cards AE, DC, MC, V
Children welcome
Disabled not suitable
Pets small dogs accepted
Closed Jun and Nov
Proprietor Adriano Lorenzi

The north-east

Country villa, Dolo

Villa Ducale

Driving along the N11 highway from Padua to Venice, you follow an old canal whose banks are scattered with beautiful 18thC villas, where wealthy Venetians used to escape from the city in summer. Villa Ducale is one of them – surrounded by formal gardens, with statues, a fountain, ancient trees and arbours.

The entrance to the hotel is rather grand. The marble-floored reception area leads into a vast chandeliered dining-hall, with a more modest breakfast room to one side. A grand staircase leads to the bedrooms. Upstairs, the floors are the original decorative wooden parquet, overlaid with patterned rugs. In the bedrooms, much of the furniture is antique and in some the original softly painted walls and ceilings remain. The larger rooms have balconies, and are a generous size. Bathrooms have decorative tiles and gilt fittings, which in lesser surroundings might seem pretentious. Smaller rooms at the rear overlook horse-chestnut trees.

The hotel was extensively refurbished in 1993 and the new management, appears to be more interested in business travellers than holiday guests. The restaurant specializes in fish dishes. Reports, please.

Nearby Venice (20 km); Padua (21 km); Treviso (33 km).

Riviera Martiri della Liberta 75, Dolo 30031 Venezia
Tel & Fax (041) 5608020/5608004
Location 2 km E of Dolo
Food & drink breakfast
Prices rooms LLL; special rates for weekends, and for honeymoon couples
Rooms 11 double, 3 with bath, 8 with shower; one single; all rooms have phone, minibar, safe, air conditioning, terrace

Facilities sitting-room, bar, satellite TV room, dining-room, games room
Credit cards AE, DC, V
Children accepted
Disabled not suitable
Pets accepted if small
Closed never
Manager Marco Fogarin

The north-east

Village hotel, Follina

Villa Abbazia

This is a pleasantly polished bed-and-breakfast hotel, recently recommended to us by a well-satisfied reader. Abbazia, a former 17thC nobeleman's palace, is situated on the Strada del Prosecco, one of the Veneto's food and wine routes, and conveniently situated for the local sights of Asolo, Vittorio Veneto and Possagno.

The building itself is a pleasing double-cube structure, with a charming columned *loggia* giving on to a well-watered lawn and colourful garden. The interior decoration is elegant, perhaps somewhat British, with a predominance of reds and rather masculine vertical stripes, especially in the reception area. Gleaming antiques abound and the lighting is good. Some of the bedrooms have sloping ceilings and exposed beams, but these are used to great effect and the rooms don't feel cramped.

The atmosphere is friendly and aims to be as much like a private house as possible. You can't eat dinner here, but see our recommendation in Solighetto, page 82; or, closer, Da Gigetto in Miane.

Nearby Vittorio Veneto, Asolo, Treviso; villas and medieval towns of the Veneto; Venice.

Piazza IV Novembre, 31051 Follina (Treviso)
Tel (0438) 971277/970535
Fax (0438) 970001
Location in village, with own grounds, ample car parking
Food & drink breakfast only
Prices LL-LLL with breakfast
Rooms 17, all with bath or shower, minibar, satellite TV
Facilities sitting-room, breakfast room, tea room, garden; free green fees for hotel guests at the nearby

Asolo Golf Club
Credit cards AE, DC, MC, V
Children accepted
Disabled no elevator
Pets not accepted
Closed never
Proprietor Ivana Zanon De Marchi

The north-east

Restaurant with rooms, Masi

Mas del Saügo

Secluded hostelries don't come much more remote than this. A good 2 km up a winding forest track that leads to nowhere but the Lagorai mountains, the Mas del Saügo is surrounded by nothing but open meadow, forest, and fresh air.

The state of the derelict barn adjacent to this immaculately renovated 17thC farmhouse gives some idea of the scale of the restoration that the Mas del Saügo needed in the late 1980s – a project undertaken by the previous owners, Donatella Zampoli and Lorenzo Bernardini, a painter and designer. Inside, Lorenzo combined original features with his own distinctive Tyrolean-Cubist styles. The smaller dining-room is all wood, with the original decorated plaster ceiling and traditional ceramic boiler, while the larger dining-room is more formal. A wooden staircase leads down to the enchanting bar in the converted cattle stalls below – an extraordinarily sophisticated affair for such a small and rustic place. Everywhere there are gorgeous smells of wood or herbs – or food. The four bedrooms are individually decorated: some with stone walls and exposed beams, others wood-panelled, all offering peace and tranquillity. The Vinante family took over this compelling establishment in 1991, and aim to keep it much as it was. Reports, please.

Nearby Mountain walks, winter skiing at Cavalese (4 km).

Masi 38033 Cavalese
Tel (0462) 30788
Fax (0462) 21433
Location up mountain track, 4 km SW of Cavalese, 40 km SE of Bolzano; in fields, with ample car parking
Food & drink breakfast, lunch, dinner
Prices rooms LLL with breakfast; dinner LLL
Rooms 3 double, one single, all with shower; all rooms have central heating,
hairdrier
Facilities dining-room, bar
Credit cards V
Children not accepted under 8 years
Disabled no special facilities
Pets not accepted
Closed hotel never; restaurant only, Thu
Proprietors Vinante family

The north-east

Castel Labers

On the hillside to the east of Merano, Castel (or Schloss) Labers is surrounded by its own vineyards, orchards and mountain walks through alpine pastures. The hotel has been in the Neubert family since 1885, but the building itself dates back to the 11th century.

An impressive stone staircase with wrought-iron balustrades leads from the white-walled entrance hall and up to the bedrooms. These all have charming wooden double doors, with sealed wooden floors, simple old furniture, and goose feather duvets in crisp white cotton covers.

The castle gardens are packed with trees and flowering shrubs, which can be admired from the conservatory restaurant, whose windows are draped in country cottons. Leading off this is another restaurant area, with a church-like vaulted wooden ceiling and old panelling round the walls. Fresh local produce is well presented and deliciously cooked.

'Absolutely fantastic, tremendous food, friendly proprietors', enthuses one guest.

Nearby promenades along the Passirio river in Merano; Tirolo Castle (5 km); Passirio valley, the Dolomites.

Via Labers 25, Merano 39012 Bolzano
Tel (0473) 234484
Fax (0473) 234146
Location 2.5 km E of Merano, with private grounds, garage and parking (locked at night)
Food & drink breakfast, lunch, dinner
Prices rooms LL-LLL; DB&B LL; menus from LL
Rooms 22 double, 20 with bath, 2 with shower; 9 single, 2 with bath, 7 with shower; 10 family rooms, all with bath; all have central heating, phone
Facilities dining-room, dining/conservatory, bar, music/reading room, conference room; outdoor heated swimming-pool, tennis
Credit cards AE, DC, MC, V
Children welcome
Disabled not suitable
Pets dogs accepted, but not in dining-room **Closed** Nov to Mar **Proprietors** Stapf-Neubert family

Medieval manor, Merano

Castell Rundegg

Despite its smart facilities, this ancient white-painted house retains a lot of charm. The pretty sitting-room, with plush seats and antiques, overlooks the garden through delicate wrought-iron gates. The restaurant has a cellar-like atmosphere, with its stone-vaulted ceiling and alcove rooms. The bedrooms are luxurious, and many of them have special features – the turret room, reached up spiral steps, commands a 360-degree view.

Nearby Promenades along Passirio river; Passirio valley; the Dolomites; 2 golf courses nearby.

Via Scena 2, Merano 39012 Bolzano
Tel (0473) 234100 **Fax** 237200
Location on E side of town; in gardens, with car parking and garages
Food & drink breakfast, lunch, dinner
Prices DB&B LLL-LLLL; reductions for children under 14
Rooms 22 double, 20 with bath, 2 with shower; 5 single, all with shower; 2 family rooms, both with bath; all rooms have central heating, colour TV, radio, minibar, phone
Facilities 3 dining-rooms, bar, sitting,-room; heated indoor swimming-pool, health and beauty farm **Credit cards** AE, DC, MC, V **Children** welcome
Disabled lift/elevator available **Pets** small dogs accepted only on request
Closed last 3 weeks Jan
Manager P. Castelforte

The north-east

Fragsburg

A lovely drive along a narrow country lane, through mixed woodland and past Alpine pastures where goats and cattle graze, brings you to the wooded outcrop, high up to the east of Merano, where sits the Hotel Fragsburg (or Castel Verruca) – 400 years old, and a hotel for over 100 years..

Externally, Fragsburg still looks very much the hunting lodge, with carved wooden shutters and balconies decked with flowering plants. It enjoys splendid views (notably of the Texel massif), shared by many of the bedrooms; these have been decorated recently in sparkling white, with abundant wood panelling, some old and some new. Downstairs, hearty meals can be enjoyed either in the low-ceilinged dining-areas which have recently been elegantly refurbished, or on one of the terraces. Below are what appear to be dolls' houses; actually they house the bees which provide honey for the wholesome buffet breakfast. In the extensive wooded garden there are areas for lazing in the sun – including a wooden shelter reserved for all-over tanning. 'Superb meals; one of our all-time favourites', enthuses a recent visitor.

Nearby Promenades along the Passirio river in Merano; Passirio valley, the Dolomites, glaciers near Merano.

Via Fragsburg 3,
39012 Merano, Bolzano
Tel (0473) 244071
Fax (0473) 244493
E-mail info@fragsburg.com
Website http://www.fragsburg.com
Location 6 km NE of Merano, with gardens; subtropical trees; ample car parking space, and garages available
Food & drink breakfast, lunch, dinner
Prices DB&B LL-LLL
Rooms 12 double; 2 single; 4 suites; all with bath or shower; all rooms have central heating, phone, TV, safe, hairdrier **Facilities** dining-rooms, sitting-room, terrace; table-tennis, heated outdoor swimming-pool, sauna, gymnasium; lift/elevator
Credit cards not accepted
Children welcome **Disabled** access possible **Pets** accepted by arrangement
Closed Nov to Easter
Proprietors Ortner family

The north-east

Country villa, Mira Porte

Villa Margherita

Yet another country villa in the Venetian hinterland, offering peace, seclusion and a lot of real estate for your money, while being well placed for excursions into Venice itself – and you don't even need to worry about parking when you get there, because there is a regular half-hourly bus service from a stop almost in front of the villa.

Villa Margherita was built in the 17thC as Villa Contarini, one of a series of grand country residences lining the Brenta river – the weekend retreats, as it were, of Venetian nobles. It has been open as a hotel only since late 1987. It is less imposing than some of its rival villa-hotels from the outside, but charmingly furnished and decorated within, particularly in the public areas. The breakfast room is gloriously light, with French windows on to the garden, while the sitting-room has *trompe l'oeil* frescos and an open fireplace. Bedrooms are plainer, perhaps lacking character, but thoroughly comfortable (and some are notably spacious).

The highly regarded restaurant is a short walk from the main building. Service is exactly what you would expect: attentive, and rather formal. Several recent visitors were thoroughly impressed.
Nearby Venice (10 km), Padua (20 km).

Via Nazionale 416, Mira Porte
30030 Venezia
Tel (041) 426 5800
Fax (041) 426 5838
Location on banks of Brenta
river at Mira, 10 km W of
Venice; ample car parking
Food & drink breakfast,
lunch, dinner
Prices rooms LL-LLL; meals
LL
Rooms 18 double, 3 with
bath, 15 with shower; 1 single
with shower; all have central
heating, phone,
air-conditioning, TV, minibar
Facilities breakfast room,
sitting-room, bar, restaurant
(200 m walk); jogging track
Credit cards AE, DC, MC, V
Children accepted
Disabled some rooms on
ground floor
Pets by arrangement
Closed never
Proprietors Dal Corso family

The north-east

Villa Revedin

Amid open countryside just outside the little town of Gorgo al Monticano, the Villa Revedin is sheltered within its own mature, tree-screened park. Formal gardens at the front and an old fountain lead on to the park through cool tree-lined paths.

The villa dates from the 15th century, and the antique atmosphere is well preserved in the huge main salon, which has an imposing grand piano. The restaurant (which attracts local customers, particularly for its fish specialities) is more relaxed, in the familiar Italian sophisticated-rustic style, with wooden ceiling, terracotta tiled floor and cream decorations. The hotel's sitting areas have large leather sofas and chairs, and there is a pretty open fireplace for cooler evenings.

Most of the bedrooms are of generous size; all have pretty views out over the park and gardens. Although most of the furniture is modern, the tall ceilings, shuttered windows, open fireplaces and tasteful decoration lend charm.

This is a luxury hotel, but it is charming and welcoming in a way that most such hotels are not. 'Excellent value, considering the location and meals,' says a recent visitor.

Nearby Treviso (32 km); Venice within reach; Venetian villas.

Via Palazzi 4, Gorgo al Monticano, Oderzo 31040 Treviso
Tel & Fax (0422) 800033
Location 4 km E of Oderzo, signposted just N of Gorgo al Monticano; in private grounds with ample parking
Food & drink breakfast, lunch, dinner
Prices rooms LL-LLL; meals LL-LLL
Rooms 14 double, 14 single, 4 family rooms; all with bath and shower; all rooms have satellite TV, radio, phone, minibar, air-conditioning
Facilities breakfast room, dining-room, function room, bar, sitting-room, conference room (30 people)
Credit cards AE, DC, MC, V
Children very welcome
Disabled not suitable **Pets** not accepted **Closed** restaurant only, 2 weeks in Jan and Aug
Management Programma Revedin s.r.l

The north-east

Villa Quaranta

Ospedaletto earned its name as a stopping-off point on the way to and from the Brenner pass; the Chapel of Santa Maria di Mezza Campagna was where travellers stayed. The original 13thC chapel, with its Ligozzi frescos, now forms one side of the Villa Quaranta's pretty inner courtyard; the remainder of the buildings are 17thC. The main house is rather imposing, but the hotel's reception, dotted with antiques, is in the less intimidating parts behind, with the bedrooms set around the courtyard. The bedrooms are scrupulously clean, with plain carpets, polished stained-wood furniture, and bright shower rooms of pine and white ceramics. Downstairs, there is a snug little converted cellar where the splendid buffet breakfast is served. The staff are generally eager to please, and the manager keeps an eye on things from his garden office.

The formal dining-halls in the main house form the restaurant: awe-inspiring frescoed walls, stone-arched doors and tiled floors, appropriately furnished with red leather straight-back chairs. The food here is an excellent mix of regional and international cuisine. There is no longer a shortage of garden chairs from which to enjoy the wonderful grounds.

Nearby Verona (minibus service to opera); Lake Garda (12 km).

Via Brennero, Ospedaletto di Pescantina 37026 Verona
Tel (045) 6767300
Fax (045) 6767301
Location on SS12, 15 km NW of Verona
Food & drink breakfast, lunch, dinner
Prices rooms LL-LLL with breakfast; suites LLL-LLLL; DB&B LL-LLL
Rooms 14 double, 4 single, 11 family rooms, all with bath; all rooms have central

heating, air-conditioning, phone, TV, radio, minibar
Facilities 4 dining-rooms, bar, TV room; Club House with swimming-pool, 2 tennis courts, sauna and beauty centre; disco
Credit cards AE, DC, MC, V
Children no special facilities
Disabled lift/elevator
Pets not accepted
Closed hotel never; restaurant Mon
Manager Michael Trüb

The north-east

Country hotel, Rasun di Sopra

Ansitz Heufler

This converted 16thC castle is a bit too close to the road up the Anterselva valley to rate as truly idyllic. But it is undoubtedly one of the most beautiful buildings in the area, inside and out. Fir trees shelter the chairs and tables scattered on the lawn in front; once inside, traffic is soon forgotten: a large pine table serves as reception where guests are met by young and cheerful staff.

All the public rooms are pine-panelled, with rugs and skins, rustic wooden tables, benches and amply cushioned sofas and armchairs. The main sitting-room on the first floor is the real gem: here the panelling is intricately inlaid, and there is a vast traditional ceramic stove reminiscent of a castle tower. Breakfast is taken in the snug bar, while other meals are served by smart, lace-aproned waitresses in the equally cosy dining-rooms. The *carte* offers good solid Tyrolean fare, with liberal use of alcohol. Chocolate truffles in Grand Marnier can be just what the doctor ordered when it's snowing outside. The bedrooms, set around a large open hall and gallery, are all of ample size, though you have to mind your head on low door lintels at times. In the majority, the pine fixtures are original.

Nearby Walking, cycling, and winter skiing at Brunico.

39030 Rasun di Sopra
Tel (0474) 46288
Fax (0474) 48199
Location in wooded Anterselva valley, 10 km E of Brunico; with garden and car parking
Food & drink breakfast, lunch, dinner
Prices rooms LL-LLL with breakfast; DB&B LL
Rooms 9 double, 3 with bath, 6 with shower; all rooms have central heating, telephone

Facilities dining-room, sitting-room, breakfast room, bar
Credit cards MC, V
Children accepted
Disabled no special facilities
Pets accepted
Closed November; 15 May to 15 Jun
Manager Valentin Pallhuber

The north-east

Converted castle, San Paolo

Schloss Korb

Rising up above the fertile vineyards and orchards that surround the outskirts of Bolzano is the 11thC medieval tower which forms the centrepiece of Schloss Korb.

The entrance to the hotel is a riot of colour – flowering shrubs and plants set against walls of golden stone and whitewash. Inside, furnishings and decorations are in traditional style, and antiques and fresh flowers abound. Reception is a cool, dark, tiled hall, set about with brass ornaments and armoury – the oldest part of the hotel. Surrounding the main restaurant areas is a terrace, hanging out over the valley and awash with plants, where breakfast and drinks can be enjoyed.

The bedrooms in the castle are generous in size, with separate sitting-areas and lovely views out over the vineyards. Duvet covers give a warm, friendly feel. The detached annexe behind the main building has a heated indoor pool and lift/elevator – the latter being the attraction for some of the guests.

The daughter of the family (shadowed everywhere by her enormous Great Dane) speaks fluent English.

Nearby sights of Bolzano; Merano within reach; the Dolomites.

Missiano, San Paolo 39050 Bolzano
Tel (0471) 636000
Fax (0471) 636033
Location 8 km W of Bolzano, in gardens, large car park
Food & drink breakfast, lunch, dinner
Prices rooms LLL with breakfast; DB&B LLL-LLLL; meals LL; reductions for children in family room
Rooms 55 double, 2 single, 3 suites all with bath or shower; all rooms have central heating, phone, TV
Facilities dining-room, conference rooms, bar, sitting-rooms (one with TV); sauna, beauty salon, outdoor and heated indoor swimming-pools, tennis **Credit cards** not accepted **Children** welcome
Disabled lift to annexe bedrooms; awkward for wheelchairs **Pets** accepted
Closed Nov to Mar
Proprietors Dellago family

The north-east

Lakeside inn, San Vigilio

Locanda San Vigilio

In general the east side of Lake Garda is more downmarket than the west. A conspicuous exception is the Punta de San Vigilio; this verdant peninsula, dotted with olive trees and grazing ponies, is entirely owned by Count Agostino Guarienti, who lives in the impressive 16thC villa that dominates the headland. To the left of the big house, down a cobbled lane, nestling between the hillside and a miniature harbour, is this secluded inn of more modest proportions, which a recent visitor recommends for its complete peacefulness. Inside, blue carpets lend sophistication to the rustic furniture, white walls and wooden doors. Bedrooms are decorated in suitable antique style.

It is in the evening that the Locanda really comes into its own. With the day-trippers departed, guests are free to wander the peninsula, take a drink at one of the tables on the harbour wall, or join the Count for the evening meal in the Locanda (he eats here practically every night). The restaurant is candle-lit, and there is a walled garden dining-terrace with giant canvas parasols; both overlook the lake. The menu is recited to guests by the smart, cheerful staff. Lake Garda carp is an inevitable house speciality, but there can be no better setting for it.

Nearby Garda (2 km).

San Vigilio 37016 Garda
Tel (045) 725 6688
Fax (045) 6551
Location 2 km W of Garda, on promontory; parking available 150 metres away
Food & drink breakfast, lunch, dinner
Prices rooms LLL-LLLL with breakfast
Rooms 7 double, 4 suites, all with bath and shower; all rooms have central heating, air-conditioning, phone, TV

Facilities restaurant, dining-terrace, sitting-room, bar; walled garden
Credit cards AE, DC, V
Children accepted if well behaved
Disabled no special facilities
Pets accepted if well behaved
Closed Dec to Mar
Proprietor Count Agostino Guarienti

The north-east

Gardesana

Torri del Benaco is one of the showpiece villages of Lake Garda – a picturesque fishing port of immaculately restored medieval houses, a 14thC castle and an attractive waterfront with beautiful lake views. The Gardesana has a plum position on the main piazza, facing the busy little harbour.

The building has a long history, as its exterior would suggest, with its stone arcades and mellow stucco walls; but the entire interior was recently smartly modernized to produce an essentially modern and rather smart hotel. Bedrooms have been refurbished and are almost all identical – wooden furnishings, soft green fabrics, comfortable beds, and plenty of little extras – and most have views of the lake, sufficiently beautiful to have elicited a poem from Stephen Spender when he stayed here in 1959 and 1988. The historic Hall of the Ancient Council makes a suitably elegant dining-room, with Venetian-style mosaic flooring, and there are a few tables for *à la carte* meals on the balcony which overlooks the lake. There is a much more extensive ground-floor terrace for drinks. Breakfast includes ham, cheese, pâté, yoghurt, fresh fruit and home-made jams.

Nearby Bardolino (11 km), Malcesine (21 km).

Piazza Calderini 20, 37010 Torri del Benaco, Lago di Garda (Verona)
Tel (045) 722 5411
Fax (045) 722 5771
E-mail gardesana@easynet.it
Location in middle of resort, on waterfront; private car parking 150 m away
Food & drink buffet breakfast, dinner *à la carte*
Prices rooms LL-LLL; reduction for children sharing parents' room; dinner L-LL
Rooms 31 double, 4 with bath, 27 with shower; 3 single, all with shower; all rooms have central heating, air-conditioning, phone, satellite TV **Facilities** dining-room, bar, lakeside terrace **Credit cards** AE, DC, MC, V
Children welcome
Disabled no special facilities
Pets not accepted **Closed** Nov and Dec **Proprietor** Giuseppe Lorenzini

The north-east

Accademia

The old centre of Trento is much quieter now that traffic restrictions are in force, and this recently converted medieval house lies on a tiny street right in the heart of it. Quaint wooden shutters and geranium-filled window boxes break up the four storeys of the elegant cream-stucco façade. Inside, all is in the best contemporary taste: white vaulted chambers, parquet floors, classic modern furniture, and strategically placed antique pieces and old maps. There are plenty of comfortable sofas, some on a small wooden gallery above the bar – ideal for a quiet drink. The smart staff have an air of calm efficiency about them. The atmosphere is carried through to the bedrooms which are bright and airy, only the singles being a bit on the small side. You will find all the facilities you could wish for – tastefully presented, of course – right down to the electric shoe polishing machine on the landing. Breakfast is a particular pleasure when taken on the walled terrace, shaded by a giant horse-chestnut tree. The restaurant – another white vaulted room, with crisp white table-cloths and simple wooden and wicker chairs – is a Trento favourite. The *gnochetti di ricotta* are not to be missed.

Nearby Church of Santa Maria, Piazza del Duomo.

Vicolo Colico 4/6, 38100 Trento
Tel (0461) 233600
Fax (0461) 230174
Location in historic middle of town, between *duomo* and Piazza Dante
Food & drink breakfast, lunch, dinner
Prices rooms LL-LLL; meals L
Rooms 32 double, 16 with bath, 16 with shower; 9 single with shower; 2 family rooms with bath; all rooms have central heating, telephone, air-conditioning, TV, minibar, hairdrier
Facilities dining-room, sitting-room, bar, breakfast room, terrace
Credit cards AE, DC, V
Children accepted
Disabled lift/elevator
Pets accepted
Closed Christmas; restaurant Mon
Proprietor Sig. Fambri

The north-east

Town guest-house, Venice

Accademia

Though it is not quite the bargain it used to be, the Accademia is still a place of immense charm and character with prices that most people can afford and a very convenient but tranquil location. But what really distinguishes the *pensione* is its gardens – the spacious patio facing the canal, where tables are scattered among potted plants and classical urns, and the grassy garden at the back where wisteria, roses and fruit trees flourish. 'Wonderful,' reports one visitor. 'To return from a day of crowded sightseeing and enter the garden patio is like entering a private retreat.'

It was originally built as a private mansion, and earlier this century housed the Russian consulate. There are still touches of grandeur, and the furnishings for the most part are classically Venetian. But there is no trace whatever of formality. Reception is a spacious hallway-cum-salon, with ample seating, stretching between two gardens. The airy breakfast room has chandeliers and a beamed ceiling supported by columns; but, weather permitting, guests will inevitably opt to start their day in the garden, and end it there with evening drinks. 'Delightful staff' says one recent report; 'service can be less than obliging' says another.
Nearby Accademia gallery, Grand Canal.

Fondamenta Maravegie,
Dorsoduro 1058, Venice
30123
Tel (041) 523 7846
Fax (041) 523 9152
Location on side canal just S
of Grand Canal, with gardens
front and back
Food & drink breakfast
Prices rooms LLL
Rooms 20 double, 8 with
bath, 8 with shower; 6 single,
5 with bath; all rooms have
central heating, phone, TV

Facilities breakfast room, bar,
sitting-room
Credit cards AE, DC, MC, V
Children welcome
Disabled no special facilities
Pets not accepted
Closed never
Manager Giovanna Salmaso
and Massimo Dinato

The north-east

Alboretti

Enthusiastic students of Venetian painting will find this little hotel the most convenient in Venice – it lies right alongside the gallery of the Accademia.

Like many small hotels in Venice, the Alboretti occupies a building which is several centuries old, but what distinguishes it from many others is the warm welcome and the genuine family atmosphere – something of a rarity in Venice. Reception is a cosy wood-panelled room with a model of a 17thC galleon in its window; the sitting-room is small but the upper TV room is a comfortable retreat (the TV is rarely used). The restaurant offers traditional cooking, and Signora Linguerri is proud of her range of Italian wines.

Single bedrooms and family rooms have a naval theme, while double bedrooms are equipped with antique furniture. Some bathrooms have recently been modernized and enlarged. Like the rest of the hotel, everything is well cared for and spotlessly clean.

We have received no reports recently about Alboretti, but we still believe it is thoroughly recommendable.

Nearby Accademia gallery, Zattere, Gesuati church.

Accademia 882, Venice 30123
Tel (041) 523 0058
Fax (041) 521 0158
Location between the Grand Canal and Giudecca Canal; nearest landing-stage
Food & drink breakfast, lunch, dinner
Prices rooms LL-LLL with breakfast
Rooms 13 double, 8 with bath, 5 with shower; 6 single, all with showers; one family room with bath; all rooms have central heating, air-conditioning, phone, satellite TV, hairdrier
Facilities sitting-room, dining-room, bar
Credit cards AE, DC, MC, V
Children welcome – cots on request
Disabled no special facilities
Pets small dogs only accepted
Closed restaurant only, Wed and Thur lunch
Proprietor Anna Linguerri

The north-east

Flora

Such is the popularity of this small hotel, tucked away in a cul-de-sac close to St Mark's, that to get a room here you have to book weeks or even months in advance. You only need to glimpse the garden to understand why it is so sought after. Creepers, fountains and flowering shrubs cascading from stone urns create an enchanting setting for morning coffee and croissants, or evening drinks in summer. It is undoubtedly one of the prettiest and quietest gardens in Venice – somehow far removed from the hubbub of St Mark's.

The lobby is small and inviting, enhanced by the views of the garden through a glass arch. The atmosphere is one of friendly efficiency, reception acting as a mini tourist information bureau for the many English-speaking guests. There are some charming double bedrooms with painted carved antiques and other typically Venetian furnishings, but beware of other comparatively spartan rooms, some of which are barely big enough for one, let alone two. Prices are quite steep – but a recent guest endorses our view that the setting, the intimate atmosphere and closeness to Venice make it well worth the cost.
Nearby Piazza San Marco

Calle Larga 22 Marzo 2283/a,
San Marco, Venice 30124
Tel (041) 520 5844
Fax (041) 522 8217
Location 300 m from Piazza
San Marco in cul-de-sac
Food & drink breakfast
Prices rooms LLL with
breakfast
Rooms 32 double, 6 single,
6 family rooms; all with bath
and/or shower; all rooms
have air-conditioning, phone
Facilities breakfast room, bar,

sitting-room
Credit cards AE, DC, MC, V
Children accepted
Disabled 2 ground-floor
bedrooms
Pets accepted
Closed never
Proprietor Roger Romanelli

The north-east

Town hotel, Venice

Pausania

The San Barnaba area, traditionally the home of impecunious Venetian nobility, is quiet and picturesque, and now highly desirable as the better-known San Marco area becomes increasingly tourist-ridden and overpriced. The Pausania is a small hotel lying close to the last surviving floating vegetable shop in Venice – a colourful barge on the San Barnaba canal.

The building is quintessentially Venetian, a weathered Gothic *palazzo* with distinctive ogee windows. Inside, timbered ceilings, Corinthian columns, an old well-head and a battered stone staircase are features of the original building. Bedrooms (some very small) are smartly furnished in tastefully restrained and restful blues and creams. Occupants of rooms with a view (overlooking the canal – beware mosquitoes) may be gently awakened by bells from a nearby campanile, but not indecently early. Breakfast is served in a light, modern extension overlooking a secluded garden. Unusually for a small city hotel, there are several comfortable spaces to sit, including a sunny canal-side landing and a lounge of beams and classical supporting pillars. Reasonable prices, and friendly and helpful staff – rare virtues in Venice.
Nearby Scuola dei Carmini, Accademia gallery.

Dorsoduro 2824,
Venice 30124
Tel (041) 522 2083
Location short walk W of Grand Canal; with terrace
Food & drink breakfast
Prices rooms LLL-LLLL with breakfast
Rooms 23 double, 5 with bath, 18 with shower; 3 single, all with shower; 5 family rooms, one with bath, 4 with shower; all rooms have central heating, TV, air-conditioning, phone
Facilities breakfast room, bar, reading-room
Credit cards AE, MC, V
Children welcome
Disabled not suitable
Pets only small ones accepted
Closed never
Proprietor Guido Gatto

The north-east

La Residenza

This grand Gothic *palazzo* dominates the quiet, neglected square of Campo Bandiera e Moro. Just to enter is an experience: press the button on the lion's mouth on the left of the huge entrance doors and they swing open to reveal an ancient covered courtyard. A wrought-iron gate moves to one side to admit you up the ancient stone steps to the reception and sitting-room – a vast hall with mullioned windows, furnished with soft couches and antiques. The soft pastel shades of the walls add to the feeling of faded grandeur and immersion in Venice's history. Our inspector was not allowed to see any bedrooms; look before you leap.
Nearby Scuola di San Giorgio degli Schiavoni.

Campo Bandiera e Moro
3608, Castello, Venice 30122
Tel (041) 528 5315
Fax (041) 523 8859
Location on a small square,
100m back from the main
waterfront; nearest
landing-stage Arsenale
Food & drink breakfast
Prices rooms LL-LLL with
breakfast
Rooms 13 double, 3 with
bath, 10 with shower; 2 single,
with shower; all rooms have
air-conditioning, phone,
TV, minibar
Facilities large
sitting- room
Credit cards AE, DC, MC, V
Children not accepted
Disabled not suitable
Pets not accepted
Closed never
Proprietor Sg Ballestra

The north-east

Santo Stefano

If you follow the popular route from Piazza San Marco to the Accademia gallery you will walk across the Campo Santo Stefano (which, just to confuse you, is also called the Campo Francesco Morosini). It is a large, lively and rambling square whose best-known features are the alarmingly tilted *campanile* of the church of Santo Stefano and the once-famed café/*gelateria* Paolin.

Close to all the activity lies the Santo Stefano, a welcoming and well-cared-for little hotel whose front rooms have views of the piazza. It is not a spacious place; downstairs there is only a modest reception area with a few ornate chairs, a tiny breakfast room and an even tinier courtyard terrace at the back; and upstairs the bedrooms are barely big enough for two. But lack of size is made up for in other ways. The decoration is exceptionally pretty – many of the bedrooms are decked out with painted furniture and pretty pink fabrics – and it is kept in immaculate condition throughout. Welcoming staff, and guests are offered free entrance to the Casino as well as a one-way trip to Murano Island.
Nearby Accademia gallery, Grand Canal.

Campo Santo Stefano, San Marco 2957, Venice 30124 **Tel** (041) 520 0166 **Fax** (041) 522 4460 **Location** on large square about 500 m W of Piazza San Marco; nearest landing-stage San Samuele; car park (reduction for hotel guests at Tronchetto Island Parking) **Food & drink** breakfast **Prices** rooms LLL-LLLL; air-conditioning extra L15,000	**Rooms** 6 double, 2 single, 3 family rooms, all with shower; all rooms have phone, minibar, air-conditioning, satellite TV, safe, bathroom scales **Facilities** breakfast room, hall, tiny rear courtyard **Credit cards** AE, MC, V **Children** accepted **Disabled** not suitable **Pets** not accepted **Closed** never **Manager** Roberto Quatrini

The north-east

Town guest-house, Venice

Seguso

Sitting on the wide sunny promenade of the Zattere gives you the distinct feeling of being by the seaside. The quayside is lapped by the choppy waters of the wide Guidecca canal. This open setting, with a grand panorama across the lagoon, is just one of the charms of the Seguso. A *pensione* in the old tradition, it is family-run, friendly and solidly old-fashioned, and, we are pleased to report, remains unchanged. Also (unlike most hotels in Venice) prices are modest; the Seguso is not noted for its food, but half-board here costs no more than bed and breakfast alone in hotels of similar comfort closer to San Marco.

The best bedrooms are the large ones at the front of the house, overlooking the canal – though for the privilege of the views and space you may have to forfeit the luxury of a private bathroom (only half the rooms have their own facilities). The main public rooms are the dining-room, prettily furnished in traditional style, and the modest sitting-room where you can sink into large leather chairs and peruse ancient editions of travel and guide books. Breakfast is taken on a small terrace at the front of the hotel – delightful.

Nearby Accademia gallery, Gesuati church.

Zattere 779, Dorsoduro, Venice 30123
Tel (041) 528 6858
Fax (041) 522 2340
Location 5 minutes S of Accademia, overlooking Guidecca canal; nearest landing-stage Zattere
Food & drink breakfast, lunch, dinner
Prices DB&B LL-LLL; reductions for children
Rooms 31 double, 5 single; 9 with bath, 9 with shower; all rooms have phone
Facilities dining-room, sitting-room, terrace
Credit cards AE, MC, V
Children welcome
Disabled lift/elevator
Pets accepted
Closed Dec to Feb
Proprietors Seguso family

The north-east

Villa Mabapa

Despite the extensions to the original 1930s family house, giving this comfortable hotel more rooms than we normally allow in these pages, Villa Mabapa still manages to give the impression of a private home. What is more, it is good value, particularly in comparison with the large, better-known hotels on the beach at the Lido. The hotel is set in a garden beside the lagoon, with a private landing stage (the public water-bus stop is a few minutes away). The location may be slightly out of the way, being neither on the main Lido thoroughfare nor on the beach, but has the bonus of wonderfully peaceful rooms, a garden and a summer dining terrace with wonderful sunset views.

The hotel consists of two buildings. Villa Mabapa itself contains the high-ceilinged public rooms and some traditional-style bedrooms; the best are on the first floor – as is the sitting-room, with a terrace giving views of the lagoon. Within the garden is the modern annexe of Villa Morea, with more up-to-date bedrooms.

The name? It consists of the first syllables of the words mamma, bambino and pappa. A family home indeed.
Nearby Venice.

Riviera San Nicolo' 16,
Venice Lido 30126 Venice
Tel (041) 526 0590
Fax (041) 526 9441
E-mail info@villamabapa.com
Website www.villamabapa.com
Location on the lagoon side of the Lido, with fine views of city; in gardens; parking
Food & drink breakfast, lunch, dinner
Prices rooms LL-LLLL, with buffet breakfast; meals L-LL
Rooms 50 double, 10 single, all with bath or shower; all have TV, phone, safe, hairdrier, air-conditioning
Facilities dining-room, dining terrace, bar, sitting-room; beach
Credit card AE, DC, MC, V
Children accepted
Disabled not suitable
Pets no dogs allowed in dining-room
Closed never
Proprietor Sg Vianello

Country villa, Arcugnano

Villa Michelangelo

This rather severe-looking 18thC villa was a Capuchin college before it became a hotel, and there is a monastic purity about its decorative style even now. Black slate floors and leather chairs contrast with white walls. Two restaurants, extensive grounds and swimming-pool.

■ Via Sacco 19, 36057 Arcugnano (Vicenza) **Tel** (0444) 550300 **Fax** (0444) 550490 **Meals** breakfast, lunch, dinner **Prices** rooms LL-LLLL; meals LL **Rooms** 55, all with bath or shower, central heating, air-conditioning, phone, TV, radio, minibar **Credit cards** AE, DC, MC, V **Closed** never

---

Converted castle, Bolzano

Castel Guncina

Yet another of north-east Italy's handsome hilltop castles with fine views, in this case over Bolzano. Surrounded by trees and vineyards, the hotel also offers an attractive pool and tennis courts. Comfortable and well-equipped bedrooms, varying in size and outlook. Large groups and conferences only.

■ Via Miramonti 9, Guncina, 39100 Bolzano **Tel** (0471) 285742 **Fax** (0471) 266345 **Meals** breakfast, lunch, dinner **Prices** rooms L-LLL with breakfast **Rooms** 18, all with bath, central heating, phone, TV, radio, minibar **Credit cards** MC, V **Closed** Feb; restaurant only, Tue

---

Town hotel, Bressanone

Dominik

A deeply comfortable and well-run modern hotel, close to the river on the green fringes of Bressanone. Most of the spacious and well-equipped bedrooms have been refurbished and now have jacuzzis. Public areas have more style, and the garden is pretty. Large, indoor swimming-pool.

■ Via Terzo di Sotto 13, 39042 Bressanone (Bolzano) **Tel** (0472) 830 144 **Fax** (0472) 836554 **Meals** breakfast, lunch, dinner **Prices** rooms LLL; meals LL **Rooms** 29, all with bath, central heating, phone, TV, radio, hairdrier, minibar **Credit cards** AE, MC, V **Closed** 6 Jan to Easter

---

Restaurant-with-rooms, Cividale del Friuli

Locanda al Castello

Although quite properly described as a restaurant with rooms, this crenellated hilltop building is a welcoming and restful place to stay, with a large terrace accommodating easy chairs. The two dining-rooms are uncomfortably large, but the bedrooms have a pleasantly rustic Alpine feel, and spotless bathrooms.

■ Via del Castello 20, 33043 Cividale del Friuli (Udine) **Tel** (0432) 733242 **Fax** (0432) 700901 **Meals** breakfast, lunch, dinner **Prices** rooms L-LL meals L **Rooms** 10, all with bath or shower, phone, TV **Credit cards** AE, MC, V **Closed** a few days in Nov

The north-east

Mountain chalet, Colfosco

Cappella

A typical (small) example of the classical Sud Tirol hotel – modern (late 1960s), but in Alpine chalet style; thoroughly comfortable and welcoming, with richly traditional furnishings; well equipped with sports facilities (pleasant indoor pool); spectacular scenery, with skiing or walking from the door. Adjacent to Cappella, the 'Residence' has further stylish accommodation.

■ 39030 Colfosco (Bolzano) **Tel** (0471) 836183 **Fax** (0471) 836561 **Meals** breakfast, lunch, dinner **Prices** rooms LL-LLL; meals L-LL reduction for children **Rooms** 40, all with bath or shower, central heating, phone, radio, TV **Credit cards** DC, MC, V **Closed** mid-Apr to mid-Jun, end Sep to mid-Dec

---

Country hotel, Cortina d'Ampezzo

Menardi

This old farmhouse on the northern side of Cortina has evolved over the years from country inn to pensione to polished hotel. Despite the elegant antiques and modern comforts, it retains its traditional warmth. The large garden is a secluded delight.

■ Via Majon 110, 32043 Cortina d'Ampezzo (Belluno) **Tel** (0436) 2400 **Fax** (0436) 862183 **Meals** breakfast, lunch, dinner **Prices** rooms LL-LLL with breakfast; FB LL-LLL **Rooms** 51, all with bath, central heating, phone, TV **Credit cards** V **Closed** Oct to mid-Dec; mid-Apr to mid-Jun

---

Country hotel, Fiè Allo Sciliar

Turm

A polished, warmly welcoming hotel in the best Sudtirol tradition, between Bolzano and the well-known ski resorts of Val Gardena. There are cosy sitting-rooms, a rustic bar, indoor and outdoor pools. And the proprietor has built up an impressive collection of paintings on the walls.

■ Piazza della Chiesa 9, 39050 Fiè Allo Sciliar (Bolzano) **Tel** (0471) 725014 **Fax** (0471) 725474 **Meals** breakfast, lunch, dinner **Prices** rooms LL-LL with breakfast; DB&B LL; reductions for children **Rooms** 19; 7 suites; all with bath, central heating, TV, radio, phone **Credit cards** MC, V **Closed** mid-Nov to Feb

---

Country hotel, Malcesine

Park Hotel Querceto

This stylish new hotel, opened only in 1991, has a splendid panoramic position on the slopes of Monte Baldo, overlooking lake Garda. Outside, a terrace makes the most of the view; inside, abundant rustic woodwork and traditionally furnished bedrooms.

■ Loc. Campiano, 17-19, 37018 Malcesine (Verona) **Tel** (045) 740 0344 **Fax** (045) 740 0848 **Meals** breakfast, lunch, dinner **Prices** DB&B LL-LLL **Rooms** 20, all with bath or shower, phone, minibar, radio, satellite TV **Credit cards** AE, DC, MC, V **Closed** for a period in Nov

The north-east

Country hotel, Lagundo

Der Pünthof

Part of the Pünthof dates back to the Middle Ages, when it was a farmhouse, and the breakfast rooms retain traces of the original decoration on their panelled walls. Some bedrooms also have an antique atmosphere, but most are in little, detached chalets of recent vintage, with their own kitchen facilities. Good pool.

■ Via Steinach 25, 39022 Lagundo (Bolzano) **Tel** (0473) 448553 **Fax** (0473) 449919 **Meals** breakfast, dinner **Prices** DB&B LLL; meals L **Rooms** 12, all with bath or shower, central heating, TV, radio, minibar, phone, safe **Credit cards** DC **Closed** mid-Nov to Mar

Country hotel, Merano

Villa Tivoli

This rather plain-looking hotel in 'exquisite' gardens on the outskirts of Merano has our reporter hooked: 'our corner room an oasis of calm; staff warm, welcoming, spontaneously wonderful; breakfast a mountainous buffet; dinner original, bounteous, delicious; unrivalled value'. Regional specialities in the Artemis restaurant. Indoor pool and bicycles.

■ via Verdi, 72, 39012 Merano (Bolzano) **Tel** (0473) 46282 **Fax** (0473) 46849 **Meals** breakfast, lunch, dinner **Prices** rooms LL-LLL; DB&B LL **Rooms** 21, all with bath or shower, phone **Credit cards** AE, MC, V **Closed** Nov to Mar

Country villa, Paderno di Ponzano

El Toulà

People come from far and wide to experience the restaurant of this lovingly converted old farmhouse, where classic dishes are re-interpreted according to new ideas. Bedrooms vary from extremely comfortable to extremely luxurious. An expensive treat.

Via Postumia 63, 31050 Paderno di Ponzano (Treviso) **Tel** (0422) 440751/2 **Fax** (0422) 440754 **Meals** breakfast, lunch, dinner **Prices** rooms LLLL; suites LLLL **Rooms** 10, all with bath, central heating, phone, TV, minibar **Credit cards** AE, DC, V **Closed** never

REPORTING TO THE GUIDE

Charming Small Hotel Guides are greatly strengthened by reports from people who have stayed in hotels featured in the guides, or who have found other places which deserve an entry. Particularly helpful reporters can earn a free copy of the next edition of the guide. On page 11 you will find further information about sending in reports to the publishers.

The north-east

Town hotel, Padua

Donatello

This is much the best-placed base in Padua for tourists, taking its name from the creator of the famous equestrian statue that it overlooks. The bright trattoria-style restaurant has a pavement café with a good view of the basilica. Simple, modernized rooms.

■ Via del Santo 102, 35123 Padua **Tel** (049) 875 0634 **Fax** (049) 875 0829 **Meals** breakfast, lunch, dinner **Prices** rooms LL-LLL; meals from L **Rooms** 49, all with bath or shower, phone, minibar **Credit cards** AE, DC, MC, V **Closed** mid-Dec to mid-Jan; restaurant only, Wed

---

Town hotel, Padua

Leon Bianco

'Charming' may not be quite the right word for this smart little hotel, with its plate-glass doors and smooth modern furnishings. But it has a stylish air, and a good position overlooking the famous Caffè Pedrocchi. Breakfast can be taken on a small roof terrace. Garage.

■ Piazzetta Pedrocchi 12, 35100 Padua **Tel** (049) 875 0814 **Fax** (049) 875 6184 **Meals** breakfast **Prices** rooms LL-LLL; breakfast L **Rooms** 22, all with bath or shower, TV, phone, minibar, air-conditioning **Credit cards** AE, DC, MC, V **Closed** never

---

Town hotel, Padua

Majestic Toscanelli

This 17thC building looks nothing special, but it occupies an unusually quiet spot in the heart of old Padua, and was renovated a couple of years ago in confident style. Bedrooms are carefully co-ordinated and very comfortable, with sparkling shower rooms. Tuscan proprietors hence the name.

■ Piazzetta dell'Arco 2, 35122 Padua **Tel** (049) 663244 **Fax** (049) 876 0025 **Meals** breakfast, dinner **Prices** rooms LLL; suite LLL; reduced rates between 10 Jul-29 Aug **Rooms** 32, all with bath or shower, phone, air-conditioning, TV, minibar **Credit cards** AE, DC, MC, V **Closed** never

---

Converted castle, Pergine

Castel Pergine

This conspicuous hilltop castle enjoys marvellous views in all directions. Inside, enormous vaulted rooms serve as the restaurant; bedrooms have whitewashed or wood-panelled walls, and old carved beds with bright duvets. There is a peaceful, walled garden. 'Incredible value', says a reporter.

■ Pergine (Trento) **Tel** (0461) 531158 **Fax** (0461) 531 329 **Meals** breakfast, lunch, dinner **Prices** rooms LL; 40% reduction for children under 6 **Rooms** 23, all with phone; most have shower **Credit cards** MC, V **Closed** Nov to Easter

Converted castle, San Floriano del Collio

Castello de San Floriano

The beautiful rooms of this tiny hotel, contained in two renovated houses of a fortified village, are named after prestigious wines, emphasising the vinous interest of the Formentini family. Lovely gardens, with golf, tennis and a pool. English breakfasts.

■ Via Oslavia 5, 34070 San Floriano del Collio (Gorizia) **Tel** (0481) 884051 **Fax** (0481) 884052 **Meals** breakfast **Prices** rooms LLL, suite LLLL, with breakfast **Rooms** 14, 1 suite, all with bath or shower, central heating, air-conditioning, TV, minibar, phone **Credit cards** AE, DC, MC, V **Closed** Dec to Mar

Country villa, Scorze

Villa Conestabile

Not a luxury hotel, although much renovation has taken place recently to improve comfort. It remains excellent value at half the cost of a similar standard of accommodation in Venice (20 km away). It still has touches of grandeur – elaborate chandeliers, grand stair-cases and fine pieces of furniture. Notable garden designed by Guiseppe Jappelli, dating from 1835.

■ Via Roma 1, 30037 Scorze (Venezia) **Tel** (041) 445027 **Fax** (041) 584 0088 **Meals** breakfast, lunch, dinner **Prices** rooms LL; DB&B LL **Rooms** 18, all with bath or shower, central heating, phone, TV; most with bath or shower **Credit cards** AE, DC, MC, V **Closed** restaurant only, Nov to Mar, 1 week mid-Aug

Restaurant-with-rooms, Solighetto

Locanda da Lino

Restaurant with rooms, and chalk with cheese. You eat pasta and grills in a jolly room hung with copper pans and pictures, or in a courtyard hung with vines; you sleep in a beautifully furnished modern ground-floor room with a distinctive decorative theme – perhaps the super-slick 'Marcello Mastroianni'.

■ Via Brandolini 31, 31050 Solighetto (Treviso) **Tel** (0438) 82150 **Fax** (0438) 980577 **Meals** breakfast, lunch, dinner **Prices** rooms LL; meals LL **Rooms** 17, all with bath, central heating, phone, TV, minibar **Credit cards** AE, DC, MC, V **Closed** Mon, Christmas Day, July

Mountain chalet, Tires

Stefaner

A fairly modern chalet, high up in a beautiful Dolomite valley, that is run more as a home than a hotel. Furnishings are simple and cosy, with plenty of plants and ornaments. Bedrooms are bright and airy, with geranium-decked balconies. Charming and enthusiastic proprietors.

■ San Cipriano, 39050 Tires (Bolzano) **Tel** (0471) 642175 **Fax** (0471) 642175 **Meals** breakfast, dinner **Prices** DB&B L-LL **Rooms** 15, all with bath or shower, **Credit cards** not accepted **Closed** mid-Nov to mid-Dec

The north-east

Restaurant-with-rooms, Torcello

Locanda Cipriani

The Locanda Cipriani, on the popular excursion island of Torcello, is a fashionable spot for lunch or dinner (40 minutes by water-bus, much less by water-taxi) with a large terrace area. The rustic double rooms overlook the garden whence come the salads and flowers for the tables.

■ Piazza S Fosca 29, 30012 Torcello (Venice) **Tel** (041) 730757 **Fax** (041) 735433 **Meals** breakfast, lunch, dinner **Prices** DB&B LLL; FB LLLL **Rooms** 6, all with bath, phone; double rooms have sitting-room **Credit cards** AE, MC, V **Closed** early Nov to mid-Mar

---

Country hotel, Torri del Benaco

Europa

Regular visitors to the Europa call it 'a happy, welcoming hotel', offering excellent value. An old villa, up the hillside from Lake Garda, in gardens and olive groves, with a swimming-pool. Inside, most of the character has been ironed out in favour of cleanliness and simplicity. Dinner on the stroke of 7.30.

■ Via Gabriele d'Annunzio 13-15, 37010 Torri del Benaco (Verona) **Tel** (0457) 225086 (640361 in winter) **Fax** (0456) 296 632 **Meals** breakfast, dinner **Prices** rooms LL with breakfast; DB&B LL-LLL (min stay 3 days); special rates for longer stays **Rooms** 18, all with bath or shower, central heating, phone, hairdrier **Credit cards** MC, V Closed mid-Oct to Easter

---

Restaurant-with-rooms, Treviso

Le Beccherie

Le Beccherie is an unpretentious but highly regarded restaurant at the heart of old Treviso, with a few simple rooms above it. Across the tiny piazza is the same proprietor's Albergo Campeol, containing more comfortable rooms with bathrooms. 'Superb food without being over-priced' says a recent visitor.

■ Piazza G Ancillotto 10, 31100 Treviso **Tel** (0422) 540871 **Fax** (0422) 540871 **Meals** breakfast, lunch, dinner **Prices** rooms L-LL; breakfast L **Rooms** 27, all with central heating; 16 rooms have radio and phone **Credit cards** AE, DC, MC, V **Closed** restaurant only: Sun eve, Mon

---

Town hotel, Venice

Abbazia

A stylishly converted abbey near the station – and certainly a cut above the average station hotel. The former refectory is the sitting-room (with the pulpit still intact). Bedrooms and bathrooms are somewhat monastic and austere, but perfectly well kept and comfortable. A charming garden lies behind.

■ Cannaregio 68, 30121 Venice **Tel** (041) 717333 **Fax** (041) 717949 **Meals** breakfast **Prices** rooms LLL with breakfast **Rooms** 40, all with bath or shower, central heating, air-conditioning, satellite TV, minibar, phone, hairdrier **Credit cards** AE, DC, MC, V **Closed** never

Town hotel, Venice

American

A shuttered, terraced *palazzo* tucked behind the Accademia, recently restored and converted into a hotel. Large, bright bedrooms have Venetian-style painted furniture; public areas are comfortably and tastefully done with plenty of personal touches. The canal-side location is exceptionally pleasant and peaceful.

■ San Vio 628, 30123 Venice **Tel** (041) 520 4733 **Fax** (041) 520 4048 **E-mail** hotameri@tin.it **Meals** breakfast **Prices** rooms LLL-LLLL **Rooms** 30, all with bath or shower, air-conditioning, TV, minibar, phone, hairdrier, safe **Credit cards** AE, MC, V **Closed** never

---

Town hotel, Venice

Ateneo

Another of Venice's *palazzo* hotels, decked out in a civilized, traditional style with Murano glass light fittings and painted furniture. The reception is agreeable and the lack of restaurant no problem in this area by the Fenice theatre.

■ San Marco 1876, 30124 Venice **Tel** (041) 520 0777 **Fax** (041) 522 8550 **Meals** breakfast **Prices** rooms LLL-LLLL with breakfast **Rooms** 23, all with air-conditioning, central heating, phone, TV, radio, minibar **Credit cards** AE, MC, V **Closed** never

---

Town hotel, Venice

Bel Sito

A central but reasonably priced and quiet option, well looked-after inside. A patio of potted plants and parasols makes a pleasant vantage-point for people-watching. The best rooms are at the rear; front rooms are darker and more old-fashioned.

■ Campo Santa Maria del Giglio, San Marco 2517, 30124 Venice **Tel** (041) 522 3365 **Fax** (041) 520 4083 **Meals** breakfast **Prices** rooms LL-LLLL with breakfast **Rooms** 38, all with bath or shower, phone, air-conditioning (L13,000 per day), some with TV and minibar **Credit cards** AE, MC, V **Closed** never

---

Town hotel, Venice

Bucintoro

This modest, cement-rendered block (conveniently close to the vaporetto stop at Arsenale) is currently being renovated. It shares the fine Giudecca waterfront views of many more elaborate hotels. Tables and chairs are set on the quayside, screened by tubs of flowers. Inside it is light and neat – plain, but personal and well looked-after.

■ Riva Schiavoni 2135, 30122 Venice **Tel** (041) 522 3240 **Fax** (041) 523 5224 **Meals** breakfast **Prices** rooms LL-LLL with breakfast DB&B LL **Rooms** 28, all with bath or shower, phone **Credit cards** not accepted **Closed** Dec and Jan

The north-east

Town guest-house, Venice

Calcina

Ruskin's plaque reveals the long-established enthusiasm of regular visitors to this little hotel. Today, facing the sunny straits of the Giudecca canal, it is similarly hard to resist. Inside it is simple, with wooden floors. Buffet breakfasts can be taken on the deck-terrace by the canal. Friendly and informal.

■ Zattere 780, 30123 Venice **Tel** (041) 520 6466 **Fax** (041) 522 7045 **Meals** breakfast **Prices** rooms L-LLL with breakfast **Rooms** 29, all with central heating, air-conditioning, phone; most with bath or shower **Credit cards** A E, DC, MC, V **Closed** never

---

Town hotel, Venice

Kette

Recently refurbished in an ambitiously formal style with marble and much wood panelling, this hotel is now somewhat institutional. Bedrooms and all public areas are well kept and comfortable with smartly matching uniform furnishings. Displays of Murano glass and a few *objets d'art* add some personality.

■ San Marco 2053, 30124 Venice **Tel** (041) 520 7766 **Fax** (041) 522 8964 **Meals** breakfast **Prices** rooms LLL with breakfast; suites LLLL **Rooms** 50, all with bath or shower, central heating, air-conditioning, TV, safe, minibar, hairdrier **Credit cards** AE, V **Closed** never

---

Town hotel, Venice

Nuovo Teson

In a tiny square just off the Riva degli Schiavoni (a short walk or *vaporetto* ride to San Marco), this is a modern building, recently renovated. Bedrooms are small, but pretty with Venetian furniture and glass lamps. The only public space is a plainish breakfast room enclosing a small bar-lounge area. An American family disliked their annexe room, and found the staff unhelful.

■ Riva degli Schiavoni 3980, 30122 Venice **Tel** (041) 522 9929 **Fax** (041) 528 5335 **Meals** breakfast **Prices** rooms LL-LLL with breakfast **Rooms** 30, all with shower, central heating, radio, music **Credit cards** AE, DC, MC, V **Closed** Nov to Jan

---

Town hotel, Venice

Paganelli

This modest, friendly place gives itself no airs at all, but shares approximately the same lagoon views as much more august and expensive hotels on the Riva degli Schiavoni. Breakfast is served in a nearby annexe in the adjoining side-street. Largest and smartest bedrooms face the waterfront.

■ Riva degli Schiavoni 4687, 30122 Venice **Tel** (041) 522 4324 **Fax** (041) 523 9267 **Meals** breakfast **Prices** rooms LL-LLL with breakfast; 30% reduction for young children **Rooms** 23, all with phone, most with bath or shower, air-conditioning, satellite TV, hairdrier **Credit cards** AE, MC, V **Closed** never

The north-east

Town hotel, Venice

Do Pozzi

Quietly located in a tiny enclosed square near San Marco, this neat little hotel has fairly standardized furnishings and modern bedrooms, though beware the tiny bathrooms. The palm-fringed courtyard set with café tables is a popular spot; so too is the adjoining Raffaele restaurant, festooned with copper utensils and antique weaponry.

■ Via XXII Marzo, 30124 Venice **Tel** (041) 520 7855 **Fax** (041) 522 9413 **Meals** breakfast; bar service **Prices** rooms LL-LLL meals L **Rooms** 35, all with bath or shower, central heating, minibar, air-conditioning, phone, TV **Credit cards** AE, DC, MC, V **Closed** Jan

---

Town hotel, Venice

Salute da Cici

This calm, civilized place has a classically elegant lobby of columns and marble floors beneath exposed rafters. It lies in an interesting part of Venice, between the Salute basilica and the Accademia. Furnishings are quietly tasteful. A tiny, sheltered garden offers a few sunny tables for a drink.

■ Fondamenta Ca Balla 222, 30123 Venice **Tel** (041) 523 5404 **Fax** (041) 522 2271 **Meals** breakfast **Prices** rooms LL-LLL **Rooms** 50, all with central heating, phone; 34 rooms with bath or shower **Credit cards** not accepted **Closed** early Nov to Feb

---

Town hotel, Venice

San Cassiano

A gorgeous Gothic façade faces the Grand Canal and Ca d'Oro; access, via tortuous, narrow alleyways from the nearest *raghetto* point, can be tricky. Inside the *palazzo* is handsomely furnished with Murano chandeliers and antique-look pieces. It retains many original features and timbered ceilings. The light, elegant breakfast room with waterfront views is the main focal point.

■ Santa Croce 2232, 30135 Venice **Tel** (041) 5241768 **Fax** (041) 721033 **Meals** breakfast **Prices** LL-LLL **Rooms** 35, all with bath or shower, air-conditioning, TV, radio, phone, minibar, hairdrier **Credit cards** AE, DC **Closed** never

---

Town hotel, Venice

San Fantin

An intriguing façade, studded with cannonballs and guarded by a whimsical lion, distinguishes this hotel, in a quiet corner near the Fenice theatre. Amicably run by a mother-and-daughter team, the hotel is simple but cared-for, as indicated by a profusion of pictures.

■ Campiello de la Fenice 1930/a, San Marco, 30124 Venice **Tel & Fax** (041) 523 1401 **Meals** breakfast **Prices** rooms LL-LLL with breakfast **Rooms** 14, all with central heating, phone; most with shower **Credit cards** MC, V **Closed** winter

The north-east

Town hotel, Venice

San Moisé

A delightful canalside location near San Marco is an obvious attraction. Warbling gondoliers glide past within inches. This newly restored place has intrinsic good points too, and is sprucely kitted out in a mix of modern furnishings given period Venetian flavour with rugs and elaborate glass chandeliers.

■ San Marco 2058, 30124 Venice **Tel** (041) 520 3755 **Fax** (041) 521 0670 **Meals** breakfast **Prices** LL-LLLL **Rooms** 16, all with bath or shower, all rooms have phone, satellite TV, hairdrier, minibar, safe **Credit cards** AE, DC, MC, V **Closed** never

---

Town hotel, Venice

Santa Marina

An attractive, yellow-washed building on a corner-site of a relatively untouristy square near the Rialto, near several pleasant cafés. Inside decorations and furnishings are predictably hotel-like, but the welcome is civil and the ambience relaxing. Bedrooms are light and clean, modern lines softened by occasional Venetian flourishes.

■ Castello, Campo Santa Maria 6068, 30122 Venice **Tel** (041) 523 9202 **Fax** (041) 520 0907 Meals breakfast **Prices** rooms LLL-LLLL with breakfast **Rooms** 16, all with bath or shower, central heating, air-conditioning , phone, TV, minibar **Credit cards** AE, DC, MC, V **Closed** never

---

Town hotel, Venice

Scandinavia

The rambling piazza is lively on market-days, but the hotel is formal and almost hushed inside, decorated with much marble, walnut veneer and Murano glassware. The solid antique-style furnishings and many paintings give it an air of superiority. A nearby trattoria is under the same management.

■ Campo Santa Maria Formosa, Castello 5240, 30122 Venice **Tel** (041) 522 3507 **Fax** (041) 523 5232 **Meals** breakfast **Prices** rooms LL-LLLL with breakfast **Rooms** 34, all with central heating, phone, minibar, air-conditioning; all with bath **Credit cards** AE, MC, V **Closed** never

---

Town hotel, Venice

Torino

Grander inside than its exterior suggests, this Gothic *palazzo* has kept many interesting architectural features, and the style remains firmly traditional, though a number of new bedrooms have been added with modern bathrooms.

■ Calle delle Ostreghe 2356, San Marco, 30124 Venice **Tel** (041) 520 5222 **Fax** (041) 522 8227 **E-mail** info@hoteltorino.it **Website** www.hoteltorino.it **Meals** breakfast **Prices** rooms LL-LLL with breakfast **Rooms** 20, all with shower, central heating, air-conditioning, phone, radio, TV, safe, minibar **Credit cards** AE, DC, MC, V **Closed** never

The north-east

Town villa, Venice Lido

Villa Parco

A simple, reasonably priced place a few minutes away from the waterfront in a quiet residential area. The building is in art nouveau style, though furnishings are mainly modern. As well as breakfast, you can get snacks from the bar. 'Comfortable rooms and helpful staff,' reports a recent satisfied visitor.

■ Via Rodi 1, 30126 Venice Lido (Venice) **Tel** (041) 526 0015 **Fax** (041) 526 7620 **Meals** breakfast **Prices** rooms LL-LLL **Rooms** 22, all with bath or shower, central heating, phone, TV, air-condition ing, minibar **Credit cards** AE, DC, MC, V **Closed** Dec to Carnival (Feb)

Town hotel, Verona

Gabbia d'Oro

A splendid old palazzo in the pedestrian heart of Verona (a driver will take your car to and from the hotel garage – L50,000) strikingly converted into an upmarket hotel with more suites than rooms. In the public area, massive beams and bare brickwork are much in evidence; some of the bedrooms are reportedly rather severe.

■ Corso Porta Borsari, 4a, 37121 Verona **Tel** (045) 800 3060 **Fax** (045) 590293 **Meals** breakfast **Prices** rooms LLL-LLLL; suites LLLL **Rooms** 27, all with bath or shower, phone, cable TV, minibar **Credit cards** AE, DC, MC, V **Closed** never

---

Town hotel, Verona

Torcolo

A recent visitor praises the 'warmth and friendliness of the welcome' at this faded ochre building offering solid value in an excellent location close to the Arena and the city centre. Bedrooms are decorated in a variety of styles – Italian 18thC, art nouveau and modern – and most are not as noisy as you might expect. Breakfast can be served outside on a terrace.

■ Vicolo Listone 3, 37121 Verona **Tel** (045) 800 7512 **Meals** breakfast **Prices** rooms LL-LLL with breakfast **Rooms** 19, all with bath or shower, central heating, air-conditioning, phone, TV, hairdrier **Credit cards** AE, MC, V **Closed** 10 Jan to 30 Jan

---

Agriturismo, Villorba

Podere del Convento

A working farm producing wine and fruit, an equestrian centre and a restaurant, with six attractive bedrooms also available. These have roughcast walls and ceilings open to the tiled roof, with large beds and country furniture. Bustling restaurant, often packed with local families.

■ Via IV Novembre 16 3, 31050, Villorba Treviso **Tel & fax** (0422) 920 044 **Meals** breakfast, lunch, dinner **Prices** rooms L-LL breakfast L5,000 **Rooms** 6, all with shower **Credit cards** AE, MC, V **Closed** Aug

Emilia-Romagna

Hotels in Emilia-Romagna

The Via Emilia, the Roman road (now a motorway) stretching along the foothills of the Apennine mountains from Piacenza to Rimini, gives the region its name, and most of the main towns are located along it.

Bologna, the regional capital, is primarily a business centre with business-style hotels to match; but it is also a city of learning (it has the oldest university in Europe) and art (including beautiful Renaissance buildings) so there is much to attract the tourist, and we are able to recommend the three hotels owned by the Orsi family, described on pages 90–92.

Our only recommendation for Modena – too big for a full entry in this guide – is the Canalgrande (Tel (059) 217160, fax 221674, 78 bedrooms), a stylish, peaceful and comfortable villa set in beautiful gardens in the middle of the city.

Finding a satisfactory hotel in Parma is nearly as difficult but this year we have added on page 96 the Villa Ducale (Tel (0521) 272727, fax 70756), a 28-room hotel set in shady grounds, as an alternative to the Torino described on page 95. And for Ferrara, the luxurious Duchessa Isabella (Tel (0532) 202121, fax 202638) is worth mentioning as an alternative to the Ripagrande (page 95) although it is equally expensive.

The Adriatic coast of this region is not notable for small hotels, hence the lack of recommendations in this guide. Ravenna is the most important port – try the Bisanzio (Tel (0544) 217111, fax 32539, 38 rooms) or the simple but central Centrale Byron (Tel (0544) 212225, 54 rooms) if you need to stay there – and there are numerous beach resorts up and down the coast offering plenty of sea, sun and sand. The Albergo Caravel (Tel (0533) 330106, fax 330107) is one of the few examples of an alternative to the large, busy seaside hotels. This hotel has only 22 rooms and is set in a shady garden 100m from the beach at Lido di Spina.

Should you need a room in the backwater town of Sarsina, try the Al Piano (Tel (0547) 94848 fax 95153) – a simply furnished mansion in a splendid hillside position, dropped from the guide following reports from disappointed visitors. It has enjoyed enthusiastic support in the past, so more reports would be very welcome.

This page acts as an introduction to the features and hotels of Emilia-Romagna, and gives brief recommendations of reasonable hotels that for one reason or another have not made a full entry. The long entries for this region – covering the hotels we are most enthusiastic about – start on the next page. But do not neglect the shorter entries starting on page 95: these are all hotels that we would happily stay at.

Emilia-Romagna

Town hotel, Bologna

Commercianti

As its name suggests, the Commercianti caters primarily for the business market, but in a city with few tourist hotels it is a useful little place to know about, and several recent visitors have been impressed. It has an excellent position – right in the heart of things, just off Bologna's main piazza, next to a smart pedestrian shopping street. There is no restaurant – just a café-like breakfast room. The hotel has been completely revamped recently but with the occasional old beam to remind you that you are in a medieval building. With an air of efficiency rather than notable character, the Commercianti is a reasonably priced base and serves its purpose well. Bicycles supplied for city sightseeing.
Nearby San Petronio, Fontana and Piazza del Nettuno.

Via Pignattari 11, Bologna 40124
Tel (051) 233052
Fax (051) 224733
E-mail hotcom@tin.it
Website http://www.cnc.it/bologna
Location in middle of city, off Piazza Maggiore, with private car parking
Food & drink breakfast
Prices rooms LLL with breakfast
Rooms 25 double, 9 single, all with shower; 1 suite; all have central heating, satellite TV, minibar, phone, air-conditioning, safe
Facilities bar/breakfast room, sitting-area, TV room
Credit cards AE, DC, MC, V
Children accepted; beds and cots available
Disabled lift/elevator available
Pets small ones only
Closed never
Proprietor Paolo Orsi

Emilia-Romagna

Corona d'Oro 1890

The Corona d'Oro lies in the historic old city, close to the two famous leaning towers, in a cobbled street which for most of the time is closed to traffic. Enticing food shops (including a wonderful delicatessen) give you some idea of why the city is nicknamed Bologna La Grassa (the Fat).

The Corona d'Oro became a hotel in 1890, though the original building dates back to 1300. It is here that Italy's first printing press was established and there are still a few features surviving from the original palace. In the early 1980s the hotel was bought by a packaging magnate, who elevated it from a simple hotel to four-star status, successfully combining the old features with the stylish new. The 14thC portico and Renaissance ceilings were preserved, while the plush bedrooms were provided with all modern conveniences. The showpiece was the hallway, with its fine art nouveau frieze supported on columns. Light streaming from above, fresh flowers and lush feathery plants create a cheerful, inviting entrance.

If arriving by car, be sure to get the hotel's route-map; without it, you will never find your way through the Bologna maze.
Nearby Piazza Maggiore and Piazza del Nettuno.

Via Oberdan 12, Bologna 40126
Tel (051) 236456
Fax (051) 262679
E-mail hotcoro@tin.it
Website http://www.cnc.it/bologna
Location in middle, close to the two leaning towers, Piazza di Porta Ravegnana
Food & drink breakfast
Prices rooms LLLL
Rooms 27 double, all with shower; 8 single, all with shower; all rooms have central heating, colour TV, minibar, phone, safe, air-conditioning
Facilities bar, conference room, sitting-area, TV room
Credit cards AE, DC, MC, V
Children accepted
Disabled not suitable
Pets only small ones accepted
Closed Aug
Proprietor Mauro Orsi

Emilia-Romagna

Orologio

The Corona d'Oro (page 91), Commercianti (page 90) and the Orologio are all under the same management; of the three – all close together in central Bologna – this has in the past been the poor relation, but in 1990 the Orologio was completely renovated to bring it up to the standards of the others; unfortunately the prices now match, too.

The Orologio can (by a tiny margin) claim the best location of the three – just off the main square of Bologna, flanking a pedestrianized thoroughfare and facing the handsome Palazzo Communale. The hotel's formula is simple: freshly decorated and well-equipped bedrooms, and much better than average breakfasts served in a smart, bright little sitting/breakfast area. Recent visitors endorse our recommendation, commenting on the 'extremely pleasant and helpful staff', the 'very attractive' and 'well lit' bedrooms and the 'very good breakfast, still including the freshly squeezed orange juice'. We are pleased to report that the nearby 'noisy bell' noticed by guests in previous years, has now been silenced between the hours of midnight and six o'clock in the morning.

Nearby basilica of San Petronio, Fontana del Nettuno.

Via IV Novembre 10, Bologna 40123
Tel (051) 231253
Fax (051) 260552
E-mail hotoro@tin.it
Website http://www.cnc.it/bologna
Location in middle of city, on pedestrian thoroughfare, with private car parking and garage
Food & drink breakfast
Prices rooms LLL with breakfast
Rooms 23 double, 9 single, all with bath, some also with shower; all rooms have central heating, phone, air-conditioning, minibar, TV, safe
Facilities breakfast room, bar
Credit cards AE, DC, MC, V
Children accepted
Disabled no special facilities
Pets small ones only
Closed never
Proprietor Mauro Orsi

Emilia-Romagna

Restaurant with rooms, Brisighella

Gigiolè

Brisighella is a picturesque small town 13 km south-west of Faenza. The Gigiolè stands across from the main church – a vaguely French-looking shuttered building with a shaded terrace in front.

The French style extends to the food: Tarcisio Raccagni, the chef, has been put on a par with the famous Paul Bocuse. Like Bocuse he places great stress on using seasonal local ingredients of top quality and the results are superb: succulent meats, delicious soups and imaginative use of vegetables and herbs – top quality *nouvelle cuisine* but at prices you can afford and in helpings that don't leave you hungry. The setting is late 18thC, with stone arches, ceramics and copper pots. Table-cloths are white and crisp, and glasses gleam. Service is 'grave but efficient'.

After all this, some of the bedrooms come as a bit of an anti-climax; but they are adequate, and give little cause for complaint. The newly decorated rooms are quite pretty, with white modern furnishings and fabrics, and new bathrooms. Ask for a room at the back if peace is a priority. 'Very friendly welcome, splendid food, excellent value; I should gladly return', says one reporter. Another praised the receptionist, who helped with directions to a local vineyard, as well as setting up a computer in the bedroom.
Nearby Faenza; Florence, Ravenna, Bologna within reach.

Piazza Carducci 5, Brisighella
48013 Ravenna
Tel (0546) 81209
Location in middle of town,
13 km SW of Faenza on S302;
no private car parking, but
space available in the piazza
Food & drink breakfast,
lunch, dinner
Prices rooms LL-LLL; suite
LLLL with breakfast; DB&B
LL; meals LL
Rooms 7 double, 5 single,
2 family rooms; all with
bath or shower; all rooms
have central heating, phone,
hairdrier, minibar
Facilities dining-room, bar,
TV room
Credit cards AE, DC, MC, V
Children welcome
Disabled access difficult
Pets welcome if clean and
well behaved
Closed one week Feb, one
week Mar, one week Jul;
restaurant only, Mon
Proprietor Tarcisio Raccagni

Emilia-Romagna

Al Vecchio Convento

Portico di Romagna is a sleepy medieval village centred on a single paved street – the location of the Vecchio Convento. The house was built in 1840 and converted in the mid-1980s into a hotel – with panache that comes as a surprise in this backwater.

The dining-room, at the back of the house, is the main focus. With its beamed, pitched ceiling, tiled floor and open fireplace, it has a stylishly rustic air. There is also a stone-flagged family sitting-room, with piano, card-table, books and games, but in practice your sitting is more likely to be done on the small terrace outside the front door; the bar, just inside the door, offers standing room only.

A severe stone staircase leads up to the bedrooms. Here, the decoration is again plain and classy – but set against that is some glorious antique furniture. The beds are particularly notable – we've never seen such a collection of elaborate pieces. (The bases and mattresses, we're pleased to report, modern and firm.) Most rooms are adequately spacious, though some bathrooms at the top of the house have outrageously low ceilings. Sg Cameli cooks traditional dishes with flair – even his chips are a herby delight – while Marisa leads diners through the day's choices with great good humour (and passable English). Sumptuous breakfasts.

Nearby Faenza (46 km), Ravenna (70 km), Florence (80 km).

Via Roma 7, Portico di
Romagna 47010 Forli
Tel (0543) 967053
Fax (0543) 967157
E-mail http://www.
vecchioconvento.asianet.it
Location 30 km SE of Forli, in
village; with some private
parking in a garage
Food & drink breakfast,
lunch, dinner
Prices rooms LL; breakfast L;
meals LL
Rooms 12 double, 9 with

shower; 3 single, 2 with
shower; all rooms have phone
Facilities bar, dining-room,
breakfast room, sitting-room
Credit cards AE, DC, V
Children welcome
Disabled access difficult
Pets accepted
Closed never
Proprietors Marisa Raggi and
Giovanni Cameli

Emilia-Romagna

Town hotel, Busseto

I Due Foscari

It is hard to believe that this Gothic building is only a few decades old, so convincing are its beamed ceilings, heavy antiques and iron candelabras. The restaurant (with terrace) dominates – food and service are excellent; the equally traditional rooms are satisfactory.

■ Piazza Carlo Rossi 15, 43011 Busseto (Parma) **Tel**(0524) 92337 **Fax** (0524) 91625 **Meals** breakfast, lunch, dinner **Prices** rooms L-LLL; buffet breakfast L15,000 **Rooms** 20, all with bath or shower, phone, TV **Credit cards** AE, DC, MC, V **Closed** Aug and Jan; restaurant only, Mon

---

Country hotel, Castelfranco Emilia

Villa Gaidello Club

Paola Giovanna and her architect sister renovated this 250-year-old farmhouse in the 1970s, creating eight comfortable self-catering apartments in the old family home. The interior is appropriately furnished with country antiques, and the grounds include a small lake as well as a solarium.

■ Via Gaidello 18, 41013 Castelfranco Emilia (Modena) **Tel**(059) 926806 **Fax** (059) 926620 **Meals** breakfast, lunch, dinner **Prices** rooms LL-LLL, with breakfast **Rooms** 8 apartments with kitchen facilities, all with bath, minibar, TV **Credit cards** DC, MC, V **Closed** Aug; restaurant only, Sun dinner and Mon. Booking essential.

Town hotel, Ferrara

Ripagrande

The entrance hall of this Renaissance *palazzo*, converted in 1980, raises expectations high, with its exposed beams, glossy antiques and ancient stone columns. Bedrooms vary: some are smartly modern split-level affairs, others restored to traditional style. You eat in a canopied courtyard, or a bistro-style restaurant.

■ Via Ripagrande 21, 44100 Ferrara **Tel** (0532) 765250 **Fax** (0532) 764377 **E-mail** ripa@mbox.4net.it **Website** http://www.4net.com/business/ripa **Meals** breakfast , lunch, dinner **Prices** rooms LLL with breakfast; meals L-LL **Rooms** 42, all with bath or shower, central heating, air-conditioning, minibar, sat. TV, phone **Credit cards** AE, DC, MC, V **Closed** never

---

Town hotel, Parma

Torino

In the heart of the city, just a stone's throw from the main sights (with the bonus of a private garage – L15,000 per night) – yet remains reasonably priced. Bedrooms are spartan and small but clean, well cared-for. Choose a quieter one over the pleasant internal courtyard, which is adorned with flowers.

■ Via A Mazza 7, 43100 Parma **Tel** (0521) 281047 **Meals** breakfast **Prices** rooms LL **Rooms** 33, all with bath or shower, central heating, piped music, TV, phone **Credit cards** AE, DC, MC, V **Closed** first 3 weeks Aug, and Christmas

Emilia-Romagna

Country villa, Parma

Villa Ducale

A short taxi ride beyond the city's perimeter and conveniently positioned for the railway station, Villa Ducale is a three-storey 'villa padronale' in the Neoclassical style, set in its own grounds with avenues of poplar, lime and chestnut trees. The hotel is approached through a small garden, abundantly stocked with roses and fuschias. Bedrooms are clean and comfortable, several with small terraces. Friendly staff.

■-Via del Popolo 35, 43100 Parma **Tel** (0521) 272727 **Fax** (0521) 780756 **Meals** buffet breakfast **Prices** LLL with breakfast **Rooms** 28, all with bath or shower, central heating, air-conditioning, TV, phone, minibar **Credit cards** AE, DC, MC, V **Closed** Christmas

---

Town inn, Soragna

Locanda del Lupo

Rather large for our purposes, but an exceptionally comfortable place to stay in an area where we cannot offer many alternatives. The 18thC coaching inn, in a small town near Cremona, is quite a grand building, with spacious rooms harmoniously furnished with antiques.

■ Via Garibaldi 64, 43019 Soragna (Parma) **Tel** (0524) 690444 **Fax** (0524) 69350 **Meals** breakfast, lunch, dinner **Prices** rooms LL-LLL; suite LLL; DB&B LL **Rooms** 46, all with bath or shower, central heating, air-conditioning, phone, TV, radio **Credit cards** AE, DC, V **Closed** late Jul to late Aug

Readers' Reports

Reports from readers are of enormous interest to us in keeping up to date with the hotels in this guide - and others that should be in it. More information on p11

Tuscany

Hotels in Tuscany

No other region of Italy is as rich in good small hotels as Tuscany. The greatest concentrations of hotels are naturally around the tourist highlights of Florence, Siena and San Gimignano. But on recent visits we have been struck by the momentum that tourism is gaining in the countryside between Florence and Siena – the Chianti wine region. There have been fine hotels in this area for many years; but alongside the old favourites there are some new discoveries to which, with the new format of the guide, we are now able to give fuller descriptions on the following pages.

Finding notably welcoming places to stay along the Tuscan coast is not so easy – although many of the better hotels in resorts such as Forte dei Marmi and Marina di Pietrasanta have attractive shady gardens, few have any other distinguishing features. At Livorno is the Villa Godilonda (Tel (0586) 752032, fax 751177), a spotless, modest seaside hotel near two sandy beaches.

Further south and just off the coast (but within easy reach of the long sandy beach at Marina de Castagneto) is an old stone villa, La Torre at Castagneto Carducci (Tel (0565) 775268 and fax), which, as its name suggests, stands next to a ruined tower. It has been converted into a simple hotel with 11 rooms, offering B&B and basic evening meals.

The Tuscan island of Elba is big enough to absorb the many summer visitors it attracts without being swamped in the way that some of the smaller and more southerly islands have been. We have one clear recommendation on the island (page 141), but in general its small hotels are, to be honest, less attractive than many of the bigger ones which cannot properly be given entries here. There is a handful of charming and comfortable (but not cheap) hotels with 60 to 100 rooms within a few miles of the port of arrival, Portoferraio. High in the hills to the south, with wonderful views from its terraces and pool, is the Picchiaie (Tel (0565) 933110, fax 933186). Across the bay from Portoferraio, in leafy grounds close to the sea, is the polished Villa Ottone (Tel (0565) 933042, fax 933257). Nearby at Magazzini is the smart Fabricia (Tel (0565) 933181, fax 933185) with its own beach facilities. On the south side of the island is the Bahia at Cavoli (Tel (0565) 987055, fax 987020, 60 rooms in houses, gardens of olives and cacti).

We have entries for two hotels on the island of Giglio (page 145). Also worth considering is the Arenella – a quiet and comfortable hotel, with great views of the coast (Tel (0564) 809340, fax 809443).

This page acts as an introduction to the features and hotels of Tuscany, and gives brief recommendations of reasonable hotels that for one reason or another have not made a full entry. The long entries for this region – covering the hotels we are most enthusiastic about – start on the next page. But do not neglect the shorter entries starting on page 139: these are all hotels that we would happily stay at.

Tuscany

Country hotel, Artimino

Paggeria Medicea

Artimino is a village of some distinction, drawing visitors to see its museum and nearby Etruscan tombs. It also has a number of imposing buildings, one being a grand villa built by Ferdinand I of Medici, who was struck by the beauty of the surroundings in the 16thC. Now the outbuildings and servants' quarters of this villa have been converted into an elegant and peaceful hotel.

As befits its aristocratic pedigree, the atmosphere is classy, but unshowy. Furnishings are a stylish, unpretentious mix of new and old, and original features such as sloping rafters, chimneys and ceilings have, where possible, been retained both in bedrooms and in public areas.

A short walk across manicured lawns brings you to the restaurant Biagio Pignatta (named after a celebrated Medici chef). Its specialities are Tuscan dishes 'with a Renaissance flavour' (*pappardelle sul coniglio*, for instance – broad noodles with rabbit sauce) on a terrace overlooking hillsides of vines and olives. The estate produces its own wine, which is decanted at your table with religious reverence.

Nearby Etruscan museum; medieval village; Prato (15 km), Florence (18 km).

Viale Papa Giovanni XXIII, Artimino 59015 Firenze
Tel (055) 871 8081
Fax (055) 871 8080
Location 18 km NW of Florence, close to village, with ample car parking
Food & drink breakfast, lunch, dinner
Prices rooms LLL; meals LL
Rooms 34 double, some with bath, most with shower; 3 single with shower; 32 apartments; all have central heating, air-conditioning, minibar, TV, phone, radio
Facilities dining-room, reading-room, TV room; 2 tennis-courts, jogging, swimming-pool, mountain bikes, training ground, trekking **Credit cards** AE, DC, MC, V **Children** accepted
Disabled no special facilities
Pets accepted, but not in dining-room
Closed never
Manager Alessandro Gualtieri

Tuscany

Country villa, Candeli

Grand Hotel Villa la Massa

Standing on the banks of the Arno, surrounded by parkland and gentle hills, Villa la Massa (dating from the 17thC) used to be the country residence of one of the most powerful Florentine families. It is now one of the city's most elegant (and expensive) hotels (now under new management and undergoing extensive refurbishment.) And with its country setting, lawns, gardens overflowing with flowers, seductive pool and tennis-courts, it makes a sharp contrast to the city-centre hotels.(Not that staying here rules out sightseeing: there is a free shuttle bus into Florence.)

The main house sets the tone – a rather severe, four-square building with a grand, lofty central lobby and pillared galleries leading to the bedrooms. Some of these are individually furnished and the height of luxury, combining antique-style furniture with modern high-quality fabrics; our most recent inspector, however, stayed in one which was only adequate for the price.

The riverside restaurant (Il Verrocchio) is in a rather less grand but still impressive building; weather permitting, you can dine on a terrace lit by romantic lanterns hanging from the trees. With almost as many waiters as diners, service is immaculate.

Nearby Florence (7km).

Via La Massa 6, Candeli, Florence 50010
Tel (055) 6510101
Fax (055) 6510109
Location 7 km E of Florence, on Arno in extensive grounds with ample car parking
Food & drink breakfast, lunch, dinner
Prices rooms LLLL; suites LLLL; meals LLL
Rooms 34 double, 3 single, 5 suites, all with bath; all have central heating, phone, air-conditioning, satellite TV, minibar
Facilities dining-room, bar, piano bar, sitting-room, conference rooms; swimming-pool, fishing
Credit cards AE, DC, MC, V
Children accepted
Disabled no special facilities
Pets not accepted in dining-room
Closed never
Manager Guido Rabà

Tuscany

Country guest-house, Castellina in Chianti

Salivolpi

For no immediately obvious reason, the unremarkable Chianti village of Castellina contains a cluster of Tuscany's most appealing hotels. This welcome addition to the catalogue, open since 1983, offers a much cheaper alternative to its two illustrious neighbours – Tenuta de Ricavo (page 101) and Villa Casalecchi (page 102). It occupies two well-restored farm buildings and one new bungalow in a peaceful open position on the edge of the village – supposedly the location of the ancient Etruscan Castellina – affording broad views across the countryside.

There is a Spanish feel to the older of the houses – iron fittings, exposed beams, white walls, ochre tiles – and the spacious rooms are both neat and stylish, with some splendid old beds and other antiques. The whole place is well cared-for, and has a calm, relaxed atmosphere.

The garden is well tended, with plenty of space, some furniture and a fair-sized swimming-pool. Breakfast (*'molto abbondante'*, claims the boss) is served in a crisp little room in the smaller of the houses.

Nearby Siena (18 km); Florence, San Gimignano and other attractions within reach.

Via Fiorentina, Castellina in Chianti 53011 Siena
Tel (0577) 740484
Fax (0577) 740998
Location 500 m from middle of village, on the road to San Donato; with gardens and ample open-air car parking
Food & drink breakfast
Prices rooms LL with breakfast
Rooms 19 double with bath; all rooms have central heating, phone; some with satellite TV
Facilities hall, breakfast room, bar; swimming-pool
Credit cards MC, V
Children accepted
Disabled some rooms with special facilities
Pets not accepted
Closed never
Manager Angela Orlandi

Tuscany

Country hotel, Castellina in Chianti

Tenuta di Ricavo

If away from it all is where you want to get – while retaining the possibility of doing some serious sightseeing – Ricavo is hard to beat. The hotel occupies an entire hamlet, which was deserted in the 1950s when people left the land for the cities in search of work.

The grouping of houses along a wooded ridge in the depth of the countryside might have been conceived as a film-set replica of a medieval hamlet. The main house, facing a little square of other mellow stone cottages, houses some of the bedrooms, and the several sitting-rooms, which are comfortably furnished with a pleasant jumble of antique chairs and sofas (one of them with a small library of English, Italian, French and German books). The hotel's restaurant, La Pecora Nera (The Black Sheep), is open to non-residents so advance booking is essential.

Breakfast can be had outdoors – perhaps in the shade of linden trees. At the right time of the year the gardens are bright with flowers – and there are plenty of secluded corners, with the result that the place seems calm and quiet even when the hotel is full. The small garden pool is ideal for quiet cooling off, the larger one is more out of the way.

A visitor pronounces the hotel 'expensive, but professional and worth it', and the food 'very satisfactory'.

Nearby Siena (22 km); San Gimignano, Florence within reach.

Localita Ricavo, Castellina in Chianti 53011 Siena
Tel (0577) 740221
Fax (0577) 741014
Location isolated in countryside, about 1 km N of Castellina; in gardens, with ample car parking
Food & drink breakfast, dinner
Prices rooms LLL-LLLL with breakfast; meals L-LL
Rooms 20 double (10 twin), 1 single, 2 family rooms; all with bath; all have central heating, phone, TV, safe, minibar
Facilities 3 sitting-rooms, bar, dining-room; 1 swimming-pool, table tennis, 1 *boccia* court, gym **Credit cards** MC, V
Children accepted
Disabled not suitable
Pets not accepted
Closed Nov to Easter; restaurant only, Tue, Wed; Mon to Thur lunch in summer **Proprietors** Scotoni and Lobrano families

Tuscany

Country villa, Castellina in Chianti

Villa Casalecchi

It is not difficult to find fault with this unassuming villa immersed in woods and vineyards in the heart of Chianti. It does not set particularly high standards of decoration, house-keeping or cuisine, and not all of those involved in its running are notably welcoming. But Casalecchi is one of those places it is always comfortable to be going back to; perhaps the fact that it does not feel the need to try too hard is part of its charm.

The house sits high on a steepish slope. There is no clearly defined front and back, but you approach from above, and below is the fair-sized pool. Bedrooms fall into two categories: the old ones in the main house, which are lofty, fairly spacious and full of lovely antique furniture; and the ones added on to the downhill side of the house overlooking the pool, which are rather cramped but which have the undeniable attraction of a terrace immediately outside where you can take breakfast with nothing but trees and vines in view – a great advance on the dreary breakfast room. The sitting-areas – one a sort of lobby and the other a more rustic affair looking out over the vineyards – are no more than adequately comfortable. The dining-room, in welcome contrast, boasts splendid old wood-panelled walls.

Nearby Florence, Siena, San Gimignano, Volterra and Perugia.

Castellina in Chianti
53011 Siena
Tel (0577) 740240
Fax (0577) 741111
Location one km S of Castellina, in countryside, with adequate car parking
Food & drink breakfast, lunch, dinner
Prices rooms LLL-LLLL with breakfast; DB&B LLL; 20% reduction for children under 6; meals L-LL
Rooms 19 double, 14 with bath, 5 with shower; all rooms have central heating, phone, hairdrier, TV
Facilities dining-room, breakfast room, bar, 2 sitting-rooms; swimming-pool, tennis court
Credit cards AE, DC, MC, V
Children accepted
Disabled access difficult
Pets accepted, but not in public rooms **Closed** Oct to Mar **Proprietor** Elvira Lecchini- Giovannoni

Tuscany

Country guest-house, Fiesole

Bencista

'Don't send us too many tourists,' the smooth Simone Simoni begged our inspector – and he genuinely meant it. It is easy to see why the Bencista is so popular. The *pensione* stands on a hillside overlooking Florence and the Tuscan hills; views from the terrace and many of the bedrooms are unforgettable. Added to this are the charms of the building, once a monastery, a handsome hallway, three salons almost entirely furnished with antiques (including a little reading-room with shelves of books and a cosy fire), plus plenty of fascinating nooks and crannies.

No two bedrooms are alike, and each one has some captivating feature – perhaps a beautiful view, a fine piece of furniture, a huge bathroom or, in some, a private terrace. They are nearly all old-fashioned, with plain whitewashed walls and solid antiques, and the accent is more on character than luxury. The dining-room is simple, light and spacious, overlooking gardens where olives, roses and magnolia flourish. Breakfast is taken *al fresco* on the terrace – a glorious spot to start (and end) the day. Dinner is on the dot at 7.30 pm and no choice is offered (except soup as an alternative to pasta); the house wine is excellent.

Nearby Roman theatre, cathedral and monastery, all at Fiesole.

Via B da Maiano 4,
Fiesole 50014
Tel & fax (055) 59163
Location 2.5 km S of Fiesole on Florence road, set in private park overlooking city; garage and ample open-air car parking
Food & drink breakfast, lunch, dinner
Prices DB&B LLL; FB LLL
Rooms 29 double, 28 with bath, 13 with shower; 13 single, 7 with bath; all rooms have central heating, phone
Facilities 3 sitting-rooms, dining-room
Credit cards not accepted
Children accepted
Disabled no special facilities
Pets no dogs in restaurant
Closed never
Proprietor Simone Simoni

Tuscany

Country villa, Fiesole

Villa San Michele

According to its brochure the Villa was designed by Michelangelo – which perhaps accounts in part for the high prices. Rooms are among the most expensive in Italy – only a fraction less than at the hotel's more swanky sister, the Cipriani in Venice – and beyond the reach of most readers; but the guide would be incomplete without this little gem on the peaceful hillside of Fiesole – originally a monastery, built in the early part of the 15th century, enlarged towards the end of it, and much expanded recently with the creation of thirteen extra suites.

What you get for your money is not extravagant decoration or ostentatious luxury but restrained good taste and an expertly preserved aura of the past. The furniture is mostly solid antiques including 17thC masterpieces (religiously maintained every winter, we are told); many of the bedrooms have tiled floors of notable antiquity. Bathrooms, on the other hand, are impressively contemporary. Views from the villa are exceptional. One of the great delights of the place is to dine *al fresco* in the loggia, gazing down slopes of olives and cypresses to the city below. The pool terraces share this glorious view. Breakfast is an American buffet feast; DB&B prices include an *à la carte* meal, lunch or dinner.
Nearby Roman theatre, cathedral and monastery of San Francesco at Fiesole.

Via Doccia 4, Fiesole 50014
Tel (055) 59451
Fax (055) 598734
Location on Florence- Fiesole road, in private grounds with car parking available
Food & drink breakfast, lunch, dinner
Prices rooms LLLLL with breakfast; DB&B LLLL
Rooms 25 double, 15 suites; all with bath and shower; all rooms have central heating, air- conditioning, music, phone; TV and minibar on request
Facilities reading-room/bar, piano bar, dining-room with loggia/terrace; heated swimming-pool (open Jun to Sep) **Credit cards** AE, DC, MC, V **Children** accepted
Disabled 1 suite, with easy access **Pets** small dogs only, but not in dining-room or in pool area
Closed mid-Nov to mid-Mar
Manager Maurizio Saccani

Tuscany

Town hotel, Florence

Hermitage

The location, just north of the Ponte Vecchio, is highly central, and highly favoured: few hotels this close to Florence's main drag could be described as peaceful, but this Lilliputian-scale retreat is not inappropriately named. There is an air of tranquillity about it – helped by a judicious, although not always sufficient, amount of double-glazing on the busier riverside aspect.

Everything about the Hermitage is small, like a doll's house – only upside down, with neat, graceful bedrooms on the lower floors while the reception desk and public rooms are on the fifth floor, overlooking the Arno. It's worth the climb: both bar-lounge and breakfast room are delightfully domestic, in cool lemony yellows made intimate and welcoming with flowers and pictures.

The Hermitage was once no more than one of the typical, older-style pensions that are becoming rare in Florence. But it has had a marked face-lift and, as a recent inspection revealed, is now more tasteful and well-kept than average. A flower-filled roof terrace offers views across the pantiles of old Florence to the Duomo – an appealing place for breakfast.

Nearby Uffizi gallery, Ponte Vecchio.

Vicolo Marzio 1, Piazza del Pesce, Florence 50122
Tel (055) 287216
Fax (055) 212208
E-mail florence@hermitagehotel.com
Website http:/www.hermitagehotel.com
Location in heart of city, facing the river; car parking difficult; garage
Food & drink breakfast, snacks
Prices rooms LLLL with breakfast
Rooms 28 double, 14 with bath and Jacuzzi shower; 7 with bath/shower; 7 with Jacuzzi shower; all rooms have central heating, phone, satellite TV, air-conditioning
Facilities breakfast room, sitting-room with bar, roof terrace
Credit cards V
Children welcome
Disabled access difficult
Pets small dogs only
Closed never
Proprietor Vincenzo Scarcelli

Tuscany

Town hotel, Florence

Hotel J and J

A converted monastery provides the setting for this cool, chic hotel some distance east of the Duomo, on the way to the Sant'Ambroggio market. The street is comparatively quiet, and inside the hotel feels a haven from heat and dust, so effective is its air-conditioning and tranquil ambience.

Many original features of the building are still intact – columns, vaulted ceilings, frescos and wooden beams – and furnishings, though stylishly modern in places, are sympathetic to the spirit of the antique setting, and certainly not lacking personality. A small, pretty patio garden at the rear of the hotel, with elegant white parasols and plants in tubs, tempts breakfast-eaters to venture out through the plate-glass doors, though the interior option is equally charming in shades of yellow and green with wicker seating.

Bedrooms vary. All are of high standard; some exceptionally spacious, with split-level floors and seating areas, and high ceilings with exposed beams. A recent visitor felt that their eclectic style made them more like private rooms than hotel ones.

We found the reception knowledgeable and efficient.

Nearby Duomo, church of Santa Croce.

Via di Mezzo 20,
50121 Florence
Tel (055) 2345005
Fax (055) 240282
Location east of the duomo, north of Santa Croce
Food & drink breakfast
Prices rooms LLLL;
suites LLLL
Rooms 18 double, 2 family rooms, all with bath; all rooms have central heating, air-conditioning, phone, hairdrier, TV, minibar

Facilities sitting-room, bar
Credit cards AE, DC, MC, V
Children welcome
Disabled no special facilities
Pets not accepted
Closed never
Proprietor Cavagnari family

Tuscany

Town hotel, Florence

Loggiato dei Serviti

One of Florence's newest charming hotels is in one of its loveliest Renaissance buildings, designed (around 1527) by Sangallo the Elder to match Brunelleschi's famous Hospital of the Innocenti, opposite. Until a few years ago the building housed a modest *pensione* and the beautiful square was a giant car park. But the Loggiato is now elegantly restored and, thanks to the city council's change of heart, much more tranquil.

The decoration is a skilful blend of old and new, all designed to complement the original vaulting and other features with a minimum of frill and fuss. Floors are terracotta tiled, walls rag painted in pastel colours. Bedrooms are individually decorated with sympathy and flair. There is a small, bright breakfast room in which to start the day (with fruit juice, cheese and ham, brioches, fruit and coffee) and a little bar where you can recover from it, browsing glossy magazines and sipping a Campari.

A recent reporter mentions the difficulty of access with luggage to the 'pedestrian only' square. Another inspector draws attention to the sought-after rooms which have unparalled views of the Duomo, and to the helpful reception staff.

Nearby church of Santissima Annunziata, Foundlings' Hospital.

Piazza SS Annunziata 3,
Florence 50122
Tel (055) 289592
Fax (055) 289595
Location a few minutes' walk
N of the *Duomo*, on W side of
Piazza SS Annunziata; garage
service on request
Food & drink breakfast
Prices rooms LL-LLLL with
breakfast; suites LLLL
Rooms 19 double, 6 single, all
with bath or shower; 4 suites,
all with bath or shower; all

rooms have air-
conditioning/heating,
satellite TV, phone, minibar,
hairdrier, safe
Facilities breakfast room, bar
Credit cards AE, DC, MC, V
Children welcome
Disabled not suitable
Pets accepted
Closed never
Proprietor Rodolfo Budini-
Gattai

Tuscany

Town villa, Florence

Monna Lisa

A recent inspection revealed what we have previously suspected from shorter visits and readers' comments – that the reception here is somewhat cool and that the hotel lacks the 'heart' of similar establishments in Florence.

Five minutes' walk from the *Duomo*, the Monna Lisa is an elegant Renaissance *palazzo* around a small courtyard set back from the unprepossessing street façade. The main rooms, on the ground floor, have polished brick floors with Oriental carpets and beamed or vaulted ceilings, plus a very individual collection of antique furniture, paintings and sculpture. In the cosy little salon is the first model for Giambologna's famous Rape of the Sabines, and there is also a collection of drawings and statues by Giovanni Dupre, the neo-classical sculptor, from whom the owner's family is descended.

Some of the bedrooms are rather run-of-the-mill but the best are huge and high-ceilinged, with old furniture; some overlook the lovely courtyard-garden – an attraction in any location but a rare bonus in Florence.

Nearby *Duomo* (about five minutes' walk), Santa Croce, Bargello, Uffizi all within easy walking distance.

Borgo Pinti 27, Florence 50121
Tel (055) 247 9751
Fax (055) 247 9755
Location about 5 minutes' walk E of the *Duomo*; with garden and private car parking
Food & drink breakfast
Prices rooms LLL-LLLL with breakfast
Rooms 30 double, 6 single; all with bath or shower; all rooms have central heating, air-conditioning, phone, minibar, colour TV, safe
Facilities sitting-rooms, bar
Credit cards AE, DC, V
Children accepted
Disabled no special facilities
Pets accepted
Closed never
Manager Agostino Cona

Tuscany

City hotel, Florence

Morandi alla Crocetta

This lovely old house, formerly a convent, is the family home of Mrs Kathleen Doyle Antuono, an Englishwoman who has lived here since the 1920s. Now widowed, Mrs Doyle Antuono, with her son and daughter, share their house with visitors, and have made a great success of it.

The house is decorated throughout with taste and care. Antique Tuscan furnishings, patterned rugs, interesting pictures and fresh flowers abound. You may spot corbels carved with coats of arms in the reception hall, ancient painted tiles or fragments of fresco in the bedrooms, or a portrait of Mrs Doyle as an 18-year-old beauty. Our most recent inspector was impressed not only by her lovely frescoed room, but by the attention to detail, such as the thoughtful lighting, heated towel rail and even a tele-phone in the bathroom. Other visitors, though, found the walk up two flights of stairs to the lobby, unaided and with luggage, a struggle. The house, which is close to the Piazza Santissima Anunziata with is famous Spedale Innocente, is convenient for exploring the historic centre of the city.
Nearby Cathedral, archaeological museum, Academy of Fine Art.

Via Laura 50, Florence 50121
Tel (055) 234 4747
Fax (055) 248 0954
Location in quiet street, NW of Piazza del Duomo; car parking on street problematic
Food & drink breakfast
Prices rooms LL (familiy rooms more); breakfast L18,000
Rooms 4 double, 2 single, 4 family rooms, all with shower; all have central heating, air-conditioning, phone, TV, hairdrier, radio, minibar, safe
Facilities breakfast room, sitting-room
Credit cards AE, DC, MC, V
Children welcome
Disabled no special facilities
Pets small well-behaved dogs accepted
Closed never
Proprietor Kathleen Doyle Antuono and family

Tuscany

Hilltop villa, Florence

Torre di Bellosguardo

Giovanni Franchetti began renovating his beautiful 16thC family home, on the hilly outskirts south of the Arno, in 1980. His aim to create 'a peaceful oasis where travellers can feel as comfortable as in their own homes' has certainly succeeded, though few visitors to Torre di Bellosguardo can be lucky enough to live in such delightful surroundings (Bellosguardo means 'beautiful view') and is an apt name.

There are sixteen luxurious guest rooms in the house which, although grand, is not at all gaunt or dreary. Each room is a separate world, as much a sitting-room as a bedroom, carefully and individually furnished with fascinating antiques; some are split-level, others have splendid inlaid panelling. The gardens of well kept lawns and lily ponds, ancient cypress trees and shady terraces (not forgetting a secluded swimming-pool), exert as much pulling power as the interior. The unassuming geniality of the owner is a refreshing contrast to many a haughty hireling in Florence's central hotels.

Energetic guests could easily walk into the city – though the gradients on the return journey may suggest a taxi-ride.
Nearby Ponte Vecchio, Pitti Palace, Passeggiata ai Colli.

Via Roti Michelozzi 2,
Florence 50124
Tel (055) 229 8145
Fax (055) 229008
Location on hill overlooking city, just S of Porta Romana; with garden and car parking
Food & drink breakfast, lunch (by swimming-pool)
Prices rooms LLL-LLLL; suites LLLL; breakfast L30,000
Rooms 8 double, 2 single, 6 suites, all with bath; all rooms have central heating, phone; 5 rooms have air-conditioning
Facilities breakfast-room, sitting- rooms, bar; swimming-pool
Credit cards AE, DC, MC, V
Children accepted
Disabled lift/elevator
Pets accepted
Closed never
Proprietor Giovanni Franchetti

Tuscany

Villa Belvedere

This family-run hotel lies in a pleasant hilly residential district on the southern outskirts of the city, commanding excellent views through classically Tuscan cypress trees when Florentine smog permits. The building itself is no great beauty, being practical and modern, but its well kept gardens and small swimming-pool are a great boon in hot weather, and its peaceful surroundings, away from any passing traffic, a relief from the city centre at any time of the year.

The Ceschi-Perotto family manage their business with welcoming enthusiasm and efficiency, and have embarked on an ambitious programme of refurbishment. Bedrooms and bathrooms are in excellent decorative order in a smart matching scheme of *fleur de lys* motifs, racing greens and high-quality solid wood furnishings. Bathrooms gleam, with white tiles offset by restrained geometric friezes. Public areas are light, spacious and comfortable – and the breakfast room makes the best of the garden.

A limited evening snack menu is available until 8.30 pm – particularly useful after a tiring day's sightseeing, since there are few restaurants within easy walking distance.

Nearby Pitti Palace, Boboli gardens.

Via Benedetto Castelli 3,
Florence 50124
Tel (055) 222501
Fax (055) 223163
Location 3 km S of city, in gardens with some private car parking
Food & drink breakfast, snacks
Prices rooms LLL with breakfast
Rooms 21 double, 19 with bath, 2 with shower; 2 single, one with bath, one with shower; 3 suites; all rooms have central heating, air-conditioning, phone, satellite TV, safe
Facilities breakfast room, 2 sitting-rooms, bar, TV room, veranda; swimming-pool, tennis
Credit cards AE, DC, MC, V
Children welcome
Disabled no special facilities
Pets not accepted
Closed Dec to Feb
Proprietors Ceschi-Perotto family

Tuscany

Country apartments, Gaiole in Chianti

Castello di Tornano

One of the countless defence and watch towers that dot Tuscany, solidly built of grey stone in positions with commandng views of the surrounding countryside, many of them in line of sight with their neighbours. Here, you find yourself in one of the wilder parts of Chianti with views of steep wooded hills, bleak in winter and, even in summer, with an air of inviolable isolation.

Most of the apartments are in a farmhouse adjoining the base of the thousand-year-old tower, and each has a living room with a kitchen area, and one or two bedrooms, furnished in a rustic style, deployed in a relatively simple manner. Some of the apartments are in the tower, and these are decorated with a more studied elegance. Each has its own entrance and a private outdoor area.

The swimming-pool is in a common area and, fittingly for the location, has been fashioned from the remains of the former moat, still spanned by a wooden bridge. Nearby is a small fishing lake and, at the bottom of the hill, a typical Tuscan *trattoria*. Produce from the estate (wine, oil, vinegar, cheese, eggs and salami) can be bought on the spot.

Nearby Siena (16 km); Florence (50 km).

Loc. Lecchi, Gaiole in Chianti, 53013 Siena
Tel (0577) 746067; (055) 6580918 (bookings)
Fax (0577) 746067; (055) 6580918 (bookings)
Location 5 km S of Gaiole; own grounds, ample car parking
Meals self-catering apartments; family *trattoria* nearby
Prices L-LL
Rooms 9 fully equipped apartments for 2-6 persons

Facilities bar, gardens; cleaners on request; swimming-pool, table-tennis; tennis court (L10,000 ph), horse riding (L25,000 ph)
Smoking permitted
Credit cards AE, DC
Children welcome
Disabled not suitable
Pets small, on request
Closed Nov to Mar
Languages English, French, some German
Manager Barbara Sevolini

Tuscany

Country village hotel, Lecchi in Chianti

San Sano

The medieval hamlet of San Sano, a clutter of stone houses with uneven terracotta roofs, has at its heart an ancient defence tower, destroyed and rebuilt many times. Now, in its latest incarnation, this imposing structure forms the core of a delightful, family-run hotel in a relatively little visited, authentic part of Chianti.

The various buildings surrounding the tower (which houses some of the bedrooms; others have direct access to the grounds) give the hotel a rambling character, connected by narrow passageways, steep stairways and unexpected courtyards. The restoration has been meticulous and restrained. The decoration is in classic, rustic Tuscan style, somewhat stark for some tastes, but with individual touches: carefully chosen antiques, colourful pottery and plenty of flowers. The dining-room, in the former stables, spanned by a massive stone arch and still with the feeding trough, is a cool haven from the summer sun. Each bedroom has its individual character (one with nesting birds in its perforated walls, now glassed off) and gleaming, almost surgical bathrooms. Outside is a stone-paved garden at the foot of the tower and, at a slight remove, a hillside swimming-pool.

Nearby Radda in Chianti (9 km); Siena (25 km); Florence (60).

Loc. San Sano, Lecchi in Chianti, 53010 Siena
Tel (0577) 746130
Fax (0577) 746156
Location hill-top hamlet in middle of countryside; own car parking
Meals breakfast, dinner
Prices LLL
Rooms 11 doubles, all with bath or shower, phone, central heating
Facilities sitting-areas, breakfast and dining-room, garden, swimming-pool
Smoking not allowed in some public areas
Credit cards AE, DC, EC, MC, V **Children** welcome
Disabled one adapted room; ground-floor rooms accessible
Pets please check first
Closed mid-Nov to mid-Mar
Languages English, German, French, Spanish
Proprietors Giancarlo and Heidi Matarazzo

Tuscany

Country estate, Mercatale Val di Pesa

Salvadonica

This delightful assembly of rustic buildings amid olive groves and vineyards will gladden the heart of any lover of Tuscan scenery. Two entrepreneurial young sisters have energetically converted a family home, on what was until recently a feudal estate, into a thriving bed-and-breakfast and 'agriturismo' business. A recent visitor was thoroughly enchanted by the place.

Now the two main buildings of the farm – one rich red stucco, the other mellow stone and brick – offer five well-equipped, comfortable guest rooms and ten apartments to let. They have clay-tiled floors and wood-beamed ceilings, and range from the merely harmonious and comfortable to the positively splendid – a brick-vaulted cowshed.

From the paved terraces surrounding the buildings, you look over an olive grove to the neat swimming-pool area with Jacuzzi. Tennis- courts and riding stables add alternative attractions. Breakfast, with a changing variety of cakes and breads is served in a pleasant stone-walled dining room or on a sunny terrace over-looking unspoilt sweeps of countryside, where the local 'Gallo Nero' Chianti wine and excellent olive oil are still produced.
Nearby Florence (20 km).

Via Grevigiana 82, 50024
Mercatale Val di Pesa
(Firenze)
Tel (055) 821 8039
Fax (055) 821 8043
Location 18km S of Florence, E of road to Siena
Food & drink breakfast
Prices rooms LL-LLL; apartment LLL; with breakfast
Rooms 5 double, 10 apartments, all with shower; all rooms have central heating, phone, TV on request; apartments have fridge
Facilities billiard-room, swimming-pool, tennis-courts, football
Credit cards AE, DC, MC, V
Children accepted
Disabled one room and one apartment
Pets not accepted
Closed Nov to Feb
Proprietors Baccetti family

Tuscany

Converted castle, Monte San Savino

Castello di Gargonza

Gargonza is not so much a castle as a whole hilltop village, perfectly preserved in a typically Tuscan landscape, encircled by walls and surrounded by cypresses. Its paved alleyways are car-free, except that you are allowed to drive in with your luggage.

Mostly dating from the 13thC, the houses offer good value for families or other small groups. They are by and large spacious, and simply furnished, and each has its own character and name (the farmer's house, the guard's house, Lucia's house). Bear in mind that this is meant to be self-catering accommodation, even if you don't plan to cater for yourself. There is no daily cleaning and bed-making, for example.

All the individual houses have kitchens but there is also a so-so restaurant just outside the walls – specialities include spinach and ricotta roulade, and wild boar; you can take breakfast in the old oil-pressing house ('il fantoio').The houses are let on a weekly basis but there is also a guest house, whose rather spartan rooms can be rented nightly. In addition to the new swimming-pool, the grounds have just been improved and the houses have undergone refurbishment; more reports please.

Nearby Arezzo (25 km); Chianti; Val di Chiana.

Gargonza, Monte San Savino 52048 Arezzo
Tel (0575) 847021
Fax (0575) 847054
Location 35 km E of Siena on SS73, 7 km W of Monte San Savino; walled village of 18 houses with garden; ample car parking outside village walls
Food & drink breakfast, lunch, dinner
Prices rooms LL-LLL with breakfast; meals L; weekly (Sat to Sat) L770,00-L2,520,000

Rooms 7 double in main guest-house; 25 self-catering houses; all rooms have phone, central heating; main guest-house rooms have minibar **Facilities** 4 sitting-rooms (2 for meetings), TV room; swimming-pool
Credit cards AE, DC, MC, V
Children accepted **Disabled** not suitable **Pets** small dogs only accepted **Closed** 3 weeks in Nov and Jan **Proprietor** Conte Roberto Guicciardini

Tuscany

Fattoria la Loggia

Montefiridolfi is set in classic Chianti countryside scattered with ancient estates producing wine and olive oil. Many of the mellow, stone farm buildings hereabouts are being turned into tourist accommodation of one sort and another, and Fattoria la Loggia is one of the most successful of its type: a range of spacious and attractive apartments agreeably housed in a hamlet-like collection of rural dwellings, in a hilltop setting with views over gloriously peaceful surroundings. The apartments are let daily or weekly. But this is not simply a self-catering complex – cooking lessons and dinners with wine tastings are sometimes organized in the cellar. Each unit is carefully furnished with country-style pieces and many personal touches; kitchens and bathrooms, however, are efficiently modern, and are finished to a very high standard. Visitors can swim, ride, or walk on the estate, which produces its own wine and olive oil. La Loggia has recently established an artists' studio, with a permananet museum of contemporary art, as well as providing a venue for concerts and live theatre.

Nearby Florence (15 km), San Gimignano (40 km), Siena (45 km), Volterra (55 km).

Via Collina 40, 50020
Montefiridolfi, Firenze
Tel (055) 824 4288
Fax (055) 824 4283
E-mail fatlaloggia@ftbcc.it
Location 15km S of Florence,
E of road to Siena
Food & drink breakfast
(dinner occasionally)
Prices apartments LLL, daily
or weekly
Rooms 11 apartments,
sleeping 2 to 6; 4 rooms; all
have central heating, fridge,
radio, phone, safe
Facilities restaurant;
swimming-pool, table-tennis,
bikes, horses, barbeque,
solarium
Credit cards not accepted
Children accepted
Disabled no special facilities
Pets by prior arrangement
Closed never
Proprietor Giulio Baruffaldi

Tuscany

Il Bottaccio

Il Bottaccio lies a couple of miles inland from the beaches of Forte dei Marmi, amid pale-coloured hill towns and grey-green olive groves. It is primarily a restaurant (Michelin-starred), serving 10-course meals of 'creative dishes inspired by Mediterranean tradition', which have earned high praise from the gourmet guides (and from our inspector). But it is a fantastic place to stay, too: overlooked by a ruined castle, it was originally an olive oil mill and the D'Anna family have successfully blended old and new in their conversion. Sitting areas are spacious and airy with black leather seating against white walls, exposed brick and rafters. Each suite is individual, vast and luxurious, combining fascinating features with great style. For example, the Appartamento delle Macine contains the original wooden workings of the mill, a 17thC fireplace, Eastern rugs and a mosaic-tiled sunken bath. Elsewhere, bathrooms combine local marble with hand-painted tiles to great effect. The dining-room is at once plain and extraordinary: bentwood chairs stand on persian rugs scattered on a traditional tiled floor beneath a beamed ceiling, and a large pool reflects the massive white marble statues.
Nearby Beaches of Forte dei Marmi; Pisa (30 km).

Via Bottaccio 1, 54038
Montignoso
Tel (0585) 340031
Fax 340103
Location 5 km SE of Massa;
with gardens and car parking
Food & drink breakfast,
lunch, dinner
Prices suites LLLL; meals LL-LLL
Rooms 8 suites, all with bath;
all rooms have phone, TV,
radio
Facilities dining-room,
terrace
Credit cards AE, DC, MC, V
Children accepted
Disabled no special facilities
Pets accepted
Closed never
Proprietors Stefano and
Elizabeth D'Anna

Tuscany

Country villa, Panzano in Chianti

Villa le Barone

Le Barone, the attractive 16thC country house of the della Robbia family (of ceramics fame), became a hotel in 1976, but still feels very much like a private home.

The small scale of the rooms helps, but there are several other factors. The antique furniture is obviously a personal collection; reception amounts to little more than a visitors' book in the hall; there are plenty of books around – including English ones – and there are always fresh flower arrangements in the elegant little sitting-rooms; and you help yourself to drinks, recording your consumption as you do so. In the past a minimum stay of three nights has further contributed to the low-key house-party atmosphere; but the rule has now been dropped.

Guests who are not out on sightseeing excursions have plenty of space to themselves in the peaceful woody garden or by the lovely pool, which gives a glorious panorama of the surrounding hills of Tuscany.

The restaurant and some of the rooms are in converted outbuildings. One of our most recent reports speaks of Villa le Barone as friendly and comfortable, at a fair price.

Nearby Siena (31 km), Florence (31 km).

Via San Leolino 19, 50020 Panzano in Chianti (Siena)
Tel (055) 852621 **Fax** 852277
Location 31 km S of Florence off SS222; covered car parking
Food & drink breakfast, lunch, dinner
Prices DB&B LLL (min 3 nights); reductions for children
Rooms 28 double, 22 with bath, 6 with shower; one single, with shower; all rooms have phone, hairdrier; 5 rooms have air-conditioning and tea/coffee kit
Facilities self-service bar, TV room, 3 sitting-rooms, dining-room, breakfast room; ping-pong, swimming-pool, tennis **Credit cards** AE, MC, V
Children welcome
Disabled not suitable
Pets not accepted
Closed Nov to Mar
Proprietor Marchesa Franca viani della Robbia

Tuscany

Country villa, Panzano in Chianti

Villa Sangiovese

The Bleulers used to manage the long-established Tenuta di Ricavo at Castellina (see page 101). They opened their doors in Panzano, a few miles to the north, in 1988 after completely renovating the building, and winning high praise from readers.

The main villa is a neat stone-and-stucco house fronting directly on to a quiet back-street; potted plants and a brass plate beside the doorway are the only signs of a hotel. Attached to this house is an old, rambling, stone building beside a flowery, gravelled courtyard-terrace offering splendid views. The landscaped garden below includes a fair-sized pool.

Inside, all is mellow, welcoming and stylish, with carefully chosen antique furnishings against plain, pale walls. Bedrooms, some with wood-beamed ceilings, are spacious, comfortable, and tastefully restrained in decoration. The dining-room is equally simple and stylish, with subdued wall lighting and bentwood chairs on a tiled floor.

A limited but interesting à la carte menu is offered, which changes each night – service on the terrace in summer. A reporter praises the food and the wine.

Nearby Greve (5 km); Siena (30 km); Florence (30 km).

Piazza Bucciarelli 5, 50020
Panzano in Chianti, Firenze
Tel (055) 852461
Fax (055) 852463
Location on edge of town,
5 km S of Greve; with large
garden and car parking
Food & drink breakfast,
lunch, dinner
Prices rooms LLL; suites
LLLL; meals LL
Rooms 15 double, one single,
3 suites, all with bath or
shower; all rooms have phone

Facilities dining-room, bar,
2 sitting-rooms, library,
terrace; swimming-pool
Credit cards MC, V
Children accepted
Disabled no special facilities
Pets not accepted
Closed Jan, Feb; restaurant
only, Wed
Proprietors Ulderico and
Anna Maria Bleuler

Tuscany

Locanda Sari

Locanda Sari has long been run by Carmen Pierangeli's family as a local inn and convenient port of call on the road over to Ravenna; but the traffic which once passed within feet of the front door now whizzes up a neo-motorway on the other side of the narrow valley, and a few years ago Carmen seized the opportunity to turn the Locanda into a place worth travelling to find.

The house has been restored with real panache in classy country style. In the bedrooms, rustic antiques and painted reproduction wardrobes sit on glistening tiled floors, with creamy rugs and bedspreads woven to a special pattern; old iron bedheads are fixed to the walls, but the beds themselves are new (and splendidly firm); the shower rooms are compact but smart. The dining-room shows the same simple good taste, but the real attraction here is Carmen's exquisite country cooking, of the kind that tourists rarely taste; most guests agree that the daily batch of ravioli, made with local ricotta, for example, is superb, though it was not to the taste of one reporter.

Carmen and English-speaking husband Pio are 'charming and hospitable' and most visitors find the proximity of the main road 'a bore but surprisingly unobjectionable'.

Nearby Sansepolcro (16 km); La Verna (20 km).

Via Tiberina km 177, Pieve Santo Stéfano, Arezzo
Tel (0575) 797053
Location in countryside 3 km N of village, on minor road; car parking across the road
Food & drink breakfast, lunch, dinner
Prices rooms L-LL; meals L
Rooms 8 double, one with bath, 7 with shower; all rooms have central heating
Facilities dining-room, lobby, bar; small terrace

Credit cards AE, DC
Children welcome
Disabled access difficult
Pets not accepted
Closed never
Proprietor Carmen Pierangeli

Tuscany

Converted monastery, Pistoia

Il Convento

A converted monastery in the verdant hills of Pistoia (between Lucca and Florence), white-painted with a tiled roof, sounds like quite a find – and so it is. Its great attraction is the setting, which is both peaceful and panoramic: you get grand views from the hotel and the terraces of its lush gardens below, which are carefully maintained and include an impressive swimming-pool (for which guests are charged) with a generous tiled surround. (It is also open to non-residents and can become crowded in summer).

Inside, Il Convento is not all that you might expect – bedrooms are uncompromisingly modern, with the emphasis firmly on efficient facilities and cleanliness rather than on antiquity or individual character. But the public rooms are more in sympathy with their surroundings – particularly the restaurant, where the original cells have been converted into tiny, intimate dining-rooms. The sitting-room has plenty of space and comfortable chairs and sofas. Several reporters recently judged the staff to be 'not particularly helpful' and the food 'limited', the wine 'expensive'. Keep us posted, please.

Nearby sights of Pistoia; Prato, Florence within reach.

Via San Quirico 33,
Pontenuovo, Pistoia 51100
Tel (0573) 452652
Fax (0573) 453758
Location 4 km E of Pistoia in Pontenuovo area, on hillside overlooking city; with car parking space
Food & drink breakfast, lunch, dinner
Prices rooms LL with breakfast; DB&B LL; meals L
Rooms 20 double, 4 single; all with bath; all rooms have central heating, phone, TV
Facilities dining-room, sitting-area, bar, games room; swimming-pool (charge)
Credit cards MC, V
Children accepted
Disabled access difficult
Pets not accepted
Closed restaurant only, Mon
Proprietor Paolo Petrini

Tuscany

Country villa, Pistoia

Villa Vannini

Here is a real gem, lying in an area which has surprisingly few small, charming places to stay – in a remote and delightfully quiet setting, high on a hill about 2 km above the small village of Piteccio and not far from the lively little city of Pistoia. To get there, you wind your way up a narrow, roughly surfaced road through unspoiled countryside. The congenial Signora Vannini offers a particularly warm welcome, and looks after her house with loving care. There are various little sitting areas with large vases of flowers, chintz or chunky modern seats, prints and water-colours, and the sort of antiques that complete an elegant family home. The dining-room, with its whitewashed walls, china plates, polished parquet floor and marble fireplace, makes a elegant setting for the excellent Tuscan specialities that are served here ('spectacular – the best we had anywhere on our travels,' says one report). 'Excellent' breakfast, too. Bedrooms are beautifully and individually furnished – many in flowery fabrics and with fine antiques. In front of the house a simple terrace provides a haven after a day's sightseeing in Pistoia, Florence or Lucca.
Nearby cathedral, Ospedale del Ceppo and church of Sant' Andrea at Pistoia.

Villa di Piteccio, 51030 Pistoia
Tel (0573) 42031
Fax (0573) 26331
Location 6 km N of Pistoia; take Abelone road from Pistoia, branch right towards Piteccio before Piazza; on hillside, in private garden, with car parking
Food & drink breakfast, lunch, dinner
Prices rooms LL with breakfast; DB&B LLL (reductions for minimum of 3 days' stay); dinner LL
Rooms 8 double with bath
Facilities 2 sitting-rooms, games room, 2 dining-rooms
Credit cards not accepted
Children not very suitable
Disabled no special facilities
Pets not accepted
Closed never
Proprietor Maria-Rosa Vannini

Tuscany

Seaside hotel, Porto Ercole

Il Pellicano

Porto Ercole is one of those fashionable little harbours where wealthy Romans moor their boats at weekends. Il Pellicano is an elegant, russet-coloured vine-clad villa with gardens tumbling down to the rocky shoreline, where the flat rocks have been designated the hotel's 'private beach'. It offers the luxury and exclusivity you might expect from a very expensive four-star seaside hotel but manages at the same time to preserve the style and informality of a private Tuscan villa – and the exposed beams, stone arches and antique features make it feel much older than it really is. Antique country-house furnishings are offset by white-washed walls, brightly coloured stylish sofas and large vases of flowers. Fish and seafood are the best things in the restaurant – if you can stomach the prices. Meals in summer are served on the delightful open-air terrace in the garden, or beside the pool where the spread of *antipasti* is a feast for the eyes. Service is impeccable. Peaceful bedrooms, many in two-storey cottages, combine antiques and modern fabrics. The majority are cool and spacious, and all of them have a terrace or balcony. Watch out for swarms of mosquitoes, warns our inspector.
Nearby Orbetello (16 km).

Cala dei Santi, 58018 Porto Ercole Grosseto
Tel (0564) 858111
Fax (0564) 833418
E-mail Pr@Pellicanohotel.com
Website http://www.Pellicanohotel.com
Location 4 km from middle of resort, in gardens overlooking the sea; car parking
Food & drink breakfast, lunch, dinner
Prices rooms LLL-LLLL; suites LLLL
Rooms 27 double; 14 suites (6 de luxe), all with bath and shower; all rooms have central heating, air-conditioning, minibar, phone, cable TV
Facilities restaurants, bars, sitting area; terraces; beauty centre, swimming-pool; clay-pigeon shooting, tennis, riding, water-skiing **Credit cards** AE, DC, V **Children** accepted over 12 **Disabled** access difficult **Pets** not accepted **Closed** Nov to Mar
Manager Mrs Cinzia Fanciulli

Tuscany

Country villa, Prato

Villa Rucellai

This is a quintessential charming small hotel. Industrial Prato creeps almost to the doors of the mellow old villa, and the railway line skirts the property, but this should not deter you from visiting a very special place.

Its origins date back to a medieval watchtower, and it has been in the venerable Rucellai family since 1740. The unsightly views from the lovely terrace – filled with lemon trees – and the loggia, are more than compensated for by the atmosphere of the house, the warm welcome and the modest prices. Behind the property rise the beautiful Pratese Hills, which can be explored on foot from the house.

Guests have the run of the main part of the house, with its baronial hall and comfortable sitting-room, filled with pictures and books. Breakfast is self-service and is taken around a communal table in the homely dining-room. The bedrooms are simply furnished and full of character; they reflect the rare attribute of the place – that of a well-run hotel which gives no hint of being anything but a cultivated family home. A recent visitor was impressed – except for some of the homemade food and wine.

Nearby Prato; Florence (20 km).

Via di Canneto 16,
59100 Prato (Florence)
Tel (0574) 460392
Location down a narrow
street, in Bisenzio river
valley, 4 km NE of Prato,
(keep parallel with river and
train tracks on your left); with
car parking and grounds
Food & drink breakfast
Prices rooms LL
Rooms 12 double, one
family room; all rooms have
bath or shower; all have
central heating;
Facilities dining-room,
sitting- room, TV room,
gymnasium, terrace;
swimming-pool
Credit cards not accepted
Children welcome; cots and
high chairs by arrangement
Disabled not suitable
Pets not usually accepted
Closed never
Proprietors Rucellai Piqué
family

Tuscany

Country bed-and-breakfast, Pugnano

Casetta delle Selve

Yet another elevated Tuscan farmhouse – but this one, first drawn to our attention by a French reader who summarized it as a 'petit paradis', has a personality all its own. Access is tricky, on an unpaved road up a steep hill. Once safely arrived, however, the gleaming white house, the peaceful surroundings, the flower-filled garden and the red-tiled terrace with wonderful views are all there, as you would hope – but the interior is stunningly different from the norm.

Not only is the whole house exceptionally well maintained, with varnished beams standing out against immaculate white paintwork, but the bedrooms have bold, bright colour schemes, involving bedheads, rugs, bedspreads (all handmade by Signora Menchi) and pictures (lots of them) – all happily rubbing along with the antique furniture. Public areas are more sober, but still full of pictures and ornaments, and gleaming antiques.

Nicla Menchi is no ordinary hotelier either – 'the most unusual hostess of any on our trip', 'quite understanding of our American inability to speak Italian or French', 'provided a breakfast difficult to fault' – and many visitors leave as her friend.
Nearby Lucca (10 km); Pisa (12 km).

Pugnano 56010 Pisa
Tel & Fax (050) 850359
Location in countryside 2 km off SS12, E of Pugnano, 10 km SW of Lucca; with car parking
Food & drink breakfast
Prices rooms LL; breakfast L15,000
Rooms 5 double, one family room, all with bath; all rooms have central heating
Facilities breakfast room, terrace

Credit cards not accepted
Children accepted
Disabled no special facilities
Pets accepted
Closed never
Proprietor Nicla Menchi

Tuscany

Country hotel, Radda in Chianti

Relais Fattoria Vignale

This has always been a favourite with our inspectors, and recent visits have left their enthusiasm undimmed. The house is built on a slope down from the middle of the village. On the main 'ground' floor are four interconnecting sitting-rooms, each on a domestic scale, and beautifully furnished with comfy sofas, antiques, muted rugs on polished terracotta floors, walls either white and dotted with paintings or covered by murals – and one or two grand stone fireplaces. The bedrooms above are similarly classy, with waxed wooden doors, white walls and antique beds. The sitting-rooms, the back bedrooms and the pool all share a grand view across the Radda Valley.

A recent addition to the Relais Fattoria Vignale is the lovely breakfast terrace; in cool weather there is a neat breakfast-room in a brick vault beneath the hotel, where an excellent buffet is set out, and coffee and extras are served by friendly waitresses. There is also a 'taverna' for light dinners.

The best-known local restaurant, serving the innovative creations of its chef-*patron*, (also called Vignale) is only 300m away; the hotel will make reservations for you.

Nearby Siena, Florence, Arezzo all within reach.

Via Pianigiani 15, Radda in Chianti 53017 Siena
Tel (0577) 738300
Fax (0577) 738592
Location in middle of village, 31 km N of Siena, with private gardens and ample car parking
Food & drink breakfast, snacks
Prices rooms LLL-LLLL with breakfast
Rooms 20 double, 4 with bath, 16 with shower; 3 suites with shower; 3 single, all with shower; 3 family rooms, all with bath; all rooms have central heating, air-conditioning, phone, minibar
Facilities 3 sitting-rooms, breakfast room, indoor and pool bars, conference room
Credit cards AE, MC, V
Children accepted, but prefer quiet ones **Disabled** access difficult **Pets** not accepted
Closed 8th to 26th Dec; 6th Jan to 25th Mar
Manager Silvia Kummer

Tuscany

Country hotel, Radda in Chianti

Vescine – Il Relais del Chianti

We list this fairly recent addition under Radda, but it is in fact miles from anywhere, and well suited to those who want peace and seclusion. When we visited, most of the guests were silently bronzing themselves by the smart pool, occasionally lifting an eye to the glorious Chianti countryside stretching away from Vescine.

Vescine is yet another little Tuscan hamlet that has been rescued from dereliction to form a hotel – in this case, opened only in 1990. Its restoration was exceptionally thorough; there is vegetation only where the architects intended vegetation – every other square inch of ground is neatly covered in brick and tile, while borders and terraces overflow with greenery and blooms. Bedrooms are in several separate houses, employing the formula of plain walls with occasional pictures, tiled floors, exposed beams and sparse furnishings. There is a stylish breakfast room, and above it a pleasant bar/sitting-room with a spacious terrace. But dining means stirring yourself for a half-mile expedition to the associated restaurant, La Cantoniera, or a longer drive into Radda or Castellina. 'Spartan, but divinely isolated, according to a recent, relaxed visitor.'

Nearby Siena, Florence, Arezzo all within reach.

Loc. Vescine, Radda in Chianti 53017 Siena
Tel (0577) 741144
Fax (0577) 740263
Location in countryside mid-way between Radda and Castellina, 30 km N of Siena, in private grounds with ample car parking
Food & drink buffet breakfast; associated restaurant 700m away (LL)
Prices rooms LLL with breakfast; suite LLL-LLLL

Rooms 19 double, all with shower; 6 suites; all rooms have central heating, phone, minibar, satellite TV
Facilities sitting-room/bar, breakfast room; swimming-pool, tennis court; horse-riding nearby
Credit cards AE, MC, V
Children accepted
Disabled access difficult
Pets accepted
Closed Nov and Feb
Manager Birgit Fleig

Tuscany

Hilltop villa, Reggello

Villa Rigacci

This creeper-covered 15thC farmhouse, opened as a hotel for just over a decade, is in a beautiful secluded spot – on a hilltop surrounded by olive groves, pines, chestnut trees and meadows – yet only a few kilometres from the Florence-Rome autostrada, and a short drive from Florence and Arezzo.

Many of the original features of the house have been preserved – arched doorways, beamed bedrooms, tiled or stone-flagged floors – and it is furnished as a cherished private house might be. The sitting-room has an open fire in chilly weather. The bedrooms – the best (though not all) of them gloriously spacious – are full of gleaming antiques, and overlook the gardens or swimming-pool, which is of fair size, with a pleasant tile-and-grass surround and woodland views. For relaxation, there are plenty of quiet, shady spots in the park, which contains some magnificent trees.

An otherwise satisfied visitor who 'enjoyed a lovely holiday here' was disappointed that the food was predominantly 'sophisticated French' in style, but we are assured that although the cuisine is international, Tuscan dishes are also offered.
Nearby Florence (35 km); Arezzo (45 km).

Vággio 76, Reggello 50066
Tel (055) 865 6718/562
Fax (055) 865 6537
Location 300m N of Vággio, 30 km SE of Florence; exit Incisa from A1; with car parking and gardens
Food & drink breakfast, lunch, dinner
Prices rooms LL-LLL; DB&B LLL
Rooms 16 double (5 superior), 4 suites; 3 single with bath; all rooms have central heating, air-conditioning, phone, TV, radio, minibar
Facilities dining-room, sitting- rooms, library; swimming- pool
Credit cards AE, DC, MC, V
Children tolerated
Disabled not suitable
Pets accepted if small and well-behaved
Closed never
Proprietors Frederic and Florence Pierazzi

Tuscany

Villa di Corliano

A sweeping, tree-lined drive leading through lawns with lofty palms to a fine late Renaissance mansion set against thickly wooded hills; then, an interior no less splendid – frescos embellishing every inch of wall and ceiling, handsome classical busts on ornate stands, antiques, chandeliers and, from the 16thC salon and its balcony, a beautiful view of the sloping lawns below. Ruinously expensive? For once, no: all this comes for less than you pay for a room in some seedy station hotel in Pisa.

The bedrooms are not quite so grand; the cheapest border on the basic, with a basin and portable bidet (hidden discreetly behind decorative screens), creaky beds and possibly a long walk to the public bathroom. But there is compensation in the sheer size of the bedrooms (most are huge, with big 1920s wardrobes). The best doubles have touches of grandeur, and their own bathrooms; and the only rooms that could be described as small are the three in the 'tower' at the top. The old cellars serve as the breakfast room, and one of the buildings next to the main house is the restaurant. A recent visitor comments: 'A memorable dinner with genuinely caring service.' Another called it 'unique'.

Nearby Pisa (10 km); Lucca (15 km).

Rigoli, San Giuliano Terme
56010 Pisa
Tel (050) 818193
Fax (050) 818897
Location 2.5 km NW of San Giuliano Terme at Rigoli; in large park with ample car parking
Food & drink breakfast, dinner
Prices rooms L-LL; suite LLL; breakfast L; meals LL
Rooms 18 double, 6 with bath, 4 with shower; all rooms have central heating, phone
Facilities sitting-rooms, bar, breakfast room, tea room, TV room, conference room
Credit cards MC, V
Children acccepted
Disabled no special facilities
Pets accepted
Closed never
Proprietor Conte Ferdinando Agostini Venerosi della Seta

Tuscany

Country hotel, San Gimignano

Pescille

The Pescille is a rambling hilltop manor house, converted to a hotel in 1970 with great taste and care, and with sufficient diversions to keep you there all day if sightseeing seems too strenuous. In 1987 its main weakness – the lack of a restaurant – was remedied in no uncertain manner by the creation of a big, independently run restaurant, the Cinque Gigli. Sadly, this restaurant has now closed.

However, Pescille remains in general a peaceful and relaxing haven, despite the increase in the number of rooms. The rustic terraced garden has plenty of secluded spots, while indoors there are several little sitting areas, which trendily mix smart modern furniture with antique agri-cultural clutter. One visitor found the swimming-pool to be less than ideal – it has a raised lip about a foot high, which makes it seem utilitarian.

Bedrooms are simple, stylish and moderately spacious, with enchanting views of open countryside or towards the distinctive skyline of San Gimignano.

We would welcome more reports.

Nearby San Gimignano; Florence, Siena, Pisa all within reach.

Localita Pescille, San Gimignano 53037 Siena
Tel (0577) 940186
Fax (0577) 943165
E-mail pescille@iol.it
Website http://web.tin.it/san gimignano
Location 3 km SW of San Gimignano, in large gardens with private car parking
Food & drink breakfast
Prices rooms LLL
Rooms 50 double; all with bath; all rooms have bath,
central heating, phone; 12 with air-conditioning
Facilities sitting-room, TV room, breakfast room, bar; swimming-pool, tennis, bowls
Credit cards AE, DC, MC, V
Children accepted, provided they are quiet
Disabled access difficult
Pets not accepted
Closed Nov to Mar
Proprietors Gigli brothers

Tuscany

Country hotel, San Gimignano

Le Renaie

A simple, well-run country hotel – built up over the years by the present owners from a simple bar and restaurant – which makes a respectable base within a short drive of San Gimignano. Outside, Le Renaie looks fairly unprepossessing: just a modern villa set back from a rural lane. Inside, it is cool and pretty with freshly painted walls, rattan furniture and traditional polished brick floors; bedrooms are spacious and immaculate, some with individual terraces. The restaurant, Da Leonetto, is popular with locals but gets mixed notices from reporters; on fine days you can eat outside on the veranda. For most holidaymakers the chief attractions are the small swimming-pool, the tranquil location ('a guest can live peaceful hours of repose', promises the brochure) and the reasonable prices.

Nearby sights of San Gimignano; hills and vineyards of Chianti; Volterra, Siena, Florence within reach.

Localita Pancole,
San Gimignano 53037 Siena
Tel (0577) 955044
Location 6 km N of San
Gimignano off road to
Certaldo; private car parking
Food & drink breakfast,
lunch, dinner
Prices rooms LL; DB&B LL;
meals L
Rooms 25 double, one single;
all with bath; all rooms have
phone, satellite TV, air-
conditioning, safe, minibar

Facilities hall, room, dining-
room, bar; swimming- pool,
tennis
Credit cards AE, DC, MC, V
Children accepted, but must
be accompanied by parents at
swimming-pool
Disabled access difficult
Pets accepted in bedrooms
Closed last 3 weeks Nov
Proprietor Leonetto Sabatini

Tuscany

Country guest-house, Sarteano

Le Anfore

The vicinity of Sarteano and Cetona is still relatively little visited, despite the unspoilt countryside and the presence of good places in which to stay and eat – people gravitate instead to the Pienza/Montepulciano area. Here, nonetheless, is a 'find': Le Anfore, at the end of a track, off the Sarteano-Chiusi road.

The hotel consists of an old farmhouse that has been restored to a high standard and decorated with taste and style. The public rooms are on the ground floor, with a sitting-room, restaurant and bar that lead naturally to each other through brick-spanned arches, which are in turn echoed by the windows.

Most of the bedrooms are upstairs and seem to have sense-less names ('Atoll', 'Arranvanna') until you realize that they have been called after horses from the riding stables. Rooms are spacious, with highly polished dark parquet floors strewn with Persian carpets; a couple have their own sitting areas and fireplaces. Each has been individually furnished with rustic and not-so-rustic antiques. Bathrooms are stylishly tiled and illuminated.

Outdoors, there is plenty to do – swimming, tennis and riding.
Nearby Chianciano Terme (14 km); Montepulciano (22 km).

Via di Chiusi 30, Sarteano, 53047 Siena
Tel (0578) 265871
Fax (0578) 265969
Location off the road between Chiusi and Sarteano; in own grounds; car parking
Meals breakfast, dinner
Prices L-LL
Rooms 7 double, 3 suites, all with bath or shower, phone, minibar
Facilities sitting-room, bar, restaurant, garden, swimming-pool, tennis, riding
Smoking permitted
Credit cards EC, MC, V
Children welcome
Disabled no special facilities; accessible ground-floor bedroom
Pets please check first
Closed never
Manager Maurizio Pozielli

Tuscany

Country hotel, Scansano

Antico Casale di Scansano

Two widely travelled readers wrote in enthusiastic terms to draw our attention to this captivating hotel in the coastal region of Tuscany known as the Maremma, south-east of Grosseto. We can scarcely improve on their verdicts: 'Rooms sweetly decorated with country antiques and a lovely restaurant with terrace overlooking a spectacular green valley with vineyards and olive groves; a truly relaxing experience.' And: 'In four months touring the country, we thought this hotel number one; we were impressed by the welcome and hospitality, the surroundings – even the beds were the best we encountered in Italy.' Other reporters, however, are critical of the food.

The Antico Casale is a beautifully restored, 200-year-old farmhouse which retains more of its origins than most such places. The Macereto estate of which it is part produces a range of *grappa*, olive oil and wines (including the Morellino di Scansano DOC); many surrounding farms produce olive oil, and the Casale's stables are in very active use: riding holidays are offered (with instruction if you need it), and the hotel even offers special 'DB&B and horse' rates. Wine-tasting courses too. **Nearby** thermal spa of Saturnia, Argentarian coast.

Scansano, 58054 Grosseto
Tel (0564) 507219
Fax (0564) 507805
Location in countryside 30 km SE of Grosseto; with garden and car parking
Food & drink breakfast, lunch, dinner, snacks
Prices LL-LLL; 20% reduction for children under 12 in parents' room; meals LL
Rooms 11 double, 3 single, one family room, all with shower; all rooms have central heating, air-conditioning, phone, TV, minibar, hairdrier
Facilities bar, sitting-room, dining-room, terrace; small swimming-pool, horse-riding, mountain bikes
Credit cards AE, DC, MC, V
Children accepted
Disabled no special facilities
Pets accepted if well behaved
Closed mid-Jan to end-Feb
Proprietor Massimo Pellegrini

Tuscany

Town villa, Sesto Fiorentino

Villa Villoresi

The aristocratic Villa Villoresi looks rather out of place in what is now an industrial suburb of Florence, but once in the house and gardens you suddenly feel a million miles away from modern, bustling Florence. Contessa Cristina Villoresi is a warm hostess who has captured the hearts of many transatlantic and other guests. It is thanks to her that the villa still has the feel of a private home – all rather grand, if a little faded.

As you make your way through the building, each room seems to have some curiosity or feature of the past. The entrance hall is a superb gallery of massive chandeliers, frescoed walls, antiques and lofty potted plants. Then there are the beautiful frescoes on the first-floor landing, the family tree in reception, the sober looking Tuscan nobility in the dining-room, and the leather-bound novels in the sitting-room. Bedrooms are remarkably varied – from the small and quite plain to grand apartments with frescoes and Venetian chandeliers. Some overlook an inner courtyard, others look out on to the pool and garden. Half- or full-board terms at the Villa Villoresi are still quite reasonable; and we are assured that the food is now better than it once was.
Nearby Florence (8 km).

Via Ciampi 2, Colonnata di
Sesto Fiorentino,
Florence 50019
Tel (055) 443692 **Fax** 442063
Location 8 km NW of
Florence; adequate car
parking
Food & drink breakfast,
lunch, dinner
Prices rooms LL-LLLL; DB&B
LLL with breakfast; meals LL;
10% reductions
mid Jul to Sept, Nov to Easter;
and for children

Rooms 18 double, 3 single,
7 suites, all with bath or
shower; all rooms have
central heating, phone
Facilities sitting-rooms, bar,
dining- room, veranda;
swimming- pool, ping-pong
Credit cards AE, DC, MC, V
Children welcome
Disabled no special facilities
Pets not accepted in public
rooms **Closed** never
Proprietor Contessa Cristina
Villoresi

Tuscany

Converted monastery, Siena

Certosa di Maggiano

A recent visit showed that all was very well here, and if you are looking for an exclusive but unostentatious hotel in Siena, this is probably it: a former Carthusian monastery – the oldest in Tuscany – secluded in a large park (yet only minutes from the enchanting old city). Although it is extremely expensive, this is not a swanky place: the calm good taste, the atmosphere of a delightful country house and the discreet service appeal mainly to those in search of peace and privacy.

Superb modern *haute cuisine* dishes are served in an exquisite dining-room, in the tranquil 14thC cloisters or under the arcades by the swimming-pool. Guests can help themselves to drinks in the book-lined library, play backgammon or chess in a little ante-room, or relax in the lovely sitting-room. Flower arrangements are just about everywhere and bowls of fresh fruit in the bed-rooms add a personal touch, although the decoration here does not quite live up to the ravishing public rooms. Bear in mind that exploration of Siena will have to be by taxi or bus – it's too far to walk, and parking is almost impossible in the centre.

Nearby sights of Siena; hills and vineyards of Chianti; San Gimignano, Florence, Arezzo within reach.

Via Certosa 82, Siena 53100
Tel (0577) 288180 **Fax** 288189
Location 1 km SE of middle of city and Porta Romana; in gardens, with car parking opposite entrance and garage available
Food & drink breakfast, lunch, dinner
Prices rooms LLLL with breakfast; suites LLLL; meals LLL
Rooms 5 double, 12 suites; all with bath; all have central heating, TV, phone, radio
Facilities dining-room, bar, library, sitting-room; tennis, heated outdoor swimming-pool, heliport
Credit cards AE, DC, MC, V
Children accepted
Disabled access possible – 3 rooms on ground floor
Pets small dogs accepted, but not in dining-room
Closed never
Managers Anna Recordati and Margherita Grossi

Tuscany

Town villa, Siena

Villa Scacciapensieri

This modest hilltop villa dating from the early 1800s has been in the Nardi family since it ceased to be a private house in the 1930s. In that time the tentacles of suburban Siena have reached out to surround it; but if the villa can no longer claim to be in the country it is certainly on the edge of it, and it is still a calm retreat from the bustle of the city.

The garden is a great asset – a neat, formal, flowery area in front of the house, and a more rustic area to the side including the swimming-pool and a leafy terrace where meals are served in summer. Inside, beyond the cool entrance hall, the dining-room is smartly traditional in style; the sitting-room is something of a disappointment, with modern furniture which is neither stylish nor comfortable – though in cooler weather there is the attraction of a roaring log fire in the grand modern fireplace.

Bedrooms are unremarkably furnished but spacious, some with views either of the roof-tops and towers of Siena, or of vineyards, olive groves and the hills beyond. 'Breakfast is simple and good,' says a recent reporter; and there is always someone on hand to give advice on what to see and do.

Nearby sights of Siena; Florence within reach.

Via di Scacciapensieri 10, Siena 53100
Tel (0577) 41442 **Fax** 270854
Location 2 km NE of middle of city, on hill; in private gardens with car parking
Food & drink breakfast, lunch, dinner
Prices rooms LL-LLLL with breakfast; suites LLLLL; DB&B LL-LLL
Rooms 22 double, 4 single, 2 suites, all with bath or shower; all rooms have central heating, minibar, colour TV, phone, air-conditioning
Facilities dining-room, hall, bar, TV room; open air swimming-pool, tennis
Credit cards AE, DC, MC, V
Children welcome
Disabled lift/elevator
Pets small ones accepted, but not in public rooms or at pool
Closed Jan to mid-Mar; restaurant only, Wed
Proprietors Emma, Riccardo and Emanuele Nardi

Tuscany

Locanda dell'Amorosa

The Locanda dell'Amorosa is as romantic as it sounds. An elegant Renaissance villa-cum-village, within the remains of 14thC walls, has been converted into a charming country inn.

The old stables, beamed and brick-walled, have been transformed into a delightful rustic (but pricey) restaurant serving refined *nouvelle*-style versions of traditional Tuscan recipes, using ingredients from the estate, which also produces wine. The restaurant can serve up to 80 people (though it is arranged to feel more intimate) but is often full.

Only a fortunate few can actually stay here – either in apartments in the houses where peasants and farmworkers once lived, or in ordinary bedrooms in the old family residence. The bedrooms are cool, airy and pretty, with whitewashed walls, terracotta floors, antique furniture and Florentine curtains and bedspreads – and immaculate modern bathrooms.

To complete the village there is a little parish church with lovely 15thC frescoes of the Sienese school. With discreet, attentive service, the Locanda is a paradise for connoisseurs of Tuscany, for gourmets and for all romantics.

Nearby Siena (45 km); Arezzo (45 km); Chianti wine country.

Sinalunga 53048 Siena
Tel (0577) 679497
Fax (0577) 632001
Location 2 km S of Sinalunga; ample car parking
Food & drink breakfast, lunch, dinner
Prices rooms LLLL; suites LLLL; meals from LL
Rooms 12 double, 5 suites, all with bathroom; all rooms have central heating, phone, colour TV, minibar, air-conditioning

Facilities dining-room, sitting-room, bar, wine bar
Credit cards AE, DC, MC, V
Children accepted
Disabled access difficult
Pets not accepted
Closed mid-Jan to end Feb; restaurant only, Mon; Tue lunch
Manager Carlo Citterio

Tuscany

Country villa, Vicchio di Mugello

Villa Campestri

Get clear directions before you set off for this hilltop villa; it is in an isolated location, some way south of the village of Vicchio di Mugello.

The house looks classically Renaissance, but actually dates back to the 13thC. It overlooks sloping hillsides of mown grass, and miles of unspoilt countryside – much of it part of the villa's own estate. Inside, many original features remain: an old chapel, 14thC frescos, massive interior doors, and timbered ceilings. Furnishings blend with this venerable setting, including some valuable antiques, notably a vast and regal four-poster bed and an 18thC sofa. Plain white walls offset the dark wood of beams and furniture. Most of the bedrooms are handsomely furnished and spacious – some might find them too grand for comfort. Bathrooms are beautifully tiled in blue and white. The open-plan sitting-room and dining-room are traditionally furnished and fairly formal; the restaurant is renowned, and local dignitaries make the long trek to sample its offerings. Breakfast was a disappointment for one visitor, though. If you're lucky the owner may regale you with a little piano music after dinner. **Nearby** Florence (35 km).

Via di Campestri 19, 50039 Vicchio di Mugello (Firenze)
Tel (055) 849 0107
Fax (055) 849 0108
Location 3 km S of Vicchio, 35km NE of Florence, in countryside
Food & drink breakfast, dinner, snacks
Prices rooms LLL suites LLLL with breakfast; meals from L-LL
Rooms 14 double; 6 suites; 1 single; all rooms have central heating, phone, satellite TV, minibar
Facilities swimming-pool; horseriding, golf nearby
Credit cards MC, V
Children welcome
Disabled 4 adapted bedrooms
Pets accepted only on request
Closed Jan to Mar
Proprietor Paolo Pasquali

Tuscany

Country villa, Balbano

Villa Casanova

An idiosyncratic place, once dropped from the guide, but restored now on the strength of reports from readers. Spacious, simply-furnished rooms in an unaffected and atmospheric old country house (plus outbuildings); satisfying country food. Some reports mention noise from a nearby quarry.

■ Via di Casanova, 55050 Balbano (Lucca) **Tel** (0583) 548429 **Fax** (0583) 368955 **Meals** breakfast, lunch, dinner **Prices** rooms LL with breakfast; DB&B L **Rooms** 50, all with bath or shower, central heating **Credit cards** AE **Closed** never

---

Country hotel, Castellina in Chianti

Belvedere di San Leonino

This 600-year-old farmhouse, about equidistant from Castellina and Siena, is a captivating little hotel. Inside, all is in simple, elegant taste, and the best of the rooms are gloriously spacious. Guests dine communally – outdoors in summer – and the modest pool enjoys views of the surrounding vineyards and olive groves.

■ San Leonino, 53011 Castellina in Chianti (Siena) **Tel** (0577) 740887 **Fax** (0577) 740924 **Meals** breakfast, dinner **Prices** rooms LLL; dinner L **Rooms** 28, all with bath, central heating, phone **Credit cards** AE, MC, V **Closed** mid-Nov to Mar

---

Country house, Castellina in Chianti

Locanda Le Piazze

A converted 17thC farmhouse in secluded countryside, reached by a long unsurfaced road. Rustic antiques and Indonesian pieces complement typical terracotta floors, exposed beams and white plaster. Lavish striped fabrics in the bedrooms; large bathrooms.

■ Locanda Le Piazze, 53011 Castellina in Chianti (Siena) **Tel** (0577) 743190 **Fax** (0577) 743191 **Meals** breakfast, light lunch and dinneron request **Prices** rooms LL-LLLL with breakfast; special discounts; meals LL **Rooms** 20, all with bath or shower, phone **Credit cards** AE, DC, MC, V **Closed** end Nov to Apr

---

Country villa, Castellina in Chianti

Villa Casafrassi

A gracious 17thC villa in rolling countryside on the way to Siena, carefully restored and opened as a hotel in 1986. The sitting-room opens on to the lawned gardens, which contain a tennis-court as well as a fair-sized swimming-pool. Bedrooms are in the main house and a separate outbuilding.

■ Via Chiantigiana 40, 53011 Castellina in Chianti (Siena) **Tel** (0577) 740621 **Fax** (0577) 741047 **Meals** breakfast, light lunch, dinner, snacks **Prices** rooms LLL with breakfast; meals LL **Rooms** 22, all with bath or shower, central heating; practically all have phone **Credit cards** AE, DC, MC, V **Closed** mid-Nov to mid-Mar

Tuscany

Village hotel, Castelnuovo Berardenga

Relais Borgo San Felice

Another beautifully restored medieval hamlet, this one larger than most. Two of the houses are let weekly as apartments, but most of the accommodation is hotel-style. Public areas and bedrooms are fresh and stylish. Pleasant pool, and two tennis courts.

■ San Felice, 53019 Castelnuovo Berardenga (Siena) **Tel** (0577) 359260 **Fax** (0577) 359089 **Meals** breakfast, lunch, dinner **Prices** rooms LLL-LLLL with breakfast; suites LLLL; DB&B LLL **Rooms** 44, all with bath or shower, phone, TV, minibar **Credit cards** AE, DC, MC, V **Closed** Nov to Mar

---

Country villa, Centoia

Villa Elisio

A peaceful old villa in the countryside a few miles west of lake Trasimeno which puts to good effect the familiar formula of white walls, tiled floors, dark beams and mellow wooden furniture – as does the associated restaurant Le Capezzine. Tennis and a swimming-pool.

■ Capezzine, 52040 Centoia (Arezzo) **Tel** (0575) 613145 **Fax** (0575) 613167 **Meals** breakfast, lunch, dinner **Prices** rooms LL; suite LLL breakfast L15,000; DB&B LL **Rooms** 11, all with bath or shower, TV, minibar **Credit cards** AE, DC, MC, V **Closed** never

---

Country inn, Certaldo

Osteria del Vicario

The basic structure of the 13thC monastery that underlies this simple inn remains, with a garden enclosed in a Romanesque cloister. Bedrooms have abundant charm. Lovely flowered terrace in summer. Owners Sara and Claudio offer wild mushrooms on the menu in autumn. Well-behaved children welcome.

■ Via Rivellino 3, 50052 Certaldo (Firenze) **Tel** (0571) 668228 **Meals** breakfast, lunch, dinner; vegetarian meals **Prices** rooms LL; DB&B LL **Rooms** 9, all with shower, TV **Credit cards** AE, DC, V **Closed** last 3 weeks of Jan

---

Country villa, Colle di Val d'Elsa

Villa Belvedere

An elegant restaurant-with-rooms – the smart dining-room is very much the heart of this handsome, weathered villa with large garden, a few miles from Siena, and its food enjoys a high reputation in the locality. Bedrooms are also stylish, though with some amusingly ornate antique furniture. Swimming-pool.

■ Localita Belvedere, 53034 Colle di Val d'Elsa (Siena) **Tel** (0577) 920966 **Fax** (0577) 924128 **Meals** breakfast, lunch, dinner **Prices** rooms from LLL with breakfast; DB&B LLL; meals L-LL **Rooms** 15, all with bath or shower, phone, TV **Credit cards** AE, DC, MC, V **Closed** never

Tuscany

Town hotel, Cortona

San Michele

A stylishly converted Renaissance palazzo, in the preserved heart of Renaissance Cortona: old tiles, polished or painted beams, white walls and occasional decorative flourishes. Bedrooms and bathrooms, though, are in need of refurbishment, according to a report just in.

■ Via Guelfa, 15, 52044 Cortona (Arezzo) **Tel** (0575) 604348 **Fax** (0575) 630147 **Meals** breakfast **Prices** rooms LLL with buffet breakfast **Rooms** 40, all with bath or shower, phone, TV, minibar **Credit cards** AE, DC, V **Closed** Jan and Feb

---

Resort village, Elba

Capo Sud

A complex of little villas in a quiet, rather remote spot, behind a private beach (with boats for hire). Rooms are modern and quite simple, scattered among trees and macchia, none of them very far away from the restaurant, bar, sitting area and terrace (with fine views of the bay). Swimming-pool. Fruit comes from local orchards.

■ Lacona, 57037 Elba (Livorno) **Tel** (0565) 964021 **Fax** (0565) 964263 **Meals** breakfast, lunch, dinner **Prices** DB&B LL; FB LL; reductions for children **Rooms** 39, all with bath or shower, phone, minibar, 12 have air-conditioning **Credit cards** not accepted **Closed** Oct to Apr

---

Town guest-house, Fiesole

Villa Bonelli

An appealing little hotel run by the friendly and helpful Bonelli family who offer delicious Tuscan specialities. Bedrooms are simple but pleasant, the public rooms rather cramped, except for the restaurant. The road to the hotel is narrow and steep, but well signposted.

■ Via Francesco Poeti 1, 50014 Fiesole (Florence) **Tel** (055) 59513 **Fax** (055) 598942 **Meals** breakfast, dinner **Prices** rooms LL-LLL with breakfast **Rooms** 20, all with shower, central heating, phone **Credit cards** DC, MC, V **Closed** restaurant only, Nov to mid-Mar

---

Town hotel, Florence

Alba

This bright, neat hotel, with new reception area and garage service available, is handy for the station and only a few minutes from the heart of the city. It lacks the antique look of several nearby competitors, but its staff are friendly and bedrooms are well equipped. Fitness centre.

■ Via della Scala 22-38, 50123 Florence **Tel** (055) 211469 **Fax** (055) 288358 **Meals** breakfast **Prices** rooms LL-LLL **Rooms** 24, all with bath or shower, air-conditioning, central heating, double glazing, phone, satellite TV, safe, minibar **Credit cards** MC, V **Closed** never

Tuscany

Town hotel, Florence

Aprile

The elegant lines of the original 15thC Medici palace are clearly visible in this attractive little hotel, furnished appropriately in a traditional but highly individual style. Guests may enjoy a fine breakfast by the shady terrace downstairs, or views of the striking church of Santa Maria Novella from upper rooms.

■ Via della Scala 6, 50123 Florence **Tel** (055) 216237 **Fax** (055) 280947 **Meals** breakfast **Prices** LL-LLL with breakfast **Rooms** 29, all with most with bath and TV, all with central heating, phone, minibar **Credit cards** AE, MC, V **Closed** never

Town hotel, Florence

Ariele

In the garden of this home-like hotel you may be able to hear music from the nearby Teatro Communale. It has a pleasantly old-fashioned and distinctly Italian atmosphere, and public areas that are more generous and elegant than the norm. Bedrooms are rather austere, but generally spacious. Parking available.

■ Via Magenta 11, 50123 Florence **Tel** (055) 211509 **Fax** (055) 26852 **Meals** breakfast **Prices** rooms LL-LLL **Rooms** 40, all with bath or shower, central heating, air-conditioning, satellite TV **Credit cards** AE, MC, V **Closed** never

Town hotel, Florence

Casci

In a relatively busy setting some way north of San Lorenzo, this simple family-run place is unusually welcoming. The building, once home to Rossini, composer of *The Barber of Seville,* has some antiquity, with intact original frescos. Rooms are fairly Spartan, but clean; those at the rear very peaceful. Garage nearby.

■ Via Cavour 13, 50129 Florence **Tel** (055) 211686 **Fax** (055) 239 6461 **E-mail** CASCI@pn.itnet.it **Website** http://www.emmeti.it/casci.html **Meals** breakfast **Prices** rooms L-LL with buffet breakfast, family rooms more **Rooms** 25, all with bath or shower, central heating, phone, TV; some with air-conditioning **Credit cards** AE, DC, MC, V **Closed** never

Town hotel, Florence

City

The interior is more smartly urban than the unassuming exterior suggests, with a mix of shiny black and bamboo furniture in the bar-lounge areas, and efforts made with rugs, urns and plants. Bedrooms are neat and attractive, and have excellent bathrooms.

■ Via S Antonino 18, 50123 Florence (Firenze) **Tel** (055) 211543 **Fax** (055) 295451 **Meals** breakfast **Prices** rooms LLL, suites LLLLL with buffet breakfast **Rooms** 18, all with bath or shower, central heating, air-conditioning, TV, minibar, phone, hairdrier, safe **Credit cards** AE, CD, MC, V **Closed** never

Tuscany

Town hotel, Florence

Principe

A graciously proportioned, somewhat faded mansion overlooking the Arno. Rooms with the view may suffer traffic noise, and rear rooms have the compensating prospect of a charming garden. Cosy rooms at the top of the house are more appealing than the high-ceilinged, old-fashioned ones on lower floors.

■ Lungarno Amerigo Vespucci 34, 50123 Florence **Tel** (055) 284848 **Fax** (055) 283458 **Meals** breakfast, snacks **Prices** rooms LL-LLLL with breakfast **Rooms** 20, all with bath, central heating, air-conditioning, phone, hairdrier, TV, radio, minibar **Credit cards** AE, DC, MC, V **Closed** never

---

Town hotel, Florence

Regency

Sister hotel of the Lord Byron in Rome, the Regency follows the same formula of intimate five-star luxury and personal service for the super-rich. Public rooms are elegantly formal; bedrooms are predictably opulent. The location is peaceful and the garden a plus point in central Florence.

■ Piazza Massimo d'Azeglio 3, 50121 Florence **Tel** (055) 245247 **Fax** (055) 2346735 **Meals** breakfast, lunch, dinner **Prices** rooms LLLL with breakfast **Rooms** 35, all with bath, phone, TV, minibar, air-conditioning, safe, hairdrier **Credit cards** AE, DC, MC, V **Closed** never

---

Town hotel, Florence

La Residenza

The homely feel of this friendly place, near the station, in one of the most beautiful streets of Florence, is instantly appealing, even if it is not especially smart. The flowery roof garden and sitting-room are sunny havens. Rooms are simple and cheerful.

■ Via Tornabuoni 8, 50123 Florence **Tel** (055) 218684 **Fax** (055) 284197 **Meals** breakfast, dinner **Prices** rooms LL-LLL with breakfast; DB&B LLL; children under three years free **Rooms** 25, all with central heating, phone, satellite TV, air-conditioning, minibar; most have bath or shower **Credit cards** AE, DC, MC, V **Closed** never

---

Town guest-house, Florence

Silla

The imposing lower courtyard and terrace overlooking the Arno are the main features of interest in this solid Florentine *palazzo*. Bedrooms are rather conventional, though most have been refurbished recently. The welcome remains courteous and unstuffy.

■ Via dei Renai 5, 50125 Florence **Tel** (055) 234 2888 **Fax** (055) 234 1437 **Meals** breakfast **Prices** rooms LLL with buffet breakfast **Rooms** 32, all with bath or shower, central heating, TV, phone; most with air-conditioning **Credit cards** AE, DC, MC, V **Closed** 2 weeks Dec

Tuscany

Town guest-house, Florence

Splendor

A peaceful and still affordable *pensione* ten minutes' walk from the Duomo. It has a sunny terrace full of plants and several historic features; furnishings and some modern additions are not entirely harmonious.

■ Via San Gallo 30, 50129 Florence **Tel** (055) 483427 **Fax** (055) 461276 **Meals** breakfast buffet **Prices** rooms LL-LLL with breakfast **Rooms** 31, all with central heating, TV, phone, safe, hairdrier; most with bath or shower; most with air-conditioning **Credit cards** AE, MC, V **Closed** never

---

Town hotel, Florence

Unicorno

Pleasant, simple, central hotel recreating something of a Florentine *palazzo* atmosphere with rag-rolled walls, vaulting and antique-look Italianate furnishings. Upstairs in a modern dining-room 'American breakfasts' (elaborate buffets) are served.

■ Via dei Fossi 27, 50123 Florence **Tel** (055) 287313 **Meals** breakfast **Prices** rooms LL-LLL with breakfast **Rooms** 28, all with bath or shower, central heating, air-conditioning, phone, hairdrier, TV, mini bar **Credit cards** AE, DC, MC,V **Closed** never

---

Town villa, Florence

Villa Azalee

West of the centre but handy for drivers and (especially) rail travellers: a 19thC villa in a leafy garden with well equipped, individually furnished rooms – plain walls, bold floral fabrics, various styles of bed including four-posters. Valet garage parking facilities, bicycles available.

■ Viale Fratelli Rosselli, 44, 50123 Florence **Tel** (055) 214242 **Fax** (055) 268264 **Meals** breakfast, brunch **Prices** rooms LL-LLL with breakfast; brunch L22,000 **Rooms** 24, all with bath or shower, air-conditioning, phone, minibar, TV **Credit cards** AE, DC, V **Closed** never

---

Town villa, Florence

Villa Carlotta

A gracious 19thC mansion standing on a hilly, tree-lined street on the south-eastern slopes of the city, now a quietly desirable residential area. Inside, style and furnishings aspire to formal elegance; many of the building's original features have been preserved. Better-than-average breakfasts are served in a plain, modern addition, or on an attractive terrace; Tuscan food in the elegant 'Il Bobolino' restaurant. Some free parking available.

■ Via Michele di Lando 3, 50125 Florence **Tel** (055) 220530 **Meals** breakfast, dinner **Prices** rooms LL-LLLL **Rooms** 32, all with bath or shower, central heating, air-conditioning, minibar, safe, TV, phone **Credit cards** AE, DC, MC, V **Closed** never

Tuscany

Converted castle, Giglio

Castello Monticello

The pretty little island of Giglio attracts many day-trippers; if you fancy an overnight stay, this 'castle' is your best bet – built as a private house, and less austere within than without. Good views of the coast from the terrace, gardens and simple rooms. Tennis.

■ Giglio Porto, 58013 Giglio (Grosseto) **Tel** (0564) 809252 **Fax** (0564) 809473 **E-mail** hmonti@nevib.it **Website** http://www.traveleurope.it/ castellomonticello **Meals** breakfast, lunch, dinner **Prices** DB&B LLL; FB LL; meals L **Rooms** 37, all with shower, central heating, phone, air-conditioning, TV, fridge **Credit cards** DC, MC, V **Closed** Oct to Mar

Seaside villa, Giglio

Pardini's Hermitage

A real retreat: Federigo Pardini's white villa, perched on a cliff above the sea, is reached only by boat from Giglio Porto (or by car and donkey; or an hour's walk). The villa is smartly modern and the bedrooms have balconies, but you will be hoping to spend most of your time on the terraces or swimming from the rocks. Home-made goats' milk cheese and yogurt.

■ 58013 Giglio (Grosseto) **Tel** (0564) 809034 **Fax** (0564) 809177 **Meals** breakfast, lunch, dinner **Prices** DB&B LLL; FB LLL; meals LL **Rooms** 11, all with bath, phone, hairdrier, TV **Credit cards** V **Closed** Oct to Mar

Farm guest-house, Greve in Chianti

La Camporena

Also known as Agriturismo Anna, located 3 km outside Greve on the road to Figline. A tree-lined drive leads up to this hilltop farmhouse, a position both peaceful and panoramic with views across the surrounding olive groves. Simple, cheap acccommodation, with access to a pleasant garden and terrace.

■ Via Figlinese 27, 50022,Greve in Chianti (Siena) **Tel** (055) 853184/ 8544765 **Fax** (055) 853184 **Meals** breakfast, dinner **Prices** rooms L **Rooms** 16, all with bath or shower **Credit cards** AE, DC, MC, V **Closed** never

Village hotel, Greve in Chianti

Albergo del Chianti

Across Greve's central piazza from the Giovanni da Verrazzano is this very different place – a cool, calm, neatly restored and well run bed-and-breakfast hotel, with the unusual feature for such a modest village hotel of an attractive swimming-pool in the back garden. Refurbished in rustic style in 1993.

■ Piazza Matteotti 86, 50022 Greve in Chianti (Firenze) **Tel** (055) 853763 **Fax** (055) 853763 **Meals** breakfast, dinner **Prices** rooms LL with breakfast; meals from L **Rooms** 16, all with shower, central heating, air-conditioning, phone **Credit cards** AE, DC, MC, V **Closed** Nov

Tuscany

Restaurant-with-rooms, Greve in Chianti

Giovanni da Verrazzano

The first-floor flower-adorned terrace of this bustling restaurant overlooks the unusual triangular piazza around which Greve revolves. Recently renovated, bedrooms here are well equipped and reasonably priced.

■ Piazza Matteotti 28, 50022 Greve in Chianti (Firenze) **Tel** (055) 853189 **Fax** (055) 853648 **Meals** breakfast, lunch, dinner **Prices** rooms L-LL breakfast L14,000; DB&B LL **Rooms** 11, all with shower, phone, minibar, TV, hairdrier **Credit cards** AE, DC, MC, V **Closed** for a period in winter; restaurant only, Sun dinner and Mon

Restaurant-with-rooms, Montefollonico

La Chiusa

La Chiusa's reputation for outstanding food remains, most of it home-grown from local farms, as does its appeal as a place to stay. It is a stylishly renovated farmhouse, with views of Montepulciano from the simple, tasteful rooms with spectacularly swish bathrooms.

■ Via della Madonnina 88, 53040 Montefollonico (Siena) **Tel** (0577) 669668 **Fax** (0577) 669593 **Meals** breakfast, dinner **Prices** rooms LLLL with breakfast; suite LLLL; meals LLL, also *à la carte* **Rooms** 12, all with bath or shower, phone, TV, minibar, hairdrier **Credit cards** AE, DC, MC, V **Closed** Nov to 26 Dec; 10 Jan to 13 Feb

Country guest-house, Pienza

La Saracina

Pienza is a neglected gem, and so in a way is this: a beautifully restored farmhouse where a limited number of guests can enjoy perfect peace. All the rooms have sitting areas and four have fireplaces. The panoramic grounds include a tennis court as well as a smart pool. The restaurants of Pienza are only a few miles away.

■ Strada Statale 146, km 29.7, 53026 Pienza (Siena) **Tel** (0578) 748022 **Fax** (0578) 748022 **Meals** breakfast **Prices** rooms LLL-LLLL with breakfast **Rooms** 6, all with bath, phone, minibar, TV **Credit cards** AE, MC, V **Closed** never

Country villa, Pievescola

Relais La Suvera

An imposing Renaissance villa (the country retreat of Pope Julius II), surrounded by olive groves, vineyards and stately cypresses. The best of the rooms – in the main house, the stables and the Oliviera – are magnificently furnished. Secluded swimming-pool, and tennis court.

■ 53030 Pievescola (Siena) **Tel** (0577) 960300 **Fax** (0577) 960220 **Meals** breakfast, lunch, dinner **Prices** rooms LLL-LLLL with breakfast; suites LLLL; meals LL **Rooms** 35, all with bath, air-conditioning, phone, TV, minibar **Credit cards** AE, DC, MC, V **Closed** beg-Nov to end-Mar

Tuscany

Town hotel, Pisa

Royal Victoria

An endearing anachronism, opened in 1842 (Dickens stayed a few years later), by the present owner's forefather and little changed since, but dating back well beyond 1350. Rooms vary considerably in size and style, but all are basic. A *palazzo* filled with distant echoes of the Grand Tour, putting you in just the right mood for seeing Pisa. Garage available (L30,000).

■ Lungarno Pacinotti 12, Pisa **Tel** (050) 940111 **Fax** (050) 940180 **Meals** breakfast **Prices** LL with breakfast **Rooms** 48, some with bath, all with central heating, phone; TV on request **Credit cards** AE, DC, E, MC, V **Closed** never

---

Country villa, Prato

Villa San Cristina

Banquets appear to be the main business of this elegant 18thC villa at the foot of wooded slopes just outside Prato – so don't expect solitude. But the bedrooms are comfortable and harmonious (and not expensive, for what you get), and there is a pleasant pool.

■ via Poggio Secco, 58, 50047 Prato (Firenze) **Tel** (0574) 595951 **Fax** (0574) 572623 **Meals** breakfast, lunch, dinner **Prices** rooms LLL; DB&B LLL **Rooms** 23, all with bath or shower, phone, minibar, TV **Credit cards** AE, DC, MC, V **Closed** mid-Aug

---

Seaside hotel, Punta Ala

Alleluja

The smallest and most inviting of the smart hotels of exclusive, sporty Punta Ala. Inside and out it is stylish and well cared for. Designs are simple, colours light and the atmosphere cheerful. Some bedrooms have their own sitting-rooms.

■ Punta Ala (Grosseto) **Tel**(0564) 922050 **Fax** (0564) 920734 **Meals** breakfast, lunch, dinner **Prices** DB&B LLLL; FB LLL-LLLL; meals LLL **Rooms** 43, all with bath or shower, air-conditioning, phone, TV, minibar, radio **Credit cards** AE, DC, MC, V **Closed** never

---

Country guest-house, Radda in Chianti

Podere Terreno

A 400-year-old farmhouse, surrounded only by fields, vineyards and woods, and run as a family home taking guests by a Franco-Italian couple. You eat together at a refectory table in the jolly beamed living room, with open fireplace. Bedrooms are simple but satisfactory.

■ Localita Volpaia, 53017 Radda in Chianti (Siena) **Tel** (0577) 738312 **Fax** (0577) 738312 **Meals** breakfast, dinner **Prices** rooms DB&B LL **Rooms** 7, all with shower, central heating **Credit cards** MC, V **Closed** never

Tuscany

Restaurant with rooms, Rocca d'Orcia

Cantina Il Borgo

Close to the thermal springs of Bagno Vignoni and not far from Pienza, you will find, in the central piazza of this well-preserved medieval hamlet, the restaurant Cantina Il Borgo, which, as well as serving delicious local food, also has a few stylishly decorated bedrooms for visitors. Used to be the coach-house.

■ Rocca d'Orcia, 53027 (Siena) **Tel & fax** (0577) 887280
Meals breakfast, lunch, dinner, **Prices** rooms L **Rooms** 3 double all with bath or shower, air conditioning **Credit cards** AE, EC, MC, V **Closed** Feb and one week Nov

---

Farmhouse, San Benedetto

Il Rosolaccio

An 18thC hilltop farmhouse just outside San Gimignano, enlarged over the centuries by different families of farmers and recently lovingly restored by English couple, Steven and Natalie Music. Swimming-pool, with spectacular views. Mountain bikes available. New to the guide; reports please.

■ San Benedetto 34, 53037 San Gimignano (Siena) **Tel** (0577) 944465 **Fax** (0577) 944467 **Meals** breakfast **Prices** 6 rooms LL; 5 apartments LLLL, with breakfast **Rooms** 5, all with bath, phone, TV on request **Credit cards** AE, DC, MC, V **Closed** never

---

Town hotel, San Gimignano

L'Antico Pozzo

A recent inspection confirms that the Antico Pozzo brings much-needed new blood to the San Gimignano scene. A 15thC house in the middle of town, beautifully restored in 1990 and furnished with fine, simple taste – quite possibly the best in town.

■ Via S Matteo 87, 53037 San Gimignano (Siena) **Tel** (0577) 942014 **Fax** (0577) 942117 **E-mail** antpozzo@tin.it **Website** http://web.tin.it/antpozzo **Meals** breakfast **Prices** rooms LLL **Rooms** 18, all with bath, central heating, air-conditioning, phone, satellite TV, radio, hairdrier, safe **Credit cards** AE, DC, MC, V **Closed** never

---

Town hotel, San Gimignano

Bel Soggiorno

Just inside the walls of San Gimignano, this 13thC house has made a very appealing small hotel. The main attraction is the restaurant, with panoramic windows and satisfying food. Rooms are modernized and lacking character, but are pleasant; some share the views.

■ Via San Giovanni 91, 53037 San Gimignano (Siena) **Tel** (0577) 940375 **Fax** (0577) 943149 **Meals** breakfast, lunch, dinner **Prices** rooms LL-LLL; meals L-LL **Rooms** 21 (4 suites), all with bath, central heating, air-conditioning, phone, satellite TV; **Credit cards** AE, DC, MC, V **Closed** restaurant only, Wed

Tuscany

Farmhouse hotel, San Gimignano

Il Casolare di Libbiano

Two enterprising and 'spontaneously welcoming' young citizens of San Gimignano have restored this captivating old house 8 km from the town. Its hallmarks are simplicity, good taste and honesty. Everything from the furniture to the cooking is carefully considered. Splendid living room, peaceful garden with fair-sized pool. 'A gem', deserving a full entry. Bikes for hire.

■ Libbiano 3, 53037 San Gimignano (Siena) **Tel & Fax** (0577) 946002 **Meals** breakfast, dinner **Prices** DB&B LLL for 2 **Rooms** 7, all with bath or shower, central heating **Credit cards** AE, MC, V **Closed** Nov to Mar

---

Town hotel, San Gimignano

La Cisterna

This popular hotel on San Gimignano's central square generates conflicting reports from readers: don't accept a room beneath the kitchens. Excellent views from the better rooms and Terrazze restaurant. Small splendid stone-arched sitting-room.

■ Piazza della Cisterna 24, 53037 San Gimignano (Siena) **Tel** (0577) 940328 **Fax** (0577) 942080 **Meals** breakfast, lunch, dinner **Prices** rooms LL; DB&B LL; FB LL-LLL suite LLL **Rooms** 49, all with bath or shower, central heating, phone, satellite TV, hairdrier, safe **Credit cards** AE, DC, MC, V **Closed** 8 Jan to 8 March; rest only, 4 Nov to 8 Mar

---

Town hotel, San Gimignano

Leon Bianco

On San Gimignano's main square, this welcoming, spick-and-span hotel offers rather better value. Rooms are generally spacious, and furnished with a bit of panache. 'Copious' buffet breakfasts are to be had on the enclosed terrace, says a reporter.

■ Piazza del Cisterna, 53037 San Gimignano (Siena) **Tel** (0577) 941294 **Fax** (0577) 942123 **Meals** breakfast **Prices** rooms LL-LLL with breakfast; suites LL **Rooms** 25, all with bath or shower, phone, air-conditioning, satellite TV **Credit cards** AE, DC, MC, V **Closed** Jan and Feb

---

Country hotel, San Gimignano

Relais Santa Chiara

The ideal for visitors to San Gimignano more interested in comfort and convenience in their accommodation than historic character: a stylish, immaculate hotel, modern but with good use made of natural materials, with a pleasant pool, only a few hundred metres outside the town gates. Private parking.

■ Via Matteotti, 15, 53037 San Gimignano (Siena) **Tel** (0577) 940701 **Fax** (057 7) 942096 **E-mail** rsc@cyber.dada.it **Website** www.cybermarket.it/rsc **Meals** breakfast, snacks **Prices** rooms LLL; suites LLL; meals L **Rooms** 41, all with bath or shower, air-conditioning, satellite TV, radio, minibar, hairdrier, safe **Credit cards** AE, CD, MC, V **Closed** mid-Jan to end Feb

Tuscany

Country villa, San Gimignano

Villa San Paolo

A French reader drew our attention to this smartly restored villa 4 km from San Gimignano, opened to guests only since 1989. Decoration is light, confident and fresh, and the rooms are well equipped. There is tennis, and a pool served by a special bar.

■ Strada Certaldo, 53037 San Gimignano (Siena) **Tel** (0577) 955100 **Fax** (0577) 955113 **E-mail** sanpaolo@iol.it **Website** http://web.tin.it/ san_gimignano **Meals** breakfast, snacks **Prices** rooms LLL with breakfast **Rooms** 18, all with bath, central heating, air-conditioning, phone, hairdrier, satellite TV, minibar, safe **Credit cards** AE, DC, MC, V **Closed** early Jan to mid-Feb

---

Country villa, San Gusmè

Villa Arceno

A handsome 17thC villa on an extensive wooded estate half-way between Siena and Arezzo. Vaulted public rooms with light decoration and comfortable Empire-style furniture, gloriously spacious bedrooms, some with terraces. Immaculate swimming-pool in a secluded courtyard.

■ Localita Arceno, 53010 San Gusmè (Siena) **Tel** (0577) 359292 **Fax** (0577) 359276 **Meals** breakfast, lunch, dinner **Prices** rooms LLLL with breakfast; suite LLLL; meals LLL **Rooms** 16, all with bath, central heating, air-conditioning, phone, TV, minibar, hairdrier **Credit cards** AE, DC, MC, V **Closed** at times from Nov to Feb

---

Town hotel, Siena

Santa Caterina

An 18thC house just outside the city walls, but only a pleasant 10 minute walk from the Campo. A recent visit found that bedrooms were straightforward, some very small, two with frescoed ceilings. The breakfast conservatory looks on to the flowery garden.

■ Via Enea Silvio Piccolomini 7, 53100 Siena **Tel** (0577) 221105 **Fax** (0577) 271087 **Meals** breakfast **Prices** rooms L-LLL **Rooms** 19, all with bath or shower, central heating, air-conditioning, phone **Credit cards** AE, DC, MC, V **Closed** early Jan to early Mar

---

Town villa, Siena

Villa Patrizia

This plain-looking villa just misses being a truly excellent little hotel: it has aristocratic style and is relaxed and dignified, but the bedrooms are routine in their furnishings, and there is no sitting-room. Breakfast is an adequate self-service buffet.

■ Via Fiorentina 58, 53100 Siena **Tel & Fax** (0577) 50431 **Meals** breakfast, lunch, dinner **Prices** LLL-LLLL **Rooms** 33, all with central heating, phone, minibar, TV, air-conditioning **Credit cards** AE, DC, MC, V **Closed** never

Tuscany

Country estate, Sovicille

Borgo Pretale

A complete hamlet, immersed in the countryside south-west of Siena. It has been restored and furnished in the best of taste, blending old and new with success. The grounds include a big, secluded swimming-pool, tennis, putting and other facilities.

■ Localita Pretale, 53018 Sovicille (Siena) **Tel** (0577) 345401 **Fax** (0577) 345625 **Meals** breakfast, lunch, dinner, snacks **Prices** rooms LLLL with breakfast; poolside cold buffet lunches LL **Rooms** 35, all with bath or shower, central heating, air-conditioning on request, phone, TV, minibar **Credit cards** AE, DC, MC, V **Closed** mid-Nov to mid-Mar

---

Village hotel, Strove

Casalta

This stylish and intimate little hotel is tucked away in the middle of the sleepy hilltop village of Strove. The cool white-walled restaurant specializes in fish. Above it is a civilized sitting-room, and off this the tastefully simple bedrooms. Gently good-humoured padrone.

■ 53035 Strove (Siena) **Tel** (0577) 301002 **Meals** breakfast, lunch (Sun only), dinner **Prices** rooms LL with breakfast; DB&B LL, meals L **Rooms** 10, all with bath, central heating **Credit cards** MC, V **Closed** mid-Nov to Feb; restaurant Wed

---

Country guest-house, Terontola di Cortona

Residenza di San Andrea

A home, not a hotel: Patrizia Nappi takes guests in only four rooms in her mellow stone-and-brick 13thC manor house, among wooded hills 8 km from Cortona and close to Lago Trasimeno. A house-party atmosphere prevails, and Patrizia serves authentic Tuscan food. She has three dogs and a cat.

■ 52044 Terontola di Cortona (Arezzo) **Tel** (0575) 677736 **Meals** breakfast, dinner, snacks **Prices** rooms LLL with breakfast; dinner LL inclusive of wine **Rooms** 4, all with bath or shower, central heating, hairdrier, radio, fans **Credit cards** not accepted **Closed** Feb

---

Country hotel, Volterra

Villa Nencini

Set just outside the hilltop town of Volterra, this mellow stone, family-run house offers impressive views of the glorious sweeping countryside. Some of its charm has been lost through the construction of a large annexe which leaves little of the previous garden. Bedrooms are small and neat. Large swimming-pool.

■ Borgo Santo Stefano 55, 56048 Volterra (Pisa) **Tel** (0588) 86386 **Fax** 80601 **Meals** breakfast **Prices** rooms L-LL **Rooms** 35, all with central heating, phone; satellite TV; most with bath or shower; some with minibar; some with balcony **Credit cards** AE, MC, V **Closed** never

Umbria and Marche

Hotels in Umbria and Marche

Visitors are increasingly discovering that there is more to Umbria than Assisi; but it remains the main tourist highlight of the region. Choice of hotel is tricky: there are many that are mediocre, and some of the more comfortable hotels are too big for a full entry here; of these, the Subasio (Tel (075) 812206, fax 816691) is a 70-room, polished, rather formal place, but notable for the views from its better bedrooms and beautiful flowery terraces. If you would rather see the sights from a base outside town, the Poppy Inn-Locanda del Papavero (Tel and fax (075) 803 8041) is a restaurant with 9 bedrooms at Petrignano, 9 km away.

Perugia is not nearly so well known as Assisi, but well worth a visit if you can penetrate the infuriating defences of its traffic system. The Brufani (page 165) lies at one end of its lively central Corso Vannucci, and just along it is another hotel worth knowing about – La Rosetta (Tel and fax (075) 5720841); it is much bigger, but not worryingly impersonal, and indisputably better value. Another possibility as a base for exploring the area is the Da Sauro (Tel (075) 826168, fax 825130), a family hotel on the peaceful island of Maggiore in Lake Trasemino.

Marche's coast, like the rest of the Adriatic, offers large resorts with plenty of hotels, but not many to suit our requirements. Pesaro, though a big town, is a more interesting mixture of old town and beach resort than many along this coastline; the Villa Serena on page 159 is our main recommendation for this area, but the Vittoria, a stylish, well-equipped hotel on the seafront in the town itself (Tel (0721) 34343, fax 68874) is another possibility. Ancona, regional capital of the Marches and a big seaport, is definitely not the place to stay but 12 km down the coast, at the popular resort of Portonovo, we have two full recommendations and can also suggest the Internazionale (Tel (071) 801001). Further south at Numana, the Eden Gigli (Tel (071) 933 0652, fax 933 0930, 30 rooms) is a smart, modern hotel in a beautiful setting overlooking the sea.

Inland from Pesaro, the Renaissance art city of Urbino is an essential place to visit, but there is no hotel to which we can wholeheartedly give a full recommendation. Our best suggestion is the Raffaello (Tel (0722) 4896, fax 328540), a straightforward 19-room hotel; it has no restaurant but this is not a problem since it is right in the middle of the town.

Gubbio is an equally compelling place to visit, and alternatives to our main recommendation – the Bosone, on page 164 – are the Torre dei Calzolari Palace (Tel (075) 925 6327, fax 925 6320) and the extravagant Park Hotel ai Cappuccini, slightly out of the town (Tel (075) 9234, fax 9220323).

This page acts as an introduction to the features and hotels of Umbria and Marche, and gives brief recommendations of reasonable hotels that for one reason or another have not made a full entry, The long entries for this region – covering the hotels we are most enthusiastic about – start on the next page. But do not neglect the shorter entries starting on page 162: these are all hotels that we would happily stay at.

Umbria and Marche

Country hotel, Assisi

Le Silve

Even if you are not planning to stay at this rustic gem, the road up to Le Silve is worth exploring for its own rewards – or perhaps avoiding if you are the nervous sort. It winds up over a series of hills and passes until you reach the house, set on its own private hill-ridge, 700m above sea level. The views are simply wonderful.

Le Silve is an old farmhouse (parts of it very old indeed – 10thC) converted to its new purpose with great sympathy and charm. There is a delightfully rambling feel to the place, with rooms on a variety of levels. The rustic nature of the building is preserved perfectly – all polished tile floors, stone or white walls, beamed ceilings, the occasional rug – and it is furnished with country antiques. Public rooms are large and airy, bedrooms stylishly simple. The self-contained suites are in villas about 1.5 km from the main house.

Food is wholesome and satisfying, using oil, cheese and meat from the associated farm. Le Silve is close enough to Assisi for sightseeing expeditions but remote enough for complete seclusion – and with good sports facilities immediately on hand (fair-sized pool). But it's not for vertigo sufferers.
Nearby sights of Assisi.

Località Armenzano, Assisi 06081 Perugia
Tel (075) 801 9000
Location in countryside 12 km E of Assisi, between S444 and S3; ample car parking
Food & drink breakfast, lunch, dinner
Prices rooms LL-LLL with breakfast; DB&B LLL; FB LLL; reductions for children
Rooms 11 double, 3 single, 4 self-contained suites; all with bath; all rooms have central heating, phone, TV, minibar, safe
Facilities dining-room, 2 sitting-rooms, bar; swimming- pool, tennis, sauna, riding, archery, mini-golf, motor-bike
Credit cards AE, DC, V
Children welcome
Disabled no special facilities
Pets not accepted
Closed 10 Nov to 10 Jan
Manager Daniela Taddia

Umbria and Marche

Town hotel, Assisi

Umbra

Tucked away down a little alley off the main square of Assisi is this delightful little family-run hotel.

The Umbra consists of several small houses – parts date back to the 13th century – with a small gravelled courtyard garden shaded by a pergola. The interior is comfortable and in parts more like a private home than a hotel; there is a bright little sitting-room with Mediterranean-style tiles and brocaded wing armchairs, and a series of bedrooms, mostly quite simply furnished but each with its own character and some with lovely views over the Umbrian plain. We like the elegant dining-room, and meals are served outside in fine weather; but this year we have had a recurrence of an old complaint – that the food is mediocre. Happily, there is no shortage of nearby alternatives in this popular tourist town.

The Umbra offers all the peace and tranquillity which you might hope to find in Assisi, and nothing is too much trouble for Alberto Laudenzi, whose family has run the hotel for more than 50 years.

Nearby basilica of St Francis, church of Santa Chiara, cathedral; medieval castle.

Via degli Archi 6, Assisi 06081 Perugia
Tel (075) 812240
Fax (075) 813653
Location in middle, off Piazza del Comune, with small garden; nearest car park some distance away
Food & drink breakfast, lunch, dinner
Prices rooms LL with breakfast; suites LLL
Rooms 16 double, 5 single, 4 suites, all with bath; all rooms have phone, central heating, TV
Facilities 3 sitting-rooms, bar, dining-room
Credit cards AE, DC, MC, V
Children tolerated
Disabled access difficult
Pets not accepted
Closed mid-Nov to mid-Dec, mid-Jan to mid-Mar
Proprietor Alberto Laudenzi

Umbria and Marche

Restaurant with rooms, Campello sul Clitunno

Le Casaline

Here is one of those restaurants out in the country which attract families from miles around on holidays; no further testimony to the quality of the food (especially the charcoal grills) is necessary.

The simple bedrooms are very much a sideline – in converted outbuildings a little way from the restaurant. 'Wished we could have stayed longer' remarked one visitor, but it is some while since we have received a report on Le Casaline, and we would welcome further comments.

Nearby Spoleto (14 km); Assisi (35 km).

Località Poreta, Campello sul Clitunno 06042 Perugia
Tel (0743) 521113
Fax (0743) 275099
Location 3 km E of Campello, isolated in countryside; in gardens, with ample car parking
Food & Drink breakfast, lunch, dinner
Prices rooms LL; breakfast L9,000; DB&B LL; meals L
Rooms 7 rooms, 2 with bath, 5 with shower; all rooms have phone
Facilities dining-room terrace, TV room
Credit cards AE, DC, V
Children welcome
Disabled access to 2 bedrooms possible
Pets accepted
Closed restaurant only, Mon
Proprietor Benedetto Zeppadoro

Umbria and Marche

La Badia

This marvellously preserved former Benedictine abbey (*badia*) dating from the 12thC is probably the best place from which to visit Orvieto, with its splendid cathedral. It is a sight worth seeing in its own right, with its 12-sided tower and beautifully harmonious Romanesque arches. The mellow stone buildings, the view across to the dramatically sited town, and the swimming-pool are powerful attractions.

An inspection visit confirmed other favourable reports, finding the rooms thoroughly comfortable, the suites notably spacious and restful; the Umbrian food excellent (grills on an open fire the speciality); and the service courteous and efficient, with English, French, German and Spanish spoken.

However, a more recent guest, while agreeing that the situation was 'beautiful' and the suite 'really excellent', judged the public rooms gloomy and uncomfortable and the staff impersonal.

Nearby cathedral in Orvieto; Lake of Bolsena; Todi (40 km).

La Badia, Orvieto Scalo 05019 Terni
Tel (0763) 90359 **Fax** 92796
Location 1 km S of Orvieto, off Viale 1 Maggio towards Viterbo; in large park with parking for 200 cars
Food & drink breakfast, lunch, dinner
Prices rooms LLL; suites LLLL; breakfast L18,000
Rooms 16 double, 14 with bath, one with shower; 3 single, 2 with bath, one with shower; 7 suites, 2 with bath, 2 with shower; 3 with Jacuzzi; all rooms have phone, air-conditioning, central heating
Facilities dining-room, bar, sitting-room with TV, conference hall; swimming-pool, 2 tennis courts
Credit cards AE, V
Children welcome **Disabled** access difficult **Pets** no dogs
Closed Jan and Feb; restaurant only, Wed
Proprietor Luisa Fiumi

Umbria and Marche

Country hotel, Orvieto

Villa Ciconia

Until a couple of years ago, Villa Ciconia was run mainly as a restaurant, with a few simple rooms above. When we first encountered it, we were doubtful about its inclusion in these pages. Now, all such doubts are banished: recent reports have confirmed that the genial Petrangeli family have re-established their 16thC home as a comfortable and welcoming country hotel, refurbished in keeping with the villa's original style.

The solid old house sits in a leafy, park-like garden watered by two streams that meet nearby, with tall pines giving plenty of shade. The spacious bedrooms are simply but tastefully furnished, with elegant iron-framed canopy beds and antique country furniture; The air-conditioning is not totally effective in all of them, though. The lofty dining-room is as splendid as ever, with its coffered ceiling and startling murals, and enormous stone fireplace; the breakfast room is more intimate, with plain white walls and mosaics. Cooking is distinctly Umbrian, using oil and wine from the adjacent family farm as well as fresh trout and shellfish. Dr Valentino Petrangeli is a wine enthusiast, always keen to share his knowledge of Orvieto and its wines with interested guests.
Nearby cathedral at Orvieto; Todi (40 km); Lake Bolsena.

Via dei Tigli 69, 05019 Orvieto
Tel (0763) 305582/3
Fax (0763) 302077
Location set in its own 5-acre park, about 2 km from Florence-Rome motorway; with private car parking
Food & drink breakfast, lunch, dinner
Prices rooms LL-LLL
Rooms 9 double, one single, all with bath (one with jacuzzi); all have central heating, air-conditioning (L20,000 per day), satellite TV, phone, minibar
Facilities dining-room, sitting-room, bar, conference room
Credit cards AE, DC, MC, V
Children accepted
Disabled no special facilities
Pets not encouraged
Closed mid-Jan to mid-Feb; restaurant only, Mon
Proprietor Dr Valentino Petrangeli

Umbria and Marche

Medieval manor, Ospedalicchio de Bastia

Lo Spedalicchio

Despite the attractions of Assisi, for the touring motorist there is much to be said for staying out of town in an hotel easily accessible by car. This one is the best around: a four-square manor house on the road to Perugia. The ground-floor rooms have high, vaulted brick ceilings and tiled floors with the occasional rug – whether you approach from the 'back' door as most drivers do or from the 'front' door opening on to the village square, the immediate impression is of centuries of calm living. The restaurant (which enjoys a high local reputation) is on one side – stylishly set out with bentwood chairs and pink napery; in contrast, the sitting-room bar area, which occupies much of the ground floor, is traditionally sparse with exposed stone walls. Bedrooms vary widely – some high-ceilinged, some two-level affairs with sitting space (an attractive possibility, given the poor public sitting area) – but all those we have seen are spacious and inviting. The staff are courteous and helpful; their French is better than their English. We are pleased to hear that the noisy church bells are now stopped during the night.

Nearby Assisi (10 km); Perugia (10 km); Gubbio, Orvieto, Todi and Spoleto all within reach.

Piazza Bruno Buozzi 3,
Ospedalicchio di Bastia 06080
Perugia
Tel and fax (075) 801 0323
Location between Assisi and
Perugia on S147; in garden
with ample car parking
Food & drink breakfast,
lunch, dinner
Prices rooms LL; meals from
L-LL
Rooms 20 double, 2 single, 3
family rooms; all with shower;
all rooms have central

heating, phone, colour TV;
some rooms have air-
conditioning
Facilities dining-room,
American bar, TV room,
conference rooms
Credit cards AE, DC, V
Children welcome; special
meals, baby-sitter, small beds
on request
Disabled no special facilities
Pets small ones only
Closed never
Manager Sg. G Costarelli

Umbria and Marche

Villa Serena

The Adriatic coast south of Rimini is not short of hotels, but it is very short of our kind of hotel, which makes this one a real find – a handsome 17thC mansion with some token castellations, standing in a wooded park high above the hubbub of the coast.

The villa has always belonged to one family – the counts Pinto de Franca y Vergaes, who used it as a summer residence until, in 1950, they turned it into a small hotel to be run like a family home. Renato Pinto does the cooking and serves up some better-than-average dishes (order in advance out of high season); Stefano and Filippo see to guests and reception; while their mother, Signora Silvana busies herself in the house and garden, with its terracotta pots and orange trees; all the family are reassuringly down-to-earth. The emphasis is on character, simplicity and tranquillity, not luxury. There are salons of baronial splendour, and corridors delightfully cluttered with bric à brac and potted plants. A few faded corners reinforce the villa's appealing air of impoverished aristocracy. No two bedrooms are alike but antiques and fireplaces feature in most. A couple could do with a lick of paint and some trees lopped to let in light.

Nearby municipal museum, at Pesaro; Ducal Palace at Urbino.

Via San Nicola 6/3, 61100 Pesaro
Tel (0721) 55211
Fax (0721) 55927
Location 4 km SE of Pesaro and beach, in a large wooded park on hillside with private car parking
Food & drink breakfast, lunch, dinner
Prices rooms LLL; meals LL
Rooms 10 double, all with bath or shower; all rooms have central heating, phone
Facilities 4 sitting-rooms, dining-room, bar, terrace; swimming-pool
Credit cards AE, DC, V
Children accepted
Disabled access difficult
Pets accepted
Closed 1st 2 weeks in Jan
Proprietor Renato Pinto

Umbria and Marche

Seaside hotel, Portonovo

Emilia

Although the Emilia is a seaside hotel, it stands aloof from the beaches south of Ancona, on the flanks of Monte Conero above the little resort of Portonovo (which is a car-journey away for all but the most energetic). It is a modern building of no great architectural merit. But its proprietors some years ago hit on a clever way of giving the hotel a distinctive appeal: they invited artists to come and stay, and to pay their way in kind. The results continue to accumulate on the walls: score upon score of paintings (none, we are assured, has ever been sold). Among the Italian signatures, our inspector spotted Graham Sutherland's.

Even without the extraordinary wall-covering, the hotel would have an attractive air. A long, low sitting-room with clusters of chunky modern armchairs links reception to the large, light, simply furnished dining-room, which has big windows looking on to a passable imitation of a *prato inglese* (a lawn). Food is taken seriously, although it no longer earns a Michelin star. Fish dominates the menu, and is competently cooked, though expensive. Bedrooms are thoroughly modern and snazzy. Most are in the older part of the hotel, ranged at an angle to give each room a sea-view and a small balcony. Recently 6 rooms were rebuilt with air-conditioning, and 2 'wonderful' suites were created.
Nearby church of Santa Maria (at Portonovo), Monte Conero; Ancona (12 km).

Via Poggio, 149/A Portonovo, Ancona 60020
Tel (071) 801145
Fax (071) 801330
Location 2 km W of Portonovo on cliffs; ample private car parking
Food & drink breakfast, lunch, dinner
Prices rooms LL-LLL
Rooms 28 double, 2 with bath, 26 with shower; 2 single with shower; 3 suites, 2 with bath and shower, 1 with shower; all rooms have central heating, air-conditioning, phone, colour TV, minibar
Facilities dining-room, TV room, conference room, bar, gazebo-bar; swimming-pool, tennis; golf club nearby
Credit cards AE, DC, MC, V
Children accepted
Disabled some ground-floor rooms **Pets** accepted
Closed Nov to Mar
Proprietor Maurizio Fiorini

Umbria and Marche

Le Tre Vaselle

On paper, the Tre Vaselle sounds disturbingly impersonal – it has more than 50 bedrooms and several conference rooms. But the hotel is entirely without ostentation, its modest entrance on a narrow street scarcely detectable, and the conference areas have now been made entirely separate. Friendly and courteous staff make you feel instantly at home, while the maze of ground-floor sitting-rooms – with its massive arches, white walls, rustic beams, terracotta floors, shabby but colourful armchairs and sofas, card-table and stone fireplaces – is immediately captivating.

Bedrooms, some in a more modern building behind the main one and others in a luxury annexe a short walk away, are smart and civilized. There are two pleasant dining-rooms but in warm weather the best place to eat is in the outdoor courtyard. The food at the Tre Vaselle is highly priced but excellent, and well complemented by the wines for which the owner, Dr Lung-arotti, has made Torgiano well known (don't miss the fascinating wine museum a street away from the hotel). 'Lavish breakfasts'. This is the sort of place which the touring visitor hesitates to leave, knowing for sure that the next night's hotel will be inferior.
Nearby Perugia; Assisi (25 km).

Via Garibaldi 48, Torgiano
06089 Perugia
Tel (075) 988 0447
Fax (075) 988 0214
Location in side street of village, 12 km SE of Perugia; ample car parking nearby
Food & drink breakfast, lunch, dinner
Prices rooms LLL-LLLL; suite LLLL
Rooms 52 double, 2 singles, 7 suites, most with bath, others with shower; all rooms have central heating, air- conditioning, phone, minibar, safe
Facilities sitting-rooms, dining-rooms, card and TV rooms, breakfast room, bar, conference rooms; outdoor pool, sauna **Credit cards** AE, DC, MC, V **Children** accepted
Disabled access possible – lift/elevator to bedrooms
Pets not accepted **Closed** never **Manager** Giovanni Margheritini

Umbria and Marche

Country hotel, Assisi

Castel San Gregorio

An eccentric place, occupying a small-scale castle-style building
in an elevated position a few miles from Assisi. Decoration falls
somewhere between Scottish baronial and chateau kitsch. Some
interesting bedrooms. You eat communally at one enormous
table.

■ San Gregorio, 06081 Assisi (Perugia) **Tel** (075) 8038009
Fax (075) 8038904 **Meals** breakfast, lunch, dinner **Prices** DB&B LL
Rooms 12, all with bath or shower, central heating, phone
Credit cards AE, DC, MC, V **Closed** late Jan

Country guest-house, Assisi

Country House

An unassuming guest-house amid fields and orchards a short
distance from the western gates of Assisi. Silvana Ciammarughi
runs an antiques business on the ground floor, and furnishes the
guest rooms from her stock. She strikes some visitors as jolly,
others as unfriendly; more reports welcome.

■ San Pietro Campagna 178, 06081 Assisi (Perugia) **Tel**(075) 816363
Fax (075) 816363 **Meals** breakfast **Prices** rooms L-LL; meals L
Rooms 15, all with bath, central heating **Credit cards** AE, V
Closed never

Town hotel, Assisi

Fontebella

An immaculately kept hotel in an old *palazzo* on one of the
well-worn routes from the central piazza to the basilica, with
some late-night noise affecting front rooms. Some other rooms
are said to be very small, but reporters speak well of the proprietors.

■ Via Fontebella 25, 06081 Assisi (Perugia) **Tel** (075) 812883
Fax (075) 812941 **Meals** breakfast, lunch, dinner **Prices** rooms LL-LLL
with breakfast; suite LLL **Rooms** 38, all with bath or shower,
central heating, phone, TV **Credit cards** AE, DC, MC, V **Closed** never

---

Town hotel, Assisi

Dei Priori

A well-run hotel in the heart of Assisi, close to all the tourist
sights and housed in an historic *palazzo*. Tastefully and comfortably furnished bedrooms, polished sitting-room and gracious,
arched dining-room – don't be put off by the modernized lobby
and bar.

■ Corso Mazzini 15, 06081 Assisi (Perugia) **Tel** (075) 812237
Fax (075) 816804 **Meals** breakfast, lunch, dinner **Prices** rooms LL-LLL;
DB&B LL **Rooms** 34, all with bath or shower, central heating, phone
Credit cards AE, DC, MC, V **Closed** mid-Nov to mid-Mar

Umbria and Marche

Country villa, Assisi

Santa Maria degli Ancillotti

An American reader recommends this country retreat, just a ten-minute drive from Assisi, perched on a hill surrounded by vineyards and olive groves. The two-room suites have sitting areas, mini kitchens and terraces with fine views. 'The family are utterly delightful. We looked forward to our meals as much for the company of Paolo, our host, as for the food, which was excellent.'

■ Sterpeto 42, 06086 Assisi (Perugia) **Tel & fax** (075) 8039764 **Meals** breakfast, lunch, dinner **Prices** rooms LL-LLL **Rooms** all with bath and shower, TV, phone, fridge **Credit cards** AE, DC, MC, V **Closed** mid-Nov to mid-Mar

---

Converted mill, Campello sul Clitunno

Il Vecchio Molino

An ancient mill set on an island in the middle of the river Clitunno, overlooked by and even more ancient (Roman) temple – of which the garden and terrace give a good view. Restrained decoration and harmonious furnishings in the spacious bedrooms.

■ Via del Tempio 34, Localita Pissignano, 06042 Campello sul Clitunno (Perugia) **Tel** (0743) 521122 F ax(0743) 275097 **Meals** breakfast **Prices** rooms LL-LLL; suite LLL **Rooms** 13, all with bath, central heating, phone, minibar; most have air-conditioning **Credit cards** AE, DC, MC, V **Closed** Nov to Mar

---

Town hotel, Città di Castello

Tiferno

On a small square close to the centre of a pleasant, untouristy Renaissance town: a 17thC convent that has recently been renovated with appropriate restraint and taste. More character in the public areas than in the spacious, well equipped rooms.

■ piazza R Sanzio, 13, 06012 Città di Castello (Perugia) **Tel** (075) 855 0331 **Fax** (075) 852 1196 **Meals** breakfast, lunch, dinner **Prices** rooms LL-LLL with breakfast; DB&B LL **Rooms** 38, all with bath, air-conditioning, radio, satellite TV, phone, minibar, hairdrier **Credit cards** AE, DC, MC, V **Closed** never

---

Converted castle, Deruta

Castello

High above Deruta (famous for its ceramics) is the walled village of Castelleone, and higher still is this neatly crenelled castle, apparently of 11thC origin. It was entirely refurbished in 1993. Good views from the shady garden.

■ Castelleone, 06053 Deruta (Perugia) **Tel** (075) 971 1302 **Meals** breakfast, lunch, dinner **Prices** DB&B LL **Rooms** 10, all with bath or shower, phone; some rooms have TV, minibar **Credit cards** AE, DC, V **Closed** Nov to Mar

Umbria and Marche

Town villa, Folignano

Villa Pigna

Business-style hotel – breakfast means pastries and coffee from the bar, taken standing up at peak times – and the bedrooms lack character. But the ground-floor sitting-rooms are exceptionally welcoming and satisfactory food is served in the modern dining-room.

■ Viale Assisi 33, 63040 Folignano (Ascoli Piceno) **Tel & Fax** (0736) 491868 **Meals** breakfast, lunch, dinner **Prices** rooms LL-LLL; meals L **Rooms** 54, all with phone, TV, minibar, balcony **Credit ards** AE, DC, V **Closed** restaurant only, 20 July to 23 Aug

Restaurant-with-rooms, Foligno

Villa Roncalli

Foligno may not be much to write home about, but this smart little villa in a woody garden certainly is. Fine regional dishes, imaginatively prepared, are served in the light vaulted dining-room. First-floor bedrooms are notably spacious. Excellent service. There should by now be a pool.

■ Via Roma 25, 06034 Foligno (Perugia) **Tel** (0742) 391091 **Meals** breakfast, lunch, dinner **Prices** rooms L-LL; DB&B LL **Rooms** 10, all with bath or shower, TV, phone **Credit cards** AE, DC, V **Closed** 2 weeks Aug; restaurant only, Mon

Town hotel, Gubbio

Bosone

The best place to stay to savour the atmosphere of historic Gubbio: the Bosone occupies a *palazzo* as old as some of the sights you have come to see. Two of the bedrooms are remarkably grand, with flamboyant decoration; the rest relatively ordinary. The Taverna del Lupo, where main meals are taken, is jolly.

■ Via XX Settembre 22, 06024 Gubbio (Perugia) **Tel** (075) 922 0688 **Fax** (075) 922 0552 **Meals** breakfast, lunch, dinner; meals taken in nearby Taverna del Lupo **Prices** rooms LL; breakfast L10,000; suite LLL; **Rooms** 30, all with bath, phone, TV, minibar **Credit cards** AE, DC, MC, V **Closed** Jan or Feb

Country villa, Gubbio

Villa Montegranelli

A rustic alternative to staying in Gubbio itself (follow signs to San Martino in Colle from town centre): a rather severe stone-built villa in hillside grounds. Rooms varying widely in size, furnishings simple, decoration restrained and stylish. The vaulted dining-room dates from the 13thC and serves excellent food and wine.

■ Monteluiano, 06024 Gubbio (Perugia) **Tel** (075) 922 0185 **Fax** (075) 927 3372 **Meals** breakfast, lunch, dinner **Prices** rooms LL-LLL with breakfast; suite LLL; DB&B LLL; meals LL **Rooms** 21, all with bath or shower, phone, minibar, TV **Credit cards** AE, DC, MC, V **Closed** never

Umbria and Marche

Converted fortress, Monte Vibiano

Castello di Monte Vibiano

Despite its size, this hilltop castle, rebuilt in the 17thC, takes only 12 guests – so there is no risk of tripping over one another in the vaulted public rooms of the house or on the immaculate lawns outside. It is run on house-party lines; all drinks are included in the price.

■ Mercatello, 06050 Monte Vibiano (Perugia) **Tel** Florence booking office (055) 218112 **Fax** (055) 287157 **Meals** breakfast, lunch, dinner **Prices** DB&B LLL; FB LLLL; single room supplement L50,000 **Rooms** 6, all with bath, central heating, air-conditioning, phone **Credit cards** not accepted **Closed** Oct to Jun

---

Country villa, Montecassiano

Villa Quiete

A substantial house of mixed merits: dreary sitting-rooms, smart café-style dining-room, bedrooms varying from ordinary to grand with antiques. Its key asset is the moderate-sized garden with its pines, palms and geraniums.

■ Vallecascia di Montecassiano, 62010 Montecassiano (Macerata) **Tel** (0733) 599559 **Meals** breakfast, lunch, dinner **Prices** rooms L-LL breakfast L10,000; suite LLL **Rooms** 38, all with bath or shower, central heating, air-conditioning, phone, TV, **Credit cards** V **Closed** never

---

Town hotel, Orvieto

Virgilio

An engaging old building (dating from 1300) whose prime virtue is its position right at the heart of things – several rooms overlook the cathedral. Inside, modernization has left it somewhat conventional for some tastes. But, it is comfortable and modestly priced.

■ Piazza del Duomo 5/6, 05018 Orvieto (Terni) **Tel** (0763) 341882 **Fax** (0763) 343797 **Meals** breakfast **Prices** rooms LL-LLL; breakfast L10,000 **Rooms** 13, all with bath or shower, phone **Credit cards** MC, V **Closed** 20 days in Jan-Feb

---

Town hotel, Perugia

Brufani

Calm and polished hotel with a splendid location atop one of the cliffs that define central Perugia, and at one end of the *corso*. Public areas are particularly attractive, with a spacious central lobby and a glossy American bar. The Collin's Restaurant features local specialities. Plans to greatly increase the number of rooms may force us to exclude it from our guide in the future.

■ Piazza Italia 12, 06100 Perugia **Tel** (075) 5732541 **Fax** (075) 5720210 **Meals** breakfast, lunch, dinner **Prices** rooms LLLL; breakfast L32,000; suites LLLL; meals LL **Rooms** 27, all with bath, central heating, air-conditioning, phone, TV, radio, hairdrier, minibar, safe **Credit cards** AE, DC, MC, V **Closed** never

Umbria and Marche

Town hotel, Perugia

Locanda della Posta

Perugia's oldest hotel, opened over 200 years ago, is now one of its most attractive, following a thorough renovation a few years ago. Bedrooms are smart and comfortable, public areas limited but elegant – and just outside the door is Perugia's famous pedestrian *corso*.

■ Corso Vannucci 97, 06100 Perugia **Tel** (075) 5728925 **Fax** (075) 5722413 **Meals** breakfast **Prices** rooms LL-LLL with breakfast, suite LLLL **Rooms** 40, all with bath, central heating, air-conditioning, phone, hairdrier, TV, minibar **Credit cards** AE, DC, MC, V **Closed** never

---

Seaside hotel, Portonovo

Fortino Napoleonico

An extremely unusual hotel, built within a single-storey seaside fortress, apparently dating (as the name suggests) from the early 19thC. The whole place is simple, clean and roomy, and suits families very well – many of the rooms (contained within the ramparts) can accommodate three or four.

■ Portonovo (Ancona) **Tel** (071) 801450 **Fax** (071) 801454 **Meals** breakfast, lunch, dinner **Prices** rooms LLL; suites LLL **Rooms** 30, all with bath or shower, central heating, phone **Credit cards** AE, DC, MC, V **Closed** Jan

---

Town hotel, Santa Vittoria in Matenano

Farfense

A friendly, simple, family-run hotel in a backwater hilltop town, surrounded by pretty and distinctive countryside with a patchwork of tiny fields. Spotless bedrooms (some with views) and a jolly little restaurant down in the brick-vaulted cellars.

■ Corso Matteoti 41, 63028 Santa Vittoria in Matenano (Ascoli Piceno) **Tel** (0734) 780171 **Meals** breakfast, lunch, dinner **Prices** rooms L; FB L; meals L **Rooms** 10, all with bath or shower, central heating; 4 have balconies **Credit cards** AE, DC, MC, V **Closed** 2 weeks end Sep/ early Oct; restaurant only, Wed

---

Converted monastery, Sirolo

Monteconero

Yet another religious house in a prime position – on the very summit of Monte Conero, 500 metres above the Adriatic, with superb views along the coast from the bar terrace, and with a swimming-pool and tennis court. Bedrooms are simple, modern, adequate. There is an atmospheric little stone-vaulted restaurant on the lower floor.

■ Monte Conero, 60020 Sirolo (Ancona) **Tel** (071) 9330592 **Fax** (071) 9330365 **Meals** breakf ast, lunch, dinner **Prices** rooms LL; suites LLL **Rooms** 50; 9 suites, all with shower, phone **Credit cards** AE, DC, MC, V **Closed** Nov to Easter

Umbria and Marche

Converted mill, Spello

La Bastiglia

A smartly restored old mill-house, with its ancient character preserved, and panoramic views from practically all its rooms; 7 of them are suites with private garden-terraces. A recent reporter alerted us to skimpy towels and difficulties with the hot water supply. More reports please.

■ Piazza Vallegloria, 06038 Spello (Perugia) **Tel** (0742) 651277 **Fax** (0742) 301159 **Meals** breakfast, lunch, dinner **Prices** rooms LL; suites LLL; DB&B LL; breakfast L10,000 **Rooms** 22, all with bath, air-conditioning, minibar, TV, phone **Credit cards** AE, DC, MC, V **Closed** restaurant only, Wed; mid-Jan to Feb

Town hotel, Spoleto

Gattapone

This smart little hotel is named after the architect of Spoleto's impressively high 14thC Bridge of Towers, of which guests get a grandstand view. The rooms are spacious and beautifully maintained in '60s-style, the position peaceful as well as panoramic. Our reporter raved about the stylish interior.

■ Via del Ponte 6, 06049 Spoleto (Perugia) **Tel** (0743) 223447 **Fax** (0743) 223448 **Meals** breakfast **Prices** rooms LLL with breakfast **Rooms** 13, all with bath or shower, minibar, TV **Credit cards** AE, DC, MC, V **Closed** never

Country hotel, Todi

Bramante

Not the last word in character, but a pleasant stopover in an ideal position, just outside Todi and in the shadow of Bramante's church of Santa Maria. At the core of the hotel is an old stone house; the modern furnishings are restrained and comfortable. Swimming-pool, tennis, mini soccer court (check on charges).

■ Via Orvietana 46, 06059 Todi (Perugia) **Tel** (075) 894 8381 **Fax** (075) 894 8074 **Meals** breakfast, lunch, dinner **Prices** rooms LL-LLL with breakfast; FB LLL **Rooms** 45, all with bath, phone, air-conditioning, satellite TV, minibar **Credit cards** AE, DC, MC, V **Closed** never

---

Readers' Reports

Reports from readers are of enormous interest to us in keeping up to date with the hotels in this guide - and others that should be in it. More information on p11

Lazio and Abruzzi

Hotels in Lazio and Abruzzi

Rome is a city of grand hotels rather than small and charming ones. Among the hotels we have looked at but not given an entry to is a simple but adequately comfortable place in the peaceful residential area of Aventino – the Sant'Anselmo (Tel (06) 574 3547, fax 578 3604). Other possibilities include the Cesari (Tel (06) 679 2386, fax 0882, 50 rooms, old-fashioned but comfortable), and the Piazza di Spagna (Tel (06) 679 6412, fax 0654). At the top end of the market (and of the Spanish Steps) is the luxurious 37-room Lord Byron (Tel (06) 322 0404, fax 0405) – certainly less impersonal than most smart Rome hotels, but still impressively ritzy and correspondingly expensive.

A few miles outside Rome is the Villa Fiorio at Grottaferrata (Tel (06) 943 15369, fax 941 3482), dropped from the guide a couple of years ago following a negative report, but still highly rated by some of our competitors. Reports welcome.

Palestrina (birthplace of the 16thC composer) and Tivoli (villas of Emperor Hadrian and the 16thC Cardinal d'Este) are within day-trip range of Rome, but if you want to stay over-night in Palestrina, go for the Stella – modern, excellent restaurant, clean spacious bedrooms (Tel (06) 953 8172, fax 957 3360). North of the capital is the pretty wooded countryside around Viterbo and Lago di Vico. An average town hotel in the heart of Viterbo is the Leon d'Oro (Tel and fax (0761) 344444).

The Abruzzi is a wild and wooded mountainous region, forming part of the Apennine mountains. Charming small hotels are hard to find and you might do best to explore the area from a base nearer Rome. We do have a couple of short-entry recommendations though – at Balsorano (page 181) and Scanno (page 184), and another Scanno hotel worth considering is the Del Lago (Tel and fax (0864) 74343), in a lakeside setting 3km outside the town.

L'Aquila, the capital of the region, is a big town further north but still in the heart of the mountains. Though mainly a business centre today, the surrounding mountains and the imposing historical buildings within the town itself still make it an interesting place to stay. Try the Grand Hotel del Parco (Tel (0862) 413248, fax 65938, 36 rooms), smaller and less business-oriented than most of the hotels in the town.

This page acts as an introduction to the features and hotels of Lazio and Abruzzi, and gives brief recommendations of reasonable hotels that for one reason or another have not made a full entry. The long entries for this region – covering the hotels we are most enthusiastic about – start on the next page. But do not neglect the shorter entries starting on page 181: these are all hotels that we would happily stay at.

Lazio and Abruzzi

Town hotel, Rome

Hotel dei Borgognoni

The understated elegance of the Hotel dei Borgognoni, and its mood of seclusion, may be the lingering legacy of the convent which previously occupied this convenient location in a quiet street just slightly closer to the Trevi Fountain than the Spanish Steps. Lacquered doors, heavy brass fittings, distressed mirrors, polished stucco and panels of maple create the image of impeccable modernity, enhanced by Old Master paintings, Oriental carpets and ceramics, marble and gilt tables, dried flower arrangements and a bed of palm trees in the centre of the main reception area. Other plants press against a glass window in the pretty breakfast room. Bedrooms continue the modern style with extensive use of mirrors and striped fabrics. The best rooms are located on the first floor where large glass windows open on to small private terraces equipped with a table, chairs and umbrella.

Evidently, such smart appointments are designed to appeal to the businessman for whom two conference rooms have been equipped, but the hotel, which takes its name from the Burgundian community which favoured this neighbourhood in the 17thC, is far too well placed to be ignored by other visitors.
Nearby Trevi Fountain, Sant' Andrea delle Fratte, via del Corso.

Via del Bufalo, 00187 Rome
Tel (06) 69941505
Fax (06) 69941501
Location between Piazza di Spagna and the Trevi Fountain; garage
Food and drink buffet breakfast
Prices LLLL with breakfast
Rooms 48 double with bath, 2 single with bath; all rooms have central heating, air-conditioning, satellite TV, radio, phone, minibar
Facilities breakfast room, bar, two conference rooms
Credit cards AE, DC, MC, V
Children accepted
Disabled lift/elevator
Pets accepted
Closed never
Manager Claudio Marca

Lazio and Abruzzi

Town hotel, Rome

Hotel Carriage

This smart little hotel stands in one of the narrow streets near the Piazza di Spagna, renowned for their elegant boutiques dealing in impossibly-priced clothes. The Carriage matches the designer style of its surroundings, though its prices for this part of Rome are not at all unreasonable. 'It is a perfect size,' comments a recent visitor, 'one feels like one is the only one there.'

The reception area of fat-cushioned, expensive-looking sofas and chairs in gold and blue stripes, the pretty breakfast room of black bentwood and rattan and twirly gilt, the cool flower arrangements – all seem to await only the photographer and slinky models. Upstairs, bedrooms are less florid in blue and white, with fine, solid reproduction French-look furnishings. Bathrooms are clean and streamlined, with spotlit mirrors and all the usual trimmings. At the top of the hotel there is a small roof terrace, slightly less orderly than the rest of the hotel, but allowing a breath of air along with your summer breakfast. From what we saw, breakfast is of above-average standard, with a range of hot and cold items. Reception was manned by a pleasantly professional English-speaker when we visited.

Nearby Piazza di Spagna, Via del Corso.

Via della Carrozze 36,
00187 Rome
Tel (06) 699 0124
Fax (06) 678 8279
Location between Via del Corso and Piazza di Spagna
Food & drink breakfast
Prices rooms LLL with breakfast
Rooms 17 double, all with bath and shower, 3 single, all with shower, 2 suites; all rooms have central heating, air-conditioning, phone,
hairdrier, TV, radio, minibar
Facilities breakfast room, seating in reception
Credit cards AE, DC, MC, V
Children accepted
Disabled no special facilities
Pets not accepted
Closed never
Manager Sg. Trau

Lazio and Abruzzi

Hotel Celio

Our attention was drawn to the Celio by its owner, Roberto Quattrini, who also owns an old favourite of ours in Venice, the Santo Stefano (see page 75). Roberto is an attentive manager, always ready to help and give advice when he is on hand, and to ensure that his guests (who have included Helena Bonham-Carter and Christopher Lee) are happy. Although it is centrally located, its charms are somewhat idiosyncratic, and we would welcome readers' opinions as well as our own.

The hotel is a stone's throw from the Colosseum and the Roman Forum, and conveniently placed for public transport. Its design is different, to say the least, and you will probably either love it or loathe it, a jolly mixture of classical pastiche, modern kitsch and run-of-the-mill. Elegant double doors lead into a red-carpeted entrance hall whose walls are clothed in a *trompe l'oeil* vision of the Colosseum, blue sea and sky, classical pillars and stone arches. Bedrooms are essentially plainly decorated, but enlivened by more paintings - often of angels and cherubs cavorting on clouds. The marble mosaic bathrooms are well-equipped with power showers.

Nearby Colosseum, Roman Forum.

Via dei Santissimi Quattro 35/c, 00184 Rome
Tel (06) 70495333
Fax ((06) 7096377
Location in a side street, close to the Colosseum; garage nearby
Food & drink breakfast
Prices rooms LLL-LLLL with breakfast
Rooms 10 double, all with bath; all rooms have phone, TV, radio, minibar, safe, trouser press, hairdrier, scales

Facilities sitting area, breakfast area, bar
Credit cards AE, DC, MC, V
Children accepted
Disabled not suitable
Pets not accepted
Closed never
Proprietor Roberto Quatrini

Lazio and Abruzzi

Town hotel, Rome

Hotel Condotti

Recently taken over and totally refurbished by new owners, this formerly modest hotel in a quiet side-street has been considerably improved without becoming too stiffly posed for comfort – and without losing its traditional shuttered façade.

The glossy little reception area is the only place to lounge, offering several squashy sofas liberally heaped with cushions. Down a marble staircase is the breakfast room, newly decorated in yellow, with frescos by a local artist, and royal blue tablecloths.

Bedrooms are reassuringly harmonious but modern, without a great deal of personality; unusually for a hotel of this category, there are no hairdriers in bathrooms. One or two have pleasant, spacious terraces – understandably in great demand among regular visitors.

Breakfast is more than minimal, with cheese and other extras. On the occasion of our inspection, the receptionist was a highly professional Canadian, and the hotel seemed to be doing a thriving transatlantic trade. The location is excellent for exploring the posh little shops off the Corso.

Nearby Spanish Steps, Via del Corso.

Via Mario De'Fiori 37, 00187 Rome

Via Mario De'Fiori 37, 00187 Rome
Tel (06) 679 4661
Fax (06) 679 0457
Location between Via del Corso and Piazza di Spagna
Food & drink breakfast
Prices rooms LLL-LLLL; suites LLLL with buffet breakfast
Rooms 17 double, 12 with bath, 5 with shower; all rooms have central heating, air-conditioning, phone, satellite TV, minibar
Facilities reception, breakfast room, bar
Credit cards AE, MC, V
Children accepted
Disabled lift/elevator
Pets not accepted
Closed never
Manager Sig Massimo Funaro

Lazio and Abruzzi

Town hotel, Rome

Hotel Raphaël

Cloaked in stalactites of ivy, the Hotel Raphaël stands back from the bustle of Piazza Navona and belongs, instead, to the quiet refinement of the antiques and antiquarian book shops and local *trattorias* of via dei Coronari which runs beside it. But the discreet façade conceals one of the most evocative and theatrical lobbies in the city. A pair of marble musical muses inside the entrance door announces an eclectic mix of Byzantine icons, Old Master paintings, prints by the Italian Futurists and ceramics by Picasso displayed in Baroque furniture. The aroma of white lillies in large vases pervades the atmosphere. It is hardly surprising that the acting profession has embraced this establishment.

The lobby is punctuated by the only disappointing feature – a functional marble and glass staircase connecting the five floors of the hotel. Other modernist features have been softened by recent sweeping redecoration. New panelled doors and stone architraves offer a more pleasing character and bedrooms drip in rich paisley fabrics, but are perhaps smaller than prices would suggest. A visit here will be as memorable as the splendid terrace view of Bramante's magnificent cupola of Santa Maria della Pace.
Nearby Piazza Navona, Palazzo Altemps, Santa Maria della Pace.

Largo Febo 2, 00186 Rome
Tel (06) 682 831
Fax (06) 687 8993
Location at the north end of via dell'Anima behind the Piazza Navona, garage 100 metres
Food and drink buffet breakfast, lunch, dinner
Prices LLLL
Rooms 53 double with bath; 12 de-luxe double with bath; 7 suites; all rooms have central heating, air-conditioning, satellite TV , radio, phone, minibar
Facilities breakfast room, dining-room, bar; summer roof terrace serving lunch and dinner; conference room, fitness room, sauna
Credit cards AE, DC, MC, V
Children accepted
Disabled no special facilities
Pets accepted
Closed never
Proprietor Roberto Vannoni

Lazio and Abruzzi

La Residenza

The Via Veneto is one of Rome's most fashionable addresses, and the location of some of its grandest hotels. The Residenza is not one of them, but its position only a block away from this sweeping tree-lined avenue gives it a head start.

The Residenza is part of the small Giannetti chain of hotels, concentrated in dreary Lido di Jesolo – not a good sign. But the atmosphere is intimate and the front desk staff are friendly and helpful.

Another key aspect of the hotel's appeal is its bar and sitting areas on the elevated ground floor, which are extensive and smartly done out, with a mixture of modern and antique furniture. A better-than-average help-yourself breakfast is served in a more ordinary, windowless room at the back of the hotel. Bedrooms are comfortable and well equipped, but uniformly furnished with no great flair or character. Those at the back are quieter than those at the front, which despite their double glazing suffer from noise from a nearby nightclub. Some have fair-sized terraces, and there is also a communal roof-top terrace with interesting views.

Nearby Spanish Steps, Villa Borghese.

Via Emilia 22, Rome 00187
Tel (06) 488 0789
Fax (06) 485721
Location in side-street off Via Veneto; limited car parking
Food & drink breakfast
Prices rooms LL-LLL; suite LLLL, with breakfast
Rooms 17 double, all with bath; 5 single; 7 suites; all with bath and shower; all rooms have central heating, minibar, satellite TV, air-conditioning, hairdrier,

phone
Facilities sitting-rooms, bar, breakfast room, patio, terrace
Credit cards AE, MC, V
Children accepted
Disabled access difficult
Pets not accepted
Closed never
Manager Vincenzo Casaburo

Lazio and Abruzzi

Town guest-house, Rome

Scalinata di Spagna

For many visitors to Rome, the Spanish Steps represent the heart of the city, a popular rendezvous at once lively and colourful. At their summit stand two hotels which represent the epitomes of their respective markets: the Hassler, one of the city's grandest establishments, and this highly individual little *pensione* which, now more than ever, wins our accolade for genuine charm.

In the previous edition of our guide, we acknowledged the hotel's attractions but expressed a reservation for the old-fashioned bedrooms and unremarkable bathrooms. A major programme of redecoration, by the proprietor's daughter, Claudia, has changed that situation in very pleasing ways. Rooms are now coated in pretty blue and gold floral fabrics and illuminated by Murano chandeliers. Neoclassical scroll sofas and small tables enhance a mood of comfort and intimacy. Bathrooms have been reappointed. The tiny entrance hall and corridors have been redesigned, too, with a new reception desk and polished stucco walls. Inevitably, prices have risen but compare favourably with other hotels of this category. Our earlier advice remains: with just 16 rooms, book well ahead, to be sure of a vacancy.

Nearby Piazza di Spagna, Villa Medici, Villa Borghese.

Piazza Trinita dei Monti 17, 00187 Rome
Tel (06) 679 3006
Fax (06) 699 40598
Location at the top of the Spanish Steps, car parking 50 m away
Food and drink buffet breakfast
Prices LLLL
Rooms 16 double with bath or shower; all rooms have central heating, air-conditioning, satellite TV, radio, phone, minibar
Facilities breakfast room, roof terrace
Credit cards AE, DC, MC, V
Children accepted
Disabled no special facilities
Pets accepted
Closed never
Proprietor Giuseppe Bellia

Lazio and Abruzzi

Town hotel, Rome

Sole al Pantheon

Complete refurbishment in 1988 gave this ancient *albergo* the decoration and atmosphere which does justice to its privileged position – to one side of the square in front of the famous Pantheon, one of Rome's few perfectly preserved ancient Roman buildings. The Sole is now unquestionably one of Rome's most delightful small hotels; unfortunately for prospective guests, it is now also one of the most expensive.

Bedrooms – each named after some famous visiting worthy – feature fascinating coffered and painted ceilings, and are gorgeously furnished in imaginative and elegant styles. Each is different and distinctive, though all have restful colour schemes, fabric-framed mirrors, and fine antiques. Many have interesting views. Public areas are equally pleasant: a salon of white leather seating on terracotta-tiled floors straight from the pages of some glossy magazine, and a small, cosy bar downstairs. Breakfast is served either on an upper courtyard terrace, or in a pleasant little room leading off it. Italianate corners throughout the hotel are thoughtfully filled with plants, urns, statuary or dribbling fountains.

Nearby Pantheon, Villa Borghese.

Piazza della Rotonda 63,
00186 Roma
Tel (06) 678 0441
Fax (06) 699 40689
Location in piazza in front of
the Pantheon
Food & drink breakfast
Prices rooms LLLL with
breakfast; suites LLLL
Rooms 22 double, 3 single,
all with bath; all rooms
have central heating,
air-conditioning, phone, TV,
hairdrier, radio, minibar

Facilities breakfast room, bar
Credit cards AE, DC, MC, V
Children accepted
Disabled lift/elevator
Pets not accepted
Closed never
Manager G. Piraino

Lazio and Abruzzi

Town hotel, Rome

Valadier

The Valadier began its metamorphosis from gracious decay into its present slick form – something like the innards of a millionaire's yacht (or our image of one) – a year or two back. The refit continues with the recent construction of an elegantly intimate restaurant, adding to an already generous assortment of smallish but very smart public rooms. Marble, mirror-glass, and highly polished wood face every surface.

The cabin-like bedrooms are what really bring the yacht image to mind. Not only are they very cleverly fitted out to make the most of their compact dimensions, but also they bristle with electronic gadgetry. Bewildering consoles of instruments await the visitor by the bedside, so that switching a light on in the middle of the night can be a baffling process of trial and error. You can even check your bill on the TV screen in your room. The ritzy gin-palace feel is reinforced by the obedient hum of the air-conditioning system, like the purr of the engine room.

Charming? Well, no. But distinctive and exceptionally comfortable – and well run by a pleasant staff. A good location, too, close to the heart of things.

Nearby Spanish Steps, Villa Borghese.

Via della Fontanella 15,
Rome 00187
Tel (06) 361 0559
Fax (06) 320 1558
Location off Via del Corso, close to Piazza del Popolo; garage 100 m away
Food & drink breakfast, lunch, dinner
Prices rooms LLL-LLLL; suites up to LLLL; meals LL
Rooms 24 double, 12 single, 3 suites, all with bath and shower; all rooms have central heating, phone, minibar, TV, piped music, air-conditioning, electronic safe, hairdrier
Facilities piano/American bar, dining-room, sitting-room, conference rooms; solarium **Credit cards** AE, DC, MC **Children** welcome
Disabled entrance difficult, but 2 lifts/elevators
Pets small ones only
Closed never
Proprietor Simonetta Battistini

Lazio and Abruzzi

Town villa, Rome

Villa Florence

On the broad Via Nomentana to the north-east of the middle of Rome, this well-run hotel has particular attractions for motorists reluctant to tangle with the worst of Rome's traffic (in addition to a convenient location, it has private parking in the garden behind the house).

The villa's other chief merit is the welcoming ambience of its public areas. Great efforts have been made to give the little sitting area (off reception) and the adjacent café-style breakfast room some interest and warmth. Dotted around all the public areas are interesting archaeological fragments which have been discovered on the site of the hotel.

There is a small, secluded terrace behind the house, with sunbeds as well as tables and chairs; smart white parasols provide shade. The bedrooms (some in outbuildings, with doors opening on to the garden) are simple and functional but comfortable. The cheerful proprietor makes an effort to see that breakfast is more than usually satisfying, with yoghurt, cheese and ham as well as the standard fare. A recent visitor, though, was disappointed by sullen staff and poor housekeeping standards.

Nearby Villa Borghese, Via Veneto, Piazza di Spagna.

Via Nomentana 28, Rome
00161 (Porta Pia)
Tel (06) 440 3036
Fax (06) 440 2709
Website http://www.venere.it/roma/villa_florence/
Location about one km NE of Via Veneto, with private car parking in garden
Food & drink breakfast
Prices rooms LL-LLL with breakfast; 30% reduction for children sharing parents' room

Rooms 32 double, one single, 4 family rooms, all with bath or shower; all rooms have colour TV, minibar, air-conditioning, phone, hairdrier; some have whirlpools
Facilities breakfast room, TV room, bar
Credit cards AE, DC, MC, V
Children accepted
Disabled no special facilities
Pets not accepted
Closed never
Proprietor Tullio Cappelli

Lazio and Abruzzi

Town Villa, Rome

Villa del Parco

This mellow, early-20thC villa is about a 20-minute bus ride from the middle of Rome, but its peaceful setting – on a tree-lined street in a pleasant residential area with parks and gardens nearby – more than makes up for this. Villa del Parco is set back from the road, partly shielded from traffic by walled gardens to either side. Inside, all is elegant and tranquil. From the welcoming reception lobby, steps lead down to a light and classily furnished two-part sitting-room, with a breakfast room at the far end. The ambience is both restful and tasteful: pale blue sofas, antiques, plants, together with a chessboard, and a mass of nicely framed pictures (fin-de-siècle theatrical memorabilia and sepia photographs of old Paris).

Bedrooms vary in size; some are quite small, others larger, with a touch of elegance. But all are well-furnished, with plain, softly textured wallcoverings and modern fittings in bathrooms. Those at the front are noisier. On sunny days the little garden comes into its own, and tables are set for alfresco breakfasts beneath parasols. A couple who stayed recently were entirely satisfied: 'The staff were very courteous and took care of our every need.'

Nearby Villa Torlonia, Villa Borghese

Via Nomentana, 110, Roma 00161
Tel (06) 4423 7773
Fax (06) 4423 7572
Location in residential area, NE of the middle of the city; with gardens and car parking
Food & drink breakfast, snacks
Prices LLL, with breakfast
Rooms 12 double, 12 single, all with bath or shower; all rooms have central heating, air-conditioning, phone, TV, radio, minibar
Facilities 2 sitting-rooms, breakfast room, small bar
Credit cards AE, DC, V
Children accepted
Disabled no special facilities
Pets accepted
Closed never
Proprietor Elisabetta Bernardini

Lazio and Abruzzi

Seaside hotel, San Felice Circeo

Punta Rossa

San Felice is an amiable village at the foot of the 550-metre Monte Circeo, which is an isolated lump of rock at the seaward point of a flat area, once marshland but now drained except for zones which have been declared a national park to preserve the flora and fauna. The Punta Rossa lies around the mountain in a secluded setting above an exposed and rocky shore.

The hotel has the form of a miniature village. Reception is in a lodge just inside an arched gateway, and beyond that is a little piazza enclosed by white-walled buildings in rough Mediterranean style. Bedrooms are spread around in low buildings at or near the top of a garden beyond the piazza which descends steeply to the sea. They are pleasant, varying in size, many with colour schemes which look a bit dated; all have balconies with sea views. The main attraction of the suites is their admirable size. The restaurant (food is 'exceptional' according to a recent report) is part-way down the garden (already bursting with colour when we visited in spring) towards the sea and pool.

Nearby Terracina (20 km); Circeo national park.

San Felice Circeo
04017 Latina
Tel (0773) 548085 **Fax** 548075
Location 4 km W of San Felice, isolated on rocky shore; in gardens, car parking
Food & drink breakfast, lunch, dinner
Prices rooms LLL-LLLL with breakfast; suites LLLL; meals LL
Rooms 27 double, 7 suites; all with bath or shower; all rooms have heating, air-conditioning, phone, minibar, colour satellite TV; all double rooms have sea- view balcony or terrace
Facilities bar, dining- room, terrace, courtyard; sea-water swimming-pool, heated indoor whirlpool**Credit cards** AE, DC, V **Children** welcome
Disabled access difficult
Pets small dogs accepted by arrangement **Closed** never
Manager Maria Fiorella Battaglia

Lazio and Abruzzi

Converted fortress, Balsorano

Castello di Balsorano

After a period of closure, this fine-looking hilltop fortress has re-opened under new ownership. As far as we know, the authentically medieval interior remains, with weapons and wall-hangings all around, and ornate antique beds. Reports on the new regime would be very welcome.

■ Piazza Piccolomini, 67052 Balsorano (L'Aquila) **Tel** (0863) 951236 **Meals** breakfast, lunch, dinner **Prices** rooms LL; suites LL **Rooms** 6, all with bath, central heating **Credit cards** V **Closed** never

---

Converted castle, Formia

Castello Miramare

This 19thC 'castle' (converted in the 1970s) stands high above Formia, with tremendous views of the vast, sweeping bay of Gaeta. Rooms are neatly furnished in Spanish style. In summer, drinks and breakfast can be enjoyed on the little garden terraces.

■ Balze di Pagnano, 04023 Formia (Latina) **Tel** (0771) 700138 **Fax** (0771) 700139 **Meals** breakfast, lunch, dinner **Prices** rooms LL-LLL; meals LL; breakfast L16,000 **Rooms** 10, all with bath or shower, minibar, TV, hairdrier, air-conditioning **Credit cards** AE, DC, MC, V **Closed** never

---

Country villa, Palo Laziale

La Posta Vecchia

Start with the prices; count the noughts before you entertain thoughts of booking. This is the most expensive hotel in these pages, by quite a margin. It was restored and furnished by the late John Paul Getty, and is as luxurious and tasteful as you would hope, but without formality. Close to perfection.

■ 00055 Palo Laziale (Rome) **Tel** (06) 994 9501 **Fax** (06) 994 9507 **E-mail** postavec@caerenet.it **Website** http://lapostavecchia.com **Meals** breakfast, lunch, dinner **Prices** rooms and suites LLLLL with breakfast **Rooms** 17, all with bath or shower, phone, TV, air-conditioning **Credit cards** AE, DC, MC, V **Closed** never

---

Cottage complex, Poggio Mirteto Scalo

Borgo Paraelios

A reader recommends this immaculately executed rustic-style development in the hills half-way between Rome and Rieti. It is almost entirely single-storey, the individually furnished rooms and suites spread around grassy gardens and flowery courtyards. Smart little pool and a gym. You'll need detailed directions.

■ Localita Valle Collichia, 02040 Poggio Mirteto Scalo (Rieti) **Tel** (0765) 26267 **Fax** (0765) 262 68 **Meals** breakfast, lunch, dinner **Prices** rooms LLLL with breakfast; meals LL **Rooms** 14, all with bath or shower, central heating, air-conditioning, private patio, phone, TV, hairdrier **Credit cards** AE, DC, V **Closed** Oct-Mar

Lazio and Abruzzi

Town guest-house, Rome

Gregoriana

A courteous welcome and highly distinctive decoration more than compensate for the lack of public spaces in this pleasant, shuttered, 300-year-old house, on a street leading to the Trinita dei Monti church at the top of the Spanish Steps. Some rooms have leafy balconies and quiet rooftop views.

■ Via Gregoriana 18, 00187 Rome **Tel** (06) 679 7988 **Fax** (06) 678 4258 **Meals** breakfast **Prices** rooms LLL-LLLL **Rooms** 19, all with bath or shower, central heating, air-conditioning, TV, phone **Credit cards** not accepted **Closed** never

---

Town hotel, Rome

Internazionale

The interconnected dining-and- sitting-rooms display the venerable pedigree of this former convent most clearly; elsewhere the rooms of this rambling hotel vary greatly in size and style, though all are comfortable – some exceptionally elegant and spacious. One visitor suffered a double booking error; reports welcome.

■ Via Sistina 79, 00187 Rome **Tel** (06) 679 3047 **Fax** (06) 678 4764 **Meals** breakfast **Prices** rooms LLL-LLLL with breakfast **Rooms** 42, all with bath or shower, central heating, air-conditioning, TV, phone, mini-bar, safe; most have hairdrier **Credit cards** AE, MC, V **Closed** never

---

Town hotel, Rome

Locarno

Recent refurbishment of most of the bedrooms, which are easeful and interesting, should further heighten the many attractions of this stylish, wisteria-covered building with fine *fin de siècle* doors, in particular its delightful sheltered terrace where breakfast is served until midday. Friendly staff. Roof garden. And free bicycles for exploring the city.

■ Via della Penna 22, 00186 Rome **Tel** (06) 321 6030 **Fax** (06) 321 5249 **E-mail** locarno@venere.it **Website** http://www.venere.it/roma/locarno **Meals** breakfast **Prices** rooms LLL with breakfast; suite LLL-LLLL **Rooms** 48, all with bath, central heating, air-conditioning, phone, satellite TV, minibar, safe, hairdrier **Credit cards** AE, DC, MC, V **Closed** never

---

Town hotel, Rome

Madrid

An elegant entrance of tubbed palms and a glimpse of classical statuary leads to a well-kept lobby and a friendly welcome. Bedrooms are inoffensively modern in style. From the white garden furniture on the roof terrace, guests can overlook the picturesque domes and pantiles of this historic central quarter.

■ Via Mario de Fiori 93-95, 00187 Rome **Tel** (06) 699 1511 **Fax** (06) 679 1653 **Meals** break fast **Prices** rooms LLL-LLLL **Rooms** 26, all with bath or shower, central heating, air-conditioning, TV, phone, hairdrier **Credit cards** AE, DC, MC, V **Closed** never

Lazio and Abruzzi

Town hotel, Rome

Mozart

An unassuming location on a narrow side-street near the Spanish Steps. Inside, the lobby is a calm expanse of cool, creamy archways and stylish parlour palms. Bedrooms are traditionally furnished but well equipped, with many mod cons.

■ Via dei Greci 23b, 00187 Rome **Tel** (06) 684 0041 **Fax** (06) 678 4271 **Meals** breakfast **Prices** rooms LL-LLL with breakfast **Rooms** 31, all with bath or shower, air-conditioning, TV, phone, minibar **Credit cards** AE, DC, MC, V **Closed** never

---

Town guest-house, Rome

Pensione Parlamento

Few would guess that many a well-known politician stays here, though it is conveniently near the parliament building. The rooms are very simple, but the atmosphere is civilized and friendly. Breakfast is served in a pleasant, personally furnished room with a terrace. Prices have shot up recently – perhaps because of the new lift.

■ Via delle Convertite 5, 00187 Rome **Tel** (06) 699 21000 **Meals** breakfast (on request only) **Prices** rooms LLL with breakfast **Rooms** 22, all with phone, satellite TV, hairdrier, safe; all double rooms with bath or shower **Credit cards** AE, DC, MC, V **Closed** never

---

Town hotel, Rome

Portoghesi

Common in Venice or Florence but rare in Rome: a central hotel that is unpretentious, attractively old-fashioned and fairly priced. The delightful Piazza Navona and stunning Pantheon are only yards away. Furnishings are simple, service helpful if not notably warm. Pleasant breakfast room with little terrace.

■ Via dei Portoghesi 1, 00186 Rome **Tel** (06) 686 4231 **Fax** (06) 687 6976 **Meals** breakfast **Prices** rooms LL-LLL with breakfast **Rooms** 27, all with bath or shower, phone, air-conditioning, satellite TV; all with bath or shower **Credit cards** MC, V **Closed** never

---

Town hotel, Rome

Teatro di Pompeo

One recent visitor begged us to remove this hotel, tucked away in a little-frequented corner off the Campo di Fiori, from our guide: he liked it so much he selfishly wishes to keep it to himself. The rough-cast barrel vaulting of bar and breakfast room impart more flavour of antiquity than its matching modern furnishings, but the interior is spotless. Periodically hosts small conferences.

■ Largo del Pallaro 8, 00186 Rome **Tel** (06) 687 2566 **Fax** (06) 6880 5531 **Meals** breakfast **Prices** rooms LLL with breakfast **Rooms** 12, all with bath or shower, air-conditioning, radio, TV, phone , minibar **Credit cards** AE, DC, MC, V **Closed** never

Lazio and Abruzzi

Serviced self-catering apartments, Rome

Villa Hapsburg

Self-catering in secluded, countrified grounds, ten minutes' walk from Colosseum, atmospherically bordered by city walls, with superb view to St Peter's. Choose from: gatehouse (pleasant; two bedrooms, no outlook); guest house (simple; basic kitchen, bathroom; two bedrooms, no outlook); and the larger west wing, suitable for 4/5 people (more comfort, but only one bedroom has outlook). The Belgian Ambassador resides in the main house.

■ Piazza di Metronia, Rome; book through proprietor Odile Taliani **Tel and fax** 00 43 1 7125091 **Meals** optional maid service for cooking and shopping **Prices** from £600 to £850 per week **Rooms** see above **Credit cards** not accepted **Closed** never

Town villa, Rome

Villa delle Rose

This calm old villa near the railway station is energetically managed by its Swiss owner. It boasts an unexpectedly grand bar-lounge of marbled columns and ceiling frescos. Bedrooms are more practical than elegant; many bathrooms and bedrooms have been renewed recently. It has a small, pretty garden.

■ Via Vicenza 5, 00185 Rome **Tel** (06) 445 1788 **Fax** (06) 445 1639 **Meals** breakfast **Prices** rooms LL-LLL **Rooms** 37, all with bath or shower, central heating, phone, TV **Credit cards** AE, DC, MC, V **Closed** never

Mountain chalet, Scanno

Mille Pini

'A very friendly place indeed', says a reader, confirming our recommendation of this simple, neat chalet at the foot of the chairlift up to Monte Rotondo, in the highest part of the Apennines. For less energetic tourists, the Lago di Scanno is nearby.

■ Via Pescara 2, 67038 Scanno (L'Aquila) **Tel** (0864) 74387 **Meals** breakfast, lunch, dinner **Prices** rooms LL-LLL with breakfast; DB&B LL; FB LL **Rooms** 21, all with bath, central heating, phone **Credit cards** not accepted **Closed** restaurant only, Tue

Seaside villa, Vasto

Villa Vignola

Here is a novelty for Italy: a truly small hotel – only five rooms – with no-compromise hotel-style services. There is a faintly Spanish-Moroccan style about the immaculate white clifftop villa, while furnishings mix English country house and Italian slick. The grounds lead down to a private beach.

■ Vignola, 66054 Vasto (Chieti) **Tel** (0873) 310050 **Fax** (0873) 310060 **Meals** breakfast, lunch, dinner **Prices** rooms LL-LLL with breakfast **Rooms** 5, all with bath or shower, phone, TV, minibar **Credit cards** AE, DC, V **Closed** never

Campania

Hotels in Campania

Campania has three components: the frantic city of Naples (where, somewhat to our surprise, we have succeeded in finding one attractive small hotel – the Miramare, page 199); the extremely popular seaside resorts to the south of Naples on the Sorrento peninsula and the islands of Capri and Ischia (where there is a super-abundance of such hotels); and the coast and countryside away from Naples, where we have drawn a complete blank – though you could try the Hermitage, just outside Avellino, a peaceful and comfortable hotel 50 km inland from Naples (Tel (0825) 674788, fax 674772, 30 rooms, swimming-pool).

Ischia is hard work for the seeker of small hotels. Tourism there was originally, and is still, closely linked with the island's thermal springs, and large hotels with spa facilities are the norm – accounting partly for the island's domination by German visitors. The Bagattella (Tel (081) 986072, fax 989637) is an ornate villa on the west coast of the island near Forio. One of the most popular excursions is to Sant'Angelo on the south coast – a tiny fishing village on a narrow isthmus. Sant'Angelo would be a pleasant place to stay for longer than an hour or two – indeed, it is at its best before the daily coaches arrive or after they depart – and apart from the San Michele (page 199) it has a couple of other hotels which make acceptable bases. The Miramare (Tel (081) 999219, fax 999325) is almost at sea level on the east side of the village, with a big terrace on the waterside which gets the morning sun. Just behind it up the steep hillside, with views over the rooftops from its little terraces, is La Palma (Tel (081) 999215, fax 999526).

On Capri, in addition to those described in more detail on pages 197 and 198, we can recommend the Pazziella (Tel (081) 837 0044, fax 0085), a smart ex-private villa with flowery terraces and gardens, or the luxurious and secluded Punta Tragara (Tel (081) 837 0844, fax 7790), built into rock high above the sea and offering magnificent views of the coast. At the other end of the scale, the simple, family-run Quattro Stagioni (Tel (081) 837 0041, 12 rooms) offers excellent value in an expensive area. Back on the mainland coast, and with excellent views of Capri, is the Delfino (Tel (081) 878 9261, fax 808 9074), peacefully set on an inlet near Massa Lubrense.

Hotels on the Sorrento peninsula are well represented in the pages which follow; the Villa Garden (Tel (081) 878 1387, fax 4192), in a quiet suburb of Sorrento itself, is yet another good possibility. It is more difficult to find hotels to recommend further south near Paestum (the site of the best preserved Greek temples on mainland Italy), but one possibility is the Schuhmann (Tel (0828) 851151, fax 851183), a modern, well- equipped hotel with glorious views along the coast.

This page acts as an introduction to the features and hotels of Campania, and gives brief recommendations of reasonable hotels that for one reason or another have not made a full entry. The long entries for this region – covering the hotels we are most enthusiastic about – start on the next page. But do not neglect the shorter entries starting on page 197: these are all hotels that we would happily stay at.

Campania

Cappuccini Convento

A rickety-seeming elevator from the roadside is your unimpressive introduction to this extraordinary hotel, perched in an apparently impossible position on the cliff face above Amalfi; not surprisingly, one of its great attractions is the superb views of the rugged Amalfi coast, shared by the flowery, creeper-covered terraces and many of the rooms.

But the other merits of this 12thC monastery soon become clear, too. The public areas are light and airy, with a striking sense of space, many original features retained, and antiques lining the wide hallways. The salon/bar has Oriental rugs on tiled floors, with comfortable pink-covered armchairs and sofas, a brick fireplace and a piano adding to the clubby atmosphere. The large dining-room is a delight, with superb vaulting and columns, crisp white tablecloths and bentwood and cane chairs on a tiled floor. The bedrooms are mostly large and charmingly furnished with antiques; most have tiled floors with rugs, and quite a few have both a sea view and a balcony. Several recent reports, however, lead us to believe that standards of service and maintenance are slipping here; we welcome further reports.

Nearby Grotta dello Smeraldo (4 km); Ravello (7 km).

Amalfi 84011 Salerno
Tel (089) 871877
Fax (089) 871886
Location 300 m from middle of Amalfi, high up on cliffs, reached by lift/elevator up from main road; garden and private car parking at road level (L30,000 per day)
Food & drink breakfast, lunch, dinner
Prices rooms LL-LLL; DB&B LL-LLL; meals LL
Rooms 43 double, 9 single, 2 suites, all with bath or shower; all rooms have phone
Facilities dining-room, sitting-rooms, bar, solarium, conference facilities; beach (L35,000 per day)
Credit cards AE, DC, V
Children accepted
Disabled no special facilities
Pets accepted
Closed never
Proprietor Alfredo Aielli

Campania

Luna Convento

The middle of Amalfi is crowded and bustling, and the most desirable hotels lie just outside it or well above it up on the rockface. The Luna Convento is one of the former – about five minutes' walk uphill from the cathedral. It occupies two separate buildings, separated by the winding coast road – one of them an old Saracen tower perched right on the sea.

The hotel opened in 1825 (it is one of the oldest in Amalfi), and has been in the same family for five generations. But you only have to step inside to see that the building's history goes back much further than the 19thC. The unique feature is the Byzantine cloister enclosing a garden and ancient well. The arcade serves as a quiet and civilized sitting area and breakfasts are served within the actual cloister – a delightful spot to start the day. You have the choice of modern or traditional bedrooms, and for a premium you can have your own private sitting-room. Lunch and dinner are taken either in the vaulted restaurant in the main building, where large arched windows give beautiful views of the bay, or better still across the road where the terrace and parasols of the tower restaurant extend to the water's edge. The swimming-pool forms part of the same complex – as does the somewhat incongruous disco.

Nearby cathedral of Sant'Andrea and cloisters of Paradise (in Amalfi); Valle dei Mulini (1 hr walk); Ravello (6 km).

Via P. Comite 33, Amalfi
84011 Salerno
Tel (089) 871002
Fax (089) 871333
Location short walk from middle of resort, overlooking sea, with private garage
Food & drink breakfast, lunch, dinner
Prices rooms LLL with breakfast; HB LL-LLL; FB LLL 20-30% reduction for children under 6, sharing parents' room; meals L-LL

Rooms 40 double, 2 single, 3 suited; family rooms also available; all with bath; all rooms have, phone, TV, hairdrier
Facilities 2 dining-rooms, 2 bars, Byzantine cloister; swimming-pool, disco
Credit cards AE, DC, MC, V
Children welcome
Disabled not suitable
Pets not accepted
Closed never
Manager A Milone

Campania

Seaside villa, Baia Domizia

Hotel della Baia

Baia Domizia is a modern and quite sophisticated seaside resort, stretching along a splendid, broad, sandy beach north of Naples. But at the Hotel della Baia you are unaware of being in a resort at all. It is a low-lying white building, standing well away from the main development, and its lush gardens lead straight past the tennis-court to the beach.

The hotel was opened about 30 years ago by the three Sello sisters from Venice, who have successfully reproduced the peaceful atmosphere of a stylish, if rather large, private villa. Spotless white stucco walls, cool quarry-tiled floors and white sofas are offset by bowls of fresh flowers and potted plants, and the antique and modern furnishings blend well together. The house feels lived-in, with books and magazines around, and an interesting range of pictures on the walls.

Bedrooms are no less attractive; all have balconies. A smartly furnished verandah links the house to the garden, and deck-chairs and extravagant white parasols are set out on the lawn.

The hotel has traditionally aimed high with its food, but we lack recent reports on the accuracy of that aim.

Nearby Gaeta (29 km); Naples within reach.

Via dell'Erica, Baia Domizia
81030 Caserta
Tel (0823) 721344
Fax (0823) 721566
Location in S part of resort, with gardens leading down to long sandy beach; ample car parking
Food & drink breakfast, lunch, dinner
Prices rooms LLL; FB LLL; reductions for children
Rooms 54 double, 18 with bath, 36 with shower; 2 single, one with bath, one with shower; all rooms have central heating, air-conditioning balcony, phone; TV on request **Facilities** 2 sitting-rooms, TV room, bar, terrace, dining- room; tennis, beach
Credit cards AE, DC, MC, V
Children welcome
Disabled no special facilities
Pets small, well-behaved ones accepted **Closed** Oct to mid-May **Proprietors** Elsa, Velia and Imelde Sello

Campania

Seaside hotel, Capri

Scalinatella

The little town of Capri is a ritzy, glossy place, full of boutiques selling clothes with designer labels. Those who feel at home in this scene may well head for the deluxe Grand Hotel Quisisana, or, if they want something smaller-scale but with the same degree of luxury, for its offspring – the Scalinatella, run by the son of the owner of the Quisisana.

No expense has been spared in the creation of this exclusive small hotel. A spotless white building with a profusion of arches and oriental ornamentation, it feels distinctly Moorish. Inside a world of cool luxury awaits you. Every corner is air-conditioned and the rooms have all the trimmings that you might expect for the very high price you will be paying – telephones in the bathroom, private terraces and beds that disappear into alcoves, converting your rooms into a sitting-room by day. Breakfast is brought to your room. Furnishings vary from the simple and refined to the extravagant and perhaps over-rich. But there are few other flaws. Its location, with beautiful views to the Carthusian monastery of San Giacomo, leaves little to be desired; the garden and pool (where buffet lunches are served) are immaculate.
Nearby Monastery of San Giacomo (overlooked by hotel).

Via Tragara 10, Capri 80073 Napoli
Tel (081) 837 0633
Fax (081) 837 8291
Location on Punta Tragara road; with garden
Food & drink breakfast, buffet lunch by pool
Prices rooms LLLL with breakfast
Rooms 30 double, all with bath and jacuzzi; all rooms have air- conditioning, phone, TV, minibar

Facilities sitting-rooms, bar; swimming-pool, tennis
Credit cards not accepted
Disabled no special facilities
Pets accepted
Closed Nov to mid-Mar
Proprietors Morgano family

Campania

Converted monastery, Ischia

Il Monastero

Ischia Ponte gets its name from the low bridge giving access from the 'mainland' of Ischia to the precipitous islet on top of which stands the original settlement of Ischia, known collectively as the Castello although it consists of several buildings. One of these is an old monastery which is now run as a simple but entirely captivating *pensione*.

A lift reached by a tunnel into the rock of the island takes you up to the Castello (though there are steps as an alternative). Discreet signs bring you to the locked door of the *pensione*, and a ring on the bell summons the amiable *padrone*. Up a final flight of stairs and at last you are there. Many paintings hang on the plain walls of the hallway and the neat little sitting-room. The dining-room, recently redecorated, has satisfyingly solid wooden furniture. Bedrooms are monastically simple; some are reached from inside, some from the outside terrace, which gives a breath-taking view of the town and island of Ischia. We have no first-hand experience of the food, and half-board is inescapable; but we know that the cooking is good enough to keep the Monastero full in spring and autumn when other hotels are half-empty.
Nearby Castello d'Ischia.

Castello Aragonese 3, Ischia Ponte 80070 Napoli
Tel (081) 992435
Location on island E of Ischia town, linked by causeway
Food & drink breakfast, dinner
Prices DB&B LL
Rooms 21 double, one single; most have bath or shower
Facilities dining-room, bar, TV room, large terrace
Credit cards not accepted
Children accepted

Disabled not suitable
Pets not accepted
Closed mid-Oct to mid-Mar
Proprietor Ciro Eletto

Campania

La Villarosa

This is a sharp contrast to the Monastero in every way: it is immersed in a jungle of a garden right in the heart of the little town of Ischia, and its great attraction – apart from the garden and pleasant thermal pool – is its series of delectable sitting-rooms, which are beautifully furnished with comfortable armchairs and ornate antiques. The bedrooms are furnished with 19thC furniture of Neopolitan, Sicilian and French origin.

The light, welcoming restaurant upstairs leads out on to a terrace overlooking the garden and the roof-tops of Ischia, and meals are served there in summer. At one time only full board terms were offered, but we are pleased to report that Sg Amalfitano now offers 'room only' and half-pension terms as we have no evidence about the standard of cooking.

Like many hotels on the island, the Villarosa offers thermal treatments of various sorts – with a private 'thermalist physician' on hand to supervise – but the atmosphere is far removed from that of the traditional spa hotel, and visitors not seeking a *kur* will not feel out of place.

Nearby port of Ischia (500 m); Castello d'Ischia (2 km).

Via Giacinto Gigante 5, Porto d'Ischia 80077 Napoli
Tel (081) 991316
Fax (081) 992425
Location 200 m from lido; with limited car parking
Food & drink breakfast, lunch, dinner
Prices rooms LL-LLL with breakfast; DB&B LL; FB LL-LLL
Rooms 37 double, 20 with bath, 14 with shower; 6 single, all with shower; all rooms have central heating, phone
Facilities sitting-room, bar, dining-room, TV room, terrace; swimming-pool, sauna
Credit cards AE, DC, MC, V
Children accepted
Disabled difficult; lift/elevator to bedrooms
Pets not accepted in public rooms or dining-room
Closed Nov to Mar
Proprietor Paolo Amalfitano

Seaside hotel, Positano

Miramare

Whatever bedroom you are given at the Miramare, it will have a private sea-facing terrace, shaded by vine or bougainvillea and furnished with table and deck chairs. The rooms are simply but elegantly furnished, with white walls and prettily tiled floors. Bathrooms (some with sea views themselves) are spacious, and decorated with hand-painted tiles.

The sitting-room is an attractive area with a vaulted ceiling, Oriental rugs, antique furniture and plenty of plants and flowers. The dining-room – where the food is prepared and presented with flair – is a delight: a glassed-in terrace with bougainvillaea hanging from the ceiling in great swathes, and views to the beach far below.

Set on the steep hill to the west of Positano's beach and the fishing boats, the Miramare is a series of old fishermen's houses joined to make a charming and thoroughly comfortable hotel, close to the centre yet away from most of the noise. Arriving by car, park at the 'Miramare Parking' sign, then walk back up the hill to a corner where the hotel is signposted down a long flight of steps. More steps lead from the hotel to the seafront.
Nearby Amalfi (17 km); Ravello (23 km).

Via Trara Genoino 25-27, Positano 84017 Salerno
Tel (089) 875002
Location 3 minutes W of main beach; with private parking for 10 cars
Food & drink breakfast, lunch, dinner
Prices rooms LL-LLLL with breakfast; dinner LL
Rooms 10 double, 3 single, 5 suites; all with bath and shower, central heating
Facilities dining-room, bar, 3 sitting-rooms
Credit cards AE, MC, V
Children not encouraged
Disabled not suitable
Pets not allowed in dining-room
Closed 1 Nov to 31 Mar
Proprietor Sg Attanasio

Campania

Palazzo Murat

Most hotels in Positano are ranged up the steep hills either side of the ravine leading down to the sea. The Palazzo Murat, in contrast, is right in the heart of things – just inland of the *duomo*, and on a pedestrian alley lined with trendy boutiques.

The main building is a grand L-shaped 18thC *palazzo*. Within the L is a charming courtyard – a well in the middle, bougainvillea trained up the surrounding walls, palms and other exotic vegetation dotted around – where you can take breakfast (though in spring early risers will find it sunless). Along one side of this courtyard run the interconnecting sitting-rooms, which are beautifully furnished with antiques.

Bedrooms in the *palazzo* itself are attractively traditional in style – some painted furniture, some polished hardwood – and have doors opening on to token balconies (standing room only). Rooms in the more modern extension on the seaward side of the main building have the attraction of bigger balconies.

Positano's many restaurants are mainly congregated behind the beach, a short stroll away. 'Excellent value, stunning location', was one visitor's verdict.

Nearby tour of Amalfi coast and Sorrento peninsula.

Via dei Mulini 23, Positano 84017 Salerno
Tel (089) 875177
Fax (089) 811419
Location in heart of resort; paying car park nearby
Food & drink breakfast
Prices rooms LLLL with breakfast; meals LL
Rooms 28 double, all with bath and shower, phone, balcony, radio, minibar, air-conditioning
Facilities sitting-room, TV room, terrace, bar
Credit cards AE, DC, MC, V
Children accepted
Disabled access difficult
Pets small ones only accepted
Closed Nov to Easter week, but open for Christmas week
Proprietor Attanasio family

Campania

Seaside hotel, Positano

Villa Franca

Provided you are not worried by heights, or by remoteness from the centre of things, this smartly traditional hotel has much to commend it. The position, high on the western side of the Positano ravine, gives an excellent view of the resort and the coast beyond from the windows and terraces – but does mean that the walk down to the resort centre and beach takes a few minutes and that the walk back up is exhausting. Happily, there is a private bus to and from the beach at certain times.

If the hotel's panoramic position is its first attraction, the second is its smart, cool sitting area – a series of interconnecting spaces with white-tiled floors and white-painted walls, linked by arched doorways. Comfortable armchairs with vivid blue covers are grouped around low tables, with enormous potted plants dotted around. The dining-room has the same decorative style.

The bedrooms are spacious and comfortable, and the best have their own sea-view terraces. The small pool also shares the view. We lack recent reports, but the visitor who originally recommended Villa Franca found the proprietors and staff welcoming, and the food satisfying and freshly-prepared.

Nearby Amalfi (17 km); Sorrento (17 km); Ravello (23 km).

Via Pasitea 318, Positano
84017 Salerno
Tel (089) 875655
Fax (089) 875735
Location on main road above middle of Positano, with fine sea views
Food & drink breakfast, snacks, dinner
Prices rooms LLLwith breakfast; meals L
Rooms 28 double, one single, all with bath or shower; all rooms have central heating,
radio, satellite TV, phone, air- conditioning
Facilities dining-room, bar/sitting-room; swimming-pool
Credit cards AE, DC, MC, V
Children welcome
Disabled not suitable
Pets accepted, but not allowed in dining-room
Closed never
Proprietor Mario Russo

Campania

Town hotel, Ravello

Caruso Belvedere

The Caruso Belvedere is one of several hotels in this justly popular beauty spot which have been converted from old *palazzi*. Ever since it opened in 1893 it has been in the hands of the Caruso family. The entrance is through a big, bare ground floor room – (the reception, sitting area and dining terrace are on the first floor; the belvedere is across the street, connected by a bridge). The grandeur may have faded somewhat and not all the rooms can be called luxurious – reporters confirm that some are smaller and simpler than you might expect at these prices – but unaffected, informal charm is the key to its success. We are assured that electrical and plumbing problems have been sorted out at last.

Many of the original features, such as the Corinthian columns and marble pillars, still survive; the antiques, faded sofas and open fireplaces are entirely in keeping with the setting. The restaurant is simple, light and spacious, but its best feature is the summer terrace with sensational views of the rugged coast and the Gulf of Salerno. A British couple report that the food is excellent and the staff truly caring; they plan to return 'again and again'. Wines come from the Caruso's own vineyards.

Nearby Villa Rufolo, Villa Cimbrone; Amalfi (7 km).

Via San Giovanni del Toro 52, Ravello 84010 Salerno
Tel (089) 857111
Fax (089) 857372
Location 500 m from the main piazza, with garden; public car parking in front of hotel
Food & drink breakfast, lunch, dinner
Prices DB&B LL-LLL; FB LL-LLL
Rooms 20 double, 2 single, all with shower; 2 suites; all rooms have central heating, phone
Facilities dining-room, bar, TV room, solarium
Credit cards AE, DC, MC, V
Children welcome
Disabled no special facilities
Pets small ones only accepted, and not in public areas
Closed never
Proprietor Gino Caruso

Campania

Town hotel, Ravello

Palumbo

A Moorish-inspired *palazzo*, built for a nobleman in the 12thC, the Palumbo was bought by a Swiss hotelier in the mid-19thC and is still run by his family. No expense has been spared in its conversion to a five-star hotel, but what distinguishes it from most other hotels of its category is its understated luxury and elegance.

Public rooms focus on a 12thC inner courtyard where Corinthian-topped columns, oriental arches and a profusion of flowing plants provide a cool, civilized sitting-area. The restaurant is equally elegant, though more French than Moorish, with its peach tablecloths, gilt mirrors, mouldings and bentwood chairs. But on fine days the choice location is the balcony, where you look down over terraced vineyards to dazzling blue seas below. Various other balconies and terraces (hung with vines and roses) share this same stunning panorama. Throughout the hotel there are beautiful antiques and paintings – including what is purported to be a Caravaggio. Bedrooms have been tastefully refurbished, with antiques, tiled floors and rugs. Those in the annexe are more modern in style, but much cheaper.

Nearby Villa Cimbrone, Villa Rufolo; Amalfi (7 km).

Via San Giovanni del Toro 16, Ravello 84010 Salerno
Tel (089) 857244
Fax (089) 858133
E-mail palumbo@amalfinet.it
Website http://www.hotel-palumbo.it
Location perched on cliffs; with garden, sun terrace and private car parking
Food & drink breakfast, lunch, dinner
Prices rooms LLLL; DB&B LLLL; 30% discount for children under 8 sharing

parents' room; meals LL
Rooms 21 double, 3 suites; all with bath; 7 rooms are in annexe close to main building; all rooms have phone, TV, minibar
Facilities sitting-rooms, bar, dining-room **Credit cards** AE, DC, MC, V **Children** accepted
Disabled not suitable
Pets dogs not allowed in dining-room **Closed** never
Proprietors Vuilleumier family

Campania

Seaside hotel, Amalfi

Lido Mare

This little hotel off Amalfi's Piazza del Duomo is in the same family as the Parsifal up in Ravello (page 197). Its arched, white-walled rooms are prettily furnished with antiques, and some of the bedrooms have views over the sea, only a few yards below.

■ Largo Ducci Piccolomene 9, 84011 Amalfi (Salerno) **Tel** (089) 871332 **Fax** (089) 871394 **Meals** breakfast **Prices** rooms L; breakfast L10,000 **Rooms** 15, all with bath or shower, air-conditioning, satellite TV **Credit cards** AE, DC, MC, V **Closed** never

---

Seaside hotel, Capri

Flora

On the edge of the fashionable little town of Capri, the Flora is immersed in greenery and flowers. It is a very well cared-for hotel, with calm and spacious bedrooms, many with balconies giving sea views, and an attractive terrace. A new restaurant and other facilities were added a couple of years ago.

Via Federico Serena 26, 80073 Capri (Napoli) **Tel** (081) 837 0211 **Fax** (081) 837 8949 **Meals** breakfast, lunch, dinner **Prices** rooms LLL-LLLL **Rooms** 24, all with bath, TV, minibar, air-conditioning; most rooms have terrace, phone **Credit cards** AE, DC, MC, V **Closed** Feb

---

Seaside hotel, Capri

Luna

A refreshing contrast to the ritzier hotels on Capri – a somewhat old-fashioned hotel in one of the island's most desirable locations, perched on the cliffs of the south coast. Bedrooms are spacious and comfortable, the pool is large by local standards.

■ Viale Matteotti 3, 80073 Capri (Napoli) **Tel** (081) 837 0433 **Fax** (081) 837 7459 **Meals** breakfast, lunch, dinner **Prices** rooms LLL-LLLL with breakfast; meals LL **Rooms** 54, all with bath, air-conditioning, phone, TV, minibar; most rooms have terrace **Credit cards** AE, DC, MC, V **Closed** Nov to Mar

---

Seaside hotel, Capri

Villa Brunella

An attractive modern hotel in a beautiful lush setting on steep terraced slopes with superb sea views shared by the light, spacious bedrooms, the dining-terrace and the pool. It is reached down steep steps (over 150 to most rooms).

■ Via Tragara 24, 80073 Capri (Napoli) **Tel** (081) 837 0122 **Fax** (081) 837 0430 **Meals** breakfast, lunch, dinner **Prices** rooms LLLL; suites LLLL; meals L-LLL **Rooms** 8, all with bath, central heating, air-conditioning, phone, TV; 12 suites **Credit cards** AE, MC, V **Closed** Nov to mid-Mar

SOUTHERN ITALY

Campania

Seaside villa, Capri

Villa Krupp

A welcome retreat from the bustle of the town, this serene white villa, where both Lenin and Gorky once lived, is set on a gentle hillside above the sheer cliffs of Marina Piccola. Bedrooms are bright, clean and mainly spacious. There is a new bar sitting area with TV.

■ Via Matteotti 12, 80073 Capri (Napoli) **Tel** (081) 837 0362 **Fax** (081) 837 6489 **Meals** breakfast **Prices** rooms LL-LLL with breakfast **Rooms** 12, all with bath or shower, balcony **Credit cards** V **Closed** never

---

Seaside villa, Capri

Villa Sarah

There is no access by road: you have to walk to this whitewashed building among the vineyards, although your luggage can be delivered from the harbour to the hotel, on request; the reward is peace and simplicity, well away from the bustle and vulgarity of the town. Rooms are neat and well-kept, with fine gardens in which to take breakfast or just soak up the sun.

■ Via Tiberio 3a, 80073 Capri (Napoli) **Tel** (081) 837 7817 **Fax** (081) 837 7215 **Meals** breakfast **Prices** rooms LL-LLL with breakfast **Rooms** 20, all with bath or shower, phone, satellite TV, hairdrier, minibar **Credit cards** AE, DC, MC, V **Closed** Nov to Mar

---

Seaside hotel, Conca dei Marini

Belvedere

There is more to the Belvedere than the belvedere; but in the end the setting is the thing – on the edge of a cliff with splendid views of the Amalfi coast. A lift takes you down to a fair-sized sea-water pool, and steps to a private rocky beach.

■ Strada Statale 163, 84010 Conca dei Marini (Salerno) **Tel** (089) 831282 **Fax** (089) 831439 **Meals** breakfast, lunch, dinner **Prices** rooms LL-LLL with breakfast; FB LLL **Rooms** 36, all with bath, balcony, central heating, air-conditioning, phone, TV **Credit cards** AE, DC, MC, V **Closed** mid-Oct to Mar

---

Country villa, Dragoni

Villa de Pertis

Originally a nobleman's country residence, dating back to the 17thC, Villa de Pertis has been restored recently to provide 5 plainly furnished but comfortable bedrooms and 2 suites. The restaurant serves regional dishes, and is a popular gathering place for the locals, so booking is advisable. Bicycles available.

■ Via Ponti 30, 81010 Dragoni **Tel & fax** (0823) 866619 **Website** http://www.pubbnet.com.villa de pertis **Meals** breakfast, lunch, dinner **Prices** rooms L-LL; suite LLL with breakfast **Rooms** 8, all with bath or shower, phone **Credit cards** AE, V **Closed** Jan; 3 weeks in Jun

Campania

Seaside hotel, Ischia

San Michele

This villa-style building is perched peacefully on the hillside above the little car-free village of Sant'Angelo, in beautiful gardens that include a splendid pool, terraces and (of course) thermal facilities. Modern, neat furnishings predominate, though the dining-room is more traditional in style.

■ Sant'Angelo, 80070 Ischia (Napoli) **Tel** (081) 999276 **Fax** (081) 999149 **Meals** breakfast; lunch and dinner in season **Prices** FB LLL **Rooms** 44, all with bath or shower, phone; some have minibar **Credit cards** not accepted **Closed** Nov to Mar

---

Town hotel, Naples

Miramare

An appealing little hotel in an excellent position, on the waterfront, handy for ferries to the islands and some of the major sights. Compact but comfortable bedrooms. Hearty breakfasts are served in a smart, light, penthouse room with views of the bay, surrounded by a roof terrace. Helpful staff. Five nearby restaurants are also owned by the family – discount for guests.

■ Via Nazario Sauro 24, 80132 Naples **Tel** (081) 7647584 **Fax** (081) 7660775 **Website** hotelmiramare.com **Meals** breakfast **Prices** rooms LLL-LLLL with breakfast **Rooms** 31, all with bath or shower, air-conditioning, phone, TV, minibar **Credit cards** AE, DC, MC, V **Closed** never

---

Seaside hotel, Positano

L'Ancora

Modern and unpretentious hotel, next door to the famous and over-priced Syrenuse, with the same enviable views and proximity to the heart of Positano. Spacious and simply furnished bedrooms, and a shady terrace. Free car parking.

■ Via C Colombo 36, 84017 Positano (Salerno) **Tel** (089) 875318 **Fax** (089) 811784 **Meals** breakfast **Prices** rooms LL-LLL with breakfast; DB&B LL **Rooms** 18, all with bath, phone, minibar, TV, some air-conditioning **Credit cards** AE, DC, MC, V **Closed** mid-Oct to Mar

---

Seaside hotel, Positano

Marincanto

The rooms in the main part of this modest hotel are surprisingly spacious and well furnished, and the views of colourful Positano from its flowery terraces (where you can take breakfast) are memorable. The car park is an asset, but it is not free. Don't worry about the lack of a restaurant – you'll enjoy eating out.

■ Positano (Salerno) **Tel** (089) 875130 **Fax** (089) 875760 **Meals** breakfast **Prices** rooms LL with breakfast; parking L10,000 **Rooms** 26, all with bath or shower, phone, minibar **Credit cards** AE, DC, MC, V **Closed** mid-Oct to week before Easter

Campania

Town villa, Ravello

Giordano Villa Maria

The shady garden restaurant of this charming old villa beside the path to the Villa Cimbrone is understandably popular, and there is a traditionally furnished dining-room for cooler days. Bedrooms are simple, but have newly equipped bathrooms. Guests can use the pool at the nearby Hotel Giordano.

■ Via Santa Chiara 2, 84010 Ravello (Salerno) **Tel** (089) 857170 **Fax** (089) 857071 **Meals** breakfast, lunch, dinner **Prices** rooms LLL with breakfast; suites LLLL; meals L-LL **Rooms** 17, all with bath or shower, central heating, phone, satellite TV, minibar, air-conditioning **Credit cards** AE, MC, V **Closed** 24 and 25 Dec

---

Town hotel, Ravello

Graal

The great attraction of this hotel, is its splendid swimming-pool, sharing the stunning view that is at the core of Ravello's appeal. Simple, good-value rooms, most with sea-view terraces.

■ Via della Republica 8, 84010 Ravello (Salerno) **Tel** (089) 857222 **Fax** (089) 857551 **Meals** breakfast **Prices** rooms LL-LLL; meals L **Rooms** 35, all with bath, central heating, phone, air-conditioning, TV ; 15 with Jacuzzi **Credit cards** AE, DC, MC, V **Closed** never

---

Seaside hotel, Ravello

Marmorata

The Marmorata is not up in the hills but down on the shoreline. It is an old paper mill, converted to a smart hotel with a nautical design theme. A waterfall still cascades down the cliff at the side. Large windows make the most of the sea views, and the main terrace is perched directly above the water. Salt water pool.

■ Strada Statale 163, Loc Marmorata, 84010 Ravello (Salerno) **Tel** (089) 877777 **Fax** (089) 851189 **E-mail** marmorata@starnet.it **Website** www.starnet.it/marmorata **Meals** breakfast, lunch, dinner **Prices** rooms LLL-LLLL with breakfast **Rooms** 41, all with bath or shower, central heating, TV, minibar, air-con, phone **Credit cards** AE, DC, MC, V **Closed** never

---

Converted monastery, Ravello

Parsifal

This little hotel retains a certain monastic simplicity along with its 13thC cloister. Bedrooms are plainly furnished, and some are on the small side: ask for the one with the terrace and sea view – which is heart-stopping, and shared by the creeper-clad terrace where honest, plain food is served.

■ Via G d'Anna 5, 84010 Ravello (Salerno) **Tel** (089) 857144 **Fax** (089) 857972 **Meals** breakfast, lunch, dinner **Prices** rooms LL with breakfast; DB&B LL **Rooms** 19, all with central heating, TV; most have bath or shower **Credit cards** AE, DC, MC, V **Closed** Oct to Mar

Campania

Town hotel, Ravello

Rufolo

The view along the coast is the great attraction of this 'wonderfully situated' hotel, where D. H. Lawrence stayed in 1926. The terraced gardens incorporate a narrow but adequately long pool. The buffet breakfast is 'plentiful', the staff 'friendly, and helpful when pressed', reports a reader.

■ Via San Francesco 3, 84010 Ravello (Salerno) **Tel** (089) 857133 **Fax** (089) 857935 **E-mail** rufolo@amalficoast.it **Website** www.hotel-rufolo.it **Meals** breakfast, lunch, dinner **Prices** rooms DB&B LLL-LLLL; suites LLLL with breakfast **Rooms** 23; 9 suites; all with bath, central heating, air-conditioning, TV, phone, hairdrier, minibar **Credit cards** AE, DC, MC, V **Closed** 10 Jan to end Feb

---

Town villa, Ravello

Villa Cimbrone

The gardens and views of Villa Cimbrone, a 10-minute walk from the centre, are one the great tourist attractions of Ravello. The villa has long been open to guests and was listed in early editions of the guide, but closed for a period of renovation in 1990. We have good reports of the results.

■ 84010 Ravello (Salerno) **Tel** (089) 857459 **Fax** (089) 857777 **Meals** breakfast **Prices** rooms LLL with breakfast; suites LLL **Rooms** 19, all with bath, phone **Credit cards** AE, MC, V **Closed** Nov to Apr

---

Seaside hotel, Sorrento

Bellevue Syrene

One of the grand old hotels of Sorrento, perched on the cliffs, with a lift/elevator down to the beach and swimming jetty. Bedrooms are large, comfortable and have a balcony or terrace, most with a view of the sea; public areas are decorated with *trompe l'oeils*. Part of the restaurant occupies a villa, once owned by Agrippa. 'Good range at breakfast', say reports. Parking (L.20,000).

■ Piazza della Vittoria 5, 80067 Sorrento (Napoli) **Tel** (081) 878 1024 **Fax** (081) 878 3963 **Meals** breakfast, lunch, dinner **Prices** rooms LLLL with breakfast; meals LL **Rooms** 73, all with bath, phone, TV, radio, air-conditioning, safe, minibar **Credit cards** AE, DC, MC, V **Closed** never

---

Seaside hotel, Vico Equense

Capo la Gala

Squeezed into the limited space below the Sorrento coast road, this is a neat modern hotel arranged in terraces stepping down from the reception level to the sea (and the restaurant). Rooms are uniformly done out with tiled floors, plain walls and pretty cane furniture, and have sea views. Fair-sized pool.

■ Via Luigi Serio 7, Capo la Gala, 80069 Vico Equense (Napoli) **Tel** (081) 801 5758 **Fax** (081) 879 8747 **Meals** breakfast, lunch, dinner **Prices** rooms LLL with breakfast; DB&B LLL;**Rooms** 18, all with bath, phone, minibar, balcony **Credit cards** AE, DC, MC, V **Closed** Nov to Mar

The heel and toe

Hotels in the heel and toe

To say that charming small hotels in the heel and toe of Italy are difficult to find is a wild understatement. It would be nearer the truth to say that they don't exist. The hotels which have full entries in the following pages are the best you will find, but some alternative recommendations may be helpful, particularly in the heel.

The San Nicola (Tel (080) 870 5199, fax 844752), a smart, 30-roomed hotel in the heart of Altamura, is one possibility, as is the Villa Ducale (Tel (080) 705055, fax 705885), a modern hotel in Martina Franca. If your ambition is to make it right to the southern tip of the heel, you could aim for the Terminal (Tel and fax (0833) 758242), a well-run seaside holiday hotel at Marina di Léuca.

None of the major cities of the area is particularly alluring; each has a handful of routine big hotels. But if circumstances dictate a night in Foggia the place to head for is the Cicolella (Tel (0881) 3890, fax 678984), which has an attractive restaurant. To the north at Peschici, on the other side of the Gargano peninsula from our Mattinata recommendation, are the Paradiso (Tel (0884) 964201, fax 964203, 50 rooms) and the Solemar (Tel (0884) 964186, fax 964188, 45 rooms), both peaceful beach hotels set amidst pine trees.

For travellers in the 'toe' heading south with time to spare, the SS18 makes a slow-paced alternative to the A3 motorway, sticking to the eastern coast south of Lagonegro where the motorway takes a long detour inland. Two of our recommended hotels are at the northern end of this stretch of coast, and there are a few places further south that are worth bearing in mind. At Diamante-is the Mediterranean-style Ferretti (Tel (0985) 81428, fax 81114), with terraces overlooking the sea and a highly reputed restaurant. The 65-room Grand Hotel San Michele (Tel (0982) 91012, fax 91430) at Cetraro is rather more swish – a well-restored old house in an attractive informal garden on cliffs above the beach. 90 km inland is the Barbieri (Tel (0981) 948072, fax 948073), worth a stop for excellent Calabrian fare and views of the medieval village of Altomonté.

The main tourist attraction of the toe, however, is on the other side of the A3 – the magnificently wild landscape of the Sila mountains east of Cosenza and north of Catanzaro. Each of these towns has a handful of acceptable hotels.

This page acts as an introduction to the features and hotels of Italy's 'heel' and 'toe', and gives brief recommendations of reaonable hotels that for one reason or another have not made a full entry. The long entreis for this region – covering the hotels we are most entusiastic about – start on the next page. But do not neglect the shorter entreis starting on page 205: these are all hotels that we would happily stay at.

The heel and toe

Trulli hotel, Alberobello

Dei Trulli

The 'heel' of Italy has only one major tourist attraction: *trulli* – tiny stone buildings with conical, pointed roofs, which are usually joined in jolly little groups to make up multi-roomed houses. In Alberobello, a whole sector of the town consists of *trulli*, making it the natural goal of most visitors to the heel – though there are plenty of *trulli* dotted around the countryside, too. The Dei Trulli offers *trulli* enthusiasts the irresistible opportunity to go the whole hog – not just to peer at these quaint dwellings but actually to stay in one. The hotel is a sort of refined holiday camp – it consists of little bungalows, each partly contained in a *trullo*, set among pines and neat flower beds. You get a small living-room as well as a spacious bedroom and compact bathroom, plus seats outside your front door. There is a rather plain restaurant staffed by waiters whose charming demeanour quickly evaporates when problems arise. The cooking is competent, and the price for half-board now (in contrast to a couple of years ago) seems quite reasonable in comparison with the bed-and-breakfast rate. But for more variety there are restaurants in the town (within walking distance, through Alberobello's main *trulli* zone).
Nearby coast (15-20 minutes by car).

Via Cadore 28, Alberobello 70011 Bari
Tel (080) 932 3555
Fax (080) 932 3560
Location 5 minutes' walk from middle of Alberobello; with private car parking
Food & drink breakfast, lunch, dinner
Prices rooms LL-LLL; DB&B LLL
Rooms 28 double apartments, 11 with bath, 17 with shower; 11 family

apartments all with bath and shower; all have TV, phone, sitting-room, minibar
Facilities dining-room, bar; swimming-pool, playground
Credit cards AE, V
Children welcome
Disabled no special facilities
Pets small ones only accepted
Closed never
Manager Riccardo Cottino

The heel and toe

Seaside hotel, Maratea

Villa Cheta Elite

The remote and mountainous region of Basilicata does not possess much coastline. But the tiny stretch of shore on the west side, where a corniche cuts through wild and beautiful cliffs, is one of the most spectacular parts of Italy's deep south. Villa Cheta Elite is set high up on this precipitous coastline, with splendid views. If the villa enjoyed no other distinction, its position would be enough to attract many travellers to the south. But this gracious art nouveau building has other attractions.

The villa is a pleasure to behold: a confection of ochre and cream stucco, decorated with ornate mouldings that would look at home in a grand Edwardian living-room. It lies among lush, flowery terraces, one of which is set out with café-style chairs and smartly laid dining tables. Inside, lace table-cloths, chintz sofas, carefully-chosen period pieces and abundant pictures create the air of a private home.

The beaches in the area are small, but the waters are clear, and reached in only a few minutes from the villa. The Aquadros are relaxed and charming hosts, who take great care over every aspect of their hotel, including the food.

Nearby Maratea (8 km); spectacular corniche road.

Via Nazionale, Acquafredda di Maratea 85041 Potenza
Tel (0973) 878134
Fax (0973) 878135
Location 1.5 km S of Acquafredda, in gardens overlooking sea; private car parking
Food & drink breakfast, lunch, dinner
Prices rooms LL-LLL DB&B LL-LLL; meals LL
Rooms 16 double, one with bath, 15 with shower; 2 family rooms, both with shower; all have central heating, phone
Facilities dining-room with sea-view terrace, TV and reading-room, bar
Credit cards AE, DC, MC, V
Children welcome if well behaved
Disabled access difficult
Pets small ones only accepted
Closed never
Proprietors Lamberto Aquadro

The heel and toe

Seaside hotel, Castro Marina

Orsa Maggiore

A straightforward place, thin on charm but certainly recommendable in this area: a modern building, high above the sea on the bottom of Italy's heel, run amiably and competently by the five Ciccarese brothers. Well kept, with a high local reputation for its food.

■ Litoranea per Santa Cesarea 303, 73030 Castro Marina (Lecce) **Tel** (0836) 97029 **Fax** (0836) 977 66 **Meals** breakfast, lunch, dinner **Prices** rooms L, with breakfast; DB&B L-LL; FB LL **Rooms** 30, all with bath or shower, central heating, phone **Credit cards** AE, DC, MC, V **Closed** never

---

Country villa, Cisternino

Villa Cenci

A peaceful, out-of-the-way alternative to the dei Trulli (page 200), with the common feature of accommodation in simply furnished *trulli*. There are also rooms in the main house, along with a stylishly furnished restaurant. The pleasant gardens include a fine swimming-pool.

■ Via per Ceglie Messapica, 72014 Cisternino (Brindisi) **Tel** (080) 718208 **Fax** (080) 718208 Meals breakfast, lunch, dinner **Prices** rooms L-LL; DB&B L-LL **Rooms** 22, all with bath or shower, central heating, TV **Credit cards** V **Closed** Oct to Apr

---

Country hotel, Fasano

La Silvana

A useful base from which to explore *trulli* country – modern, clean and spacious, with plainly furnished rooms (some with views), and run by a welcoming and helpful family. Their efforts attract many non-residents to the large restaurant. Not to be confused with the much larger Sierra Silvana, nearby.

■ Viale de Pini 87, Selva di Fasano, 72010 Fasano (Brindisi) **Tel** (080) 433 1161 **Fax** (080) 433 1980 **Meals** breakfast, lunch, dinner **Prices** rooms LL with breakfast; DB&B LL (minimum stay 3 days); meals L **Rooms** 18, all with central heating; most have bath or shower **Credit cards** V **Closed** restaurant only, Fri in winter

---

Seaside hotel, Maratea

Santavenere

One of the most refined hotels of the deep south, in a splendid position close to the rocky shore, just outside the charming old town. The low-lying, arcaded building is set amid lawns and surrounded by trees, and furnished with taste and restraint. Spacious rooms, many with sea views from their terraces.

■ Fiumicello di Santa Venere, 85040 Maratea (Potenza) **Tel** (0973) 876910 **Fax** (0973) 876985 Meals breakfast, lunch, dinner **Prices** DB&B LLL **Rooms** 44, all with bath, phone, terrace or balcony, TV, minibar **Credit cards** AE, DC, V, MC **Closed** Oct to Apr

The heel and toe

Town hotel, Mattinata

Alba del Gargano

Low-rise modern hotel in the middle of a lively little town – a short, free bus-ride (in summer) from the beach. Meals are served in the basement restaurant – fresh fish in particular. Simple but quite stylish furnishings; helpful staff.

■ Corso Matino 102, 71030 Mattinata (Foggia) **Tel** (0884) 4771 **Fax** (0884) 4772 **Meals** breakfast, lunch, dinner **Prices** rooms L-LLL with breakfast; air-conditioning L15,000; FB LL-LLL; reductions for children under 6 **Rooms** 39, all with shower, phone; 9 rooms have air-conditioning **Credit cards** V **Closed** never

---

Country villa, Monópoli

Il Melograno

'The Pomegranate', a fortified house dating from the 16thC, was a working farm until quite recently. It now has conference and banqueting facilities, but retains its charm – secluded behind white walls, the grounds dotted with quiet courtyards, the rooms beautifully decorated and furnished with antiques. Indoor and outdoor swimming-pools, tennis court and private beach.

■ Contrada Torricella 345, 70043 Monópoli (Bari) **Tel** (080) 690 9030 **Fax** (080) 747908 **Meals** breakfast, lunch, dinner **Prices** rooms LLL-LLLL with breakfast; suites LLLL; lunch/dinner LL **Rooms** 37, all with bath, central heating, air-conditioning, phone, satellite TV, hairdrier, radio, minibar, safe **Credit cards** AE, DC, MC, V **Closed** Feb

---

Town hotel, Otranto

Albania

Not so much charming as stylish and spotless – a modern hotel run with Swiss efficiency, at the extremity of the Adriatic coast, where any attractive hotel is worth noting. Public areas and bedrooms alike are spacious, light and calm. Seafood specialities.

■ Via S Francesco di Paola 10, 73028 Otranto (Lecce) **Tel** (0836) 801183 **Meals** breakfast, lunch, dinner, snacks **Prices** rooms L-LL with breakfast; meals L **Rooms** 10, all with bath or shower, central heating, air-conditioning, phone, radio, TV **Credit cards** DC, MC, V **Closed** never

---

Resort village, Parghelia

Baia Paraelios

An unusual hotel, with 72 bungalows built on a wooded hillside from the sea. The setting is superb, overlooking a bay of white sands washed by blue seas. Communal areas consist of three pools and open-air bar, and a dining-room/terrace by the sea.

■ Fornaci, 88035 Parghelia (Catanzaro) **Tel** (0963) 600300 **Fax** (0963) 600074 **Meals** breakfast, lunch, dinner **Prices** FB LLL-LLLL; reductions for children **Rooms** 72, all with bath, shower, sitting-room, terrace, phone, ceiling fan; some rooms have heating **Credit cards** AE, DC, MC, V **Closed** Oct to Apr

The heel and toe

Village hotel, Stilo

San Giorgio

This little hotel has been formed in a handsome stone-built 17thC house that was once a cardinal's palace, set in a pretty village in a scenic part of Calabria. The interior does not disappoint, and the theatrical friends of owner Francesco Careri ensure an animated atmosphere. Fine views, terrace garden and small swimming-pool. Parking is difficult.

■ Via Citarelli 8, 89049 Stilo (Reggio di Calabria) **Tel** (0964) 775047 **Fax** (0964) 629306 **Meals** breakfast, lunch, dinner, snacks **Prices** rooms L-LL; DB&B LL **Rooms** 14, all with bath or shower, central heating **Credit cards** AE, MC, V **Closed** Oct to Mar

---

Seaside hotel, Vieste del Gargano

Seggio

At the tip of the Gargano peninsula, Vieste is a tight little town, perched on cliffs; the Seggio is right on the edge, with resultant views, and a tiny terrace down on the shoreline. The hotel is mainly done out in a smart, uniform, modern style; the vaulted restaurant is more traditional. A Swiss professor gives a favourable report on the food, and found the Seggio 'good value in this pleasant town'.

■ Via Veste 7, 71019 Vieste del Gargano (Foggia) **Tel** (0884) 708123 **Fax** (0884) 708727 **Meals** breakfast, lunch, dinner **Prices** rooms LL with breakfast; meals L **Rooms** 28, all with bath, central heating, air-conditioning, phone, TV **Credit cards** AE, MC, V **Closed** mid-Oct to mid-Mar

---

Readers' Reports

Reports from readers are of enormous interest to us in keeping up to date with the hotels in this guide - and others that should be in it. More information on p11

The islands

Hotels in the islands

Sicily, the largest and most populous island in the Mediterranean, has an extraordinary mix of sightseeing interest – spectacular scenery, ancient Greek ruins, medieval towns, splendid cathedrals, busy street markets, not to mention an active volcano – and therefore attracts hordes of visitors in the summer months. Taormina is the main resort and is well represented by hotels on the following pages. Another possibility is the elegant Villa Riis (Tel (0942) 24874, fax 626254) which has its own swimming-pool. In the large cities, we have yet to find a sufficiently small and charming hotel to include for Palermo, but in this new, expanded edition we do include the luxurious Grand Hotel in Siracusa. To see the sights of Palermo, you could stay in Cefalu, a pretty fishing port 60 km to the East. The Riva del Sole (Tel (0921) 21230, fax 21984) is a comfortable hotel close to the beach and the port, or the Baia del Capitano (Tel (0921) 20003, fax 20163) is a 39-room hotel 5 km out of town.

If you plan a more peaceful holiday, you might do best to choose one of the Aeolian (or Lipari) Islands, seven beautiful volcanic islands to the North of Sicily. We have an entry for the Villa Diana on Lipari (see page 216); in addition we suggest the Villa Meligunis (Tel (090) 981 2426, fax 988 0149), the Giardino sul Mare (Tel (090) 981 1004, fax 988 0150) and the Oriente (Tel (090) 981 1493, fax 988 0198), as other possibilities on Lipari. On the neighbouring island of Salina, try a cliff-top hotel, Punta Scario (Tel (090) 984 4139), or a restaurant-with-rooms, L'Ariana (Tel (090) 980 9075, fax 980 9250).

Although about the same size as Sicily, Sardinia is completely different: its population is sparse; there are few major sightseeing attractions and no very large towns or resorts; and there are no crowds, even in the most developed area for tourists, the Costa Smeralda – which is where most of our recommendations are located. Development is gradually spreading along the coastline from there in both directions. On the north coast, in addition to the Shardana (page 216), the Li Nibbari, also at Santa Teresa Gallura (Tel (0789) 754453, 38 rooms), is a possibility.

On the east coast, the Pensione l'Oasi (Tel (0784) 93111, fax 93444) at Dorgali is a well-equipped hotel set on a hill overlooking the sea, amidst gardens and pinewoods. But if you really want to 'get away from it all', two small islands just off the south-west coast of Sardinia may appeal: Sant'Antioco – try the Club Ibisco Farm (Tel (0781) 809 003, fax 809003) – and the Isola San Pietro – try the Hieracon (Tel and fax (0781) 854028, 24 rooms) on the waterfront at Carloforte.

This page acts as an introduction to the features and hotels of Sicily and Sardinia, and the Aeolian islands, and gives brief recommendations of reasonable hotels that for one reason or another have not made a full entry. The long entries for this region – covering the hotels we are most enthusiastic about – start on the next page. But do not neglect the shorter entries on pages 215-216 and 229: these are all hotels that we would happily stay at.

Sardinia

Seaside villa, Alghero

Villa las Tronas

This castellated, 19thC folly lords it over its own bare, rocky promontory. It stands aloof from the blocks of flats that otherwise characterize this unattractive part of modern Alghero. The interior – all marble floors and ornate chandeliers – is as grand as you might expect of somewhere that was a holiday home for Italian royalty until the 1940s. Yet the unstuffy and businesslike staff ensure it is not intimidatingly formal.

Antiques abound, including in the luxurious bedrooms, which feature brass or sleigh beds and grand canopies, along with swanky marble bathrooms. Those billed as having garden views in reality overlook Alghero's apartment blocks. You pay extra to open the shutters on a view across the bay to the awesome cliff of Capo Caccia; priciest sea-facing rooms come with balconies.

There are no beaches in this part of Alghero, but the hotel has a pool, and many guests swim off the rocks and an old dockyard. Breakfast on an inspection visit was dire. For meals, you may be better off making the five-minute stroll along the seaside promenade into the magical backstreets of old Alghero, where you'll find a wide choice of cafés and restaurants.

Nearby Maria Pia, the best nearby beach, is 4 km north.

Lungomare Valencia 1, 07041 Alghero (Sassari)
Tel 079 981818
Fax 079 981044
Location in modern Alghero, 800 metres south of old Alghero; with car parking
Food & drink breakfast, lunch, dinner
Prices rooms LLL-LLLL with breakfast; dinner LL
Rooms 22 doubles and 1 suite with bath, 6 singles with shower; all with phone, TV, mini-bar, air-conditioning
Facilities bar, sitting-room, dining-room, sea-water swimming pool, gym, bicycles (free)
Credit cards AE, DC, MC, V
Children welcome
Disabled no
Pets only if small and quiet
Closed never
Manager Maria Teresa Masia

Sardinia

Su Gologone

The Barbagia is a mountainous inland region where the landscape is wild, the villages remote and bandits still thrive – though tourists are unlikely to encounter them. The hotel is a low-lying white villa, covered in creepers, surrounded by flowing shrubs and set in a landscape of rural splendour: wooded ravines, fields of olives, pinewoods and the craggy peaks of the Supramonte mountains. It feels isolated, and it is; but the Su Golognone is far from undiscovered. Once, only a few adventurous foreign travellers found their way here; now, they come for the peace, or indeed for the food alone, which is typically Sard: cuts of local meats, roast lamb and the speciality of roast suckling pig – you can watch it being cooked on a spit in front of a huge fireplace. The wines are produced in the local vineyards. The dining-room spreads in all directions – into the vine-clad courtyard, the terrace and other rooms, all in suitably rustic style. The bedrooms are light and simple, again in rustic style, in keeping with the surroundings. Walls are whitewashed, floors are tiled and there are lovely views. Despite its size, the Su Gologone still feels small and friendly, and in most respects still typically Sard.
Nearby Gennargentu mountains; Monte Ortobene (21-km).

Oliena 08025 Nuoro
Tel (0784) 287512
Fax (0784) 287668
Location 8 km NE of Oliena, in remote mountain setting with private parking
Food & drink breakfast, lunch, dinner
Prices rooms LLL DB&B LLL; FB LLL
Rooms 65 double (8 suites), 4 family rooms, all with bath; all have central heating, phone, air-conditioning, colour TV, minibar
Facilities 5 dining-rooms, 2 bars, conference room; swimming-pool, tennis, bowls, mini golf, Land Rover for excursions
Credit cards AE, MC, V
Children accepted
Disabled no special facilities
Pets accepted
Closed Nov to Feb, except Christmas
Proprietor Giuseppe Palimodde

Sardinia

Seaside hotel, Palau

Capo D'Orso

This civilized yet unpretentious waterside hotel stands in marked contrast to the flashy establishments on the nearby Costa Smeralda. It's a place for slow-paced, laid-back, water and beach-oriented holidays. Basking in mesmerising views of the verdant yet rocky coastline and offshore islands, its secluded setting – the nearest centre, the humdrum port of Palau, is a 10-minute drive away – could hardly be prettier. For chilling out, choose between two picturesque, sheltered slips of sand, a lovely amoeba-shaped pool and, in what amount to the focus of the hotel, thoroughly romantic drinks and dining terraces shaded by olive trees and tamarisks. The food is praised; breakfasts come in the form of buffets, and there is also a lunchtime pizzeria.

The simple bedrooms, in low-rise blocks, are lifted by cheerful paintings and the fact that all face the sea and have a balcony or terrace. Suites suit families: the sitting-room, connected to a bedroom by a sliding door, has a sofa bed.

If boredom sets in, the hotel can arrange diving and riding. Boat trips from its jetty visit Maddalena and Caprera, and the fleshpots of the Costa Smeralda's Porto Cervo.
Nearby The islands of Maddalena and Caprrera; Costa Smeralda.

Localita Cala Capra 07020 Palau
Tel (0789) 702000
Fax (0789) 702009
Location 6 km east of Palau
Food & drink breakfast, lunch, dinner
Prices DB&B LL-LLLL
Rooms 33 doubles, 9 family rooms, 18 suites, all with shower; all rooms have phone, TV, minibar, air-conditioning, balcony or terrace
Facilities bar, sitting-room, 2 restaurants, swimming-pool, tennis court, boat trips, watersports
Credit cards AE, DC, MC, V
Children welcome
Disabled no
Pets accepted
Closed early Oct to late Apr
Manager Alessandro Fumagalli

Sardinia

Resort village, Porto Cervo

Pitrizza

The smart playground of the Costa Smeralda is liberally endowed with luxury hotels, but there is one that stands out from the rest: the Pitrizza. What distinguishes it (apart from its small size) is its exclusive, intimate, club-like atmosphere. No shops, disco or ritzy touches here. Small private villas are scattered discreetly among the rocks and flowering gardens, overlooking a private beach. Rooms are furnished throughout with immaculate taste, some of them amazingly simple. The style is predominantly rustic, with white stucco walls, beams and locally crafted furniture and fabrics. Each villa has four to six rooms, and most have a private terrace, garden or patio. The core of the hotel is the club-house, with a small sitting-room, bar, restaurant and spacious terrace where you can sit, enjoying the company of other guests or simply watching the sunset. A path leads down to the golden sands of a small beach and a private jetty where you can moor your yacht. Equally desirable is the sea-water pool, which has been carved out of the rocky shoreline.

There is of course a hitch to the Pitrizza. The rooms here are among the most expensive on the entire Italian coastline.

Nearby beaches of the Costa Smeralda; Maddalena archipelago.

Porto Cervo 07020 Sassari
Tel (0789) 930111
Fax (0789) 930611
Location 4 km from Porto Cervo, at Liscia di Vacca; ample car parking
Food & drink breakfast, lunch, dinner
Prices DB&B LLLL; FB LLLL; reductions for children sharing parents' room
Rooms 38 double, 13 suites; all with bath; all rooms have air-conditioning, minibar, phone, TV, radio; most rooms have terrace or patio
Facilities bar, dining-room, terrace; sea-water swimming-pool; beach, water skiing, boat hire, windsurfing, private mooring; fitness centre **Credit cards** AE, DC, MC, V **Children** accepted
Disabled no special facilities
Pets not accepted
Closed mid-Oct to Apr
Manager Sg. P Tondina

Sardinia

Seaside hotel, Porto Cervo

Romazzino

Though fabulously stylish and punitively expensive, the Romazzino is a little less exclusive and pricey than its smaller sister, the Pitrizza (see page 213). It's a better choice if a beach is important in your plans, since the whitewashed, terracotta-roofed complex presides over one of the biggest on the Costa Smeralda (as well as an enormous pool). Families in particular should be more at home here.

Make no mistake, however: this is still one of Europe's most luxurious beach hotels. The interior has the airiness and under-stated elegance of a giant Moorish-cum-Mediterranean mansion. For example, whimsical, painted ceramics adorn the walls of the sitting-room, while gay colour schemes complement soothing Sardinian fabrics in the thoroughly tasteful bedrooms.

A veritable army of staff panders to your every need. At dinner, it's hard to know whether to be more impressed by the creative Franco-Italian cuisine, or the zealously attentive, multi-lingual service. Although the Romazzino exceeds our normal room limit by a considerable margin, we include it for the first time in this new edition because if has the feel of a much smaller place.

Nearby Hotel Cala di Volpe, a jaw-dropping faux-Medieval castle.

07020 Porto Cervo, Costa Smeralda
Tel (0789) 977111
Fax (0789) 96258
Location 11km from Porto Cervo
Food & drink breakfast, lunch, dinner
Prices DB&B LLLL
Rooms 77 double, 14 suites; all with bath and shower; all with phone, TV, minibar, air-conditioning
Facilities bar, sitting-room, 2 restaurants; swimming-pool, tennis court, watersports
Credit cards AE, DC, MC, V
Children accepted
Disabled access difficult
Pets not accepted
Closed mid-Oct to late Apr
Manager Carlo Ferraris

Sardinia

Seaside hotel, Santa Margherita di Pula

Is Morus

Is Morus is one of several upmarket and isolated hotels along a strip of flat coastline dotted with holiday homes and greenhouses and backed by parched, rocky hills. This is a civilized and peaceful corner of Sardinia, bereft of bright lights or of even anything amounting to a resort.

Secluded within an oleander-rich garden and a pine and eucalyptus wood, pantiled and whitewashed Is Morus is a Mediterranean rendition of a smart country-house hotel. In keeping with the fairly formal service, an understated elegance pervades the place, both in the cool, light sitting-rooms that are interconnected by arches and furnished with squashy modern soft furnishings, and in bedrooms that are almost minimalist in style. Some of these are in the main building (avoid those without a seaview or balcony), others in villas sprinkled through the wood, with two or three bedrooms per villa. The sandy beach isn't one of Sardinia's best (it can be weedy), but it is yards from the main building, private and immaculately maintained, and the swimming-pool is large and inviting.

Nearby the magnificent sand-dune beaches at Chia; the Punic and Roman ruins at Nora.

Santa Margherita di Pula, 09010 Pula
Tel (070) 921171
Fax (070) 921596
Location on the coast south of Pula
Food & drink breakfast, lunch, dinner
Prices DB&B and FB LLL-LLLL
Rooms 69 double, 49 with bath, 20 with shower; 16 single, 7 with bath, 9 with shower; 9 suites with bath; all rooms have phone, TV, mini-bar, air-conditioning
Facilities bar, sitting-room, restaurant; swimming-pool, tennis, watersports; horseriding and golf nearby
Credit cards AE, DC, MC, V
Children welcome
Disabled no special facilities
Pets accepted if small
Closed Jan to Apr
Manager Martina Ketzer

Sardinia

Town hotel, Alghero

San Francesco

This *pensione* is right in the heart of old Alghero. Its unadorned bedrooms are nothing to write home about, but they're clean, quiet and roomy, and set around Medieval cloisters. The court-yard is often used for classical concerts. There is limited private parking: street parking is a fair walk away.

■ Via Ambrogio Machin 2 07041 Alghero (Sassari) **Tel & fax** (079) 980330 **Meals** breakfast **Prices** rooms L-LL with breakfast **Rooms** 20, all with shower, phone **Credit cards** DC, M, V **Closed** never

---

Seaside hotel, Porto Cervo

Balocco

A more modest (though by no means cheap) alternative to the five-star luxury of the Costa Smeralda: a stylishly rustic modern hotel in lush gardens, only a short walk from the shops and chic harbour of Porto Cervo. Fine views, pleasant pool.

■ Via Liscia di Vacca, 07020 Porto Cervo (Sassari) **Tel** (0789) 91555 **Fax** (0789) 91510 **Meals** breakfast **Prices** rooms LLL-LLLL with breakfast **Rooms** 34, all with bath or shower, phone, TV, air-conditioning, minibar, balcony or terrace **Credit cards** AE, DC, MC, V **Closed** mid-Oct to Apr

---

Seaside hotel, Porto Cervo

Capriccioli

You don't have to spend a fortune to stay on the rugged Costa Smeralda: the Capriccioli is a simple family-run hotel standing among windswept *macchia* close to a pretty beach. The Azara family started their restaurant here over 30 years ago, and Ristorante Il Pirata is still the focus of the rustic, villa-style hotel.

■ Capriccioli, 07020 Porto Cervo (Sassari) **Tel** (0789) 96004 **Fax** (0789) 96422 **Meals** bre akfast, lunch, dinner **Prices** rooms LL-LLLL with breakfast; DB&B LL-LLL; FB LL-LLL; meals LL-LLL **Rooms** 40, all with bath or shower, central heating, air-conditioning, TV, minibar **Credit cards** AE, MC, V **Closed** Nov to Mar

---

Seaside hotel, Porto Rotondo

Sporting

An oasis of luxury, consisting of neo-rustic buildings scattered around a promontory, with sea views all around, particularly from their terraces. Everything is tastefully simple – beams, tiled floors, white walls, plain fabrics. The atmosphere is quite clubby, with a strong yachting contingent.

■ Olbia, 07026 Porto Rotondo (Sassari) **Tel** (0789) 34005 **Fax** (0789) 34383 **Meals** breakfast, lunch, dinner **Prices** FB LLLL **Rooms** 27, all with bath, minibar, phone, balcony **Credit cards** AE, DC, MC, V **Closed** mid-Oct to Apr

Sardinia

Seaside hotel, Santa Teresa Gallura

Shardana

Another affordable alternative to the Costa Smeralda norm, isolated near a sandy beach on the northern tip of Sardinia. Accommodation is mainly in separate, stylish little villas, some in the central clubhouse along with the restaurant and bar. Small, pretty pool, watersports.

■ Capo Testa, 07028 Santa Teresa Gallura (Sassari) **Tel** (0789) 754031 **Fax** (0789) 754129 **Meals** breakfast, lunch, dinner **Prices** rooms LL-LLL; FB LL-LLL **Rooms** 51, all with bath or shower, phone, TV, air-conditioning, minibar **Credit cards** AE, V **Closed** Oct to May

---

Resort village, Vaccileddi

Don Diego

Despite a reader's report critical of cleanliness of the pool and beach, the Don Diego keeps its place here on the grounds of sheer charm. It consists of comfortable, stylish cottages scattered among *macchia* and flowery gardens, each with a terrace. The dining-room and sitting-room are tastefully rustic.

■ Porto San Paolo, Costa Dorata, 07020 Vaccileddi (Sassari) **Tel** (0789) 40007 **Fax** (0789) 40026 **Meals** breakfast, lunch, dinner **Prices** DB&B LLL-LLLL **Rooms** 60, all with bath or shower, phone **Credit cards** AE **Closed** never

---

Lipari

Town guest-house, Lipari

Villa Diana

This skilfully restored villa is an oasis of quiet, with ample terraces and peaceful gardens overlooking Lipari and the surrounding bays. It is still very much a family home, furnished and looked after with care. Dinner is no longer served here. Private parking.

■ Via Tufo, Isole Eolie, 98055 Lipari (Messina) **Tel & Fax** (090) 981 1403 **Meals** breakfast **Prices** rooms LL with breakfast **Rooms** 12, all with bath or shower, **Credit cards** AE, V Closed Nov to Mar

Sicily

Foresteria Baglio della Luna

This is a memorable hotel owned by a family with deep roots in the area. Situated in Agrigento's Valley of the Temples, one of Europe's most compelling ancient sites, the Baglio (motto: Parva Domus Magna Quies), is dominated by its sturdy square tower, constructed in the 13thC and rebuilt in 1555. In the 18thC it became a private country residence. Recent restoration has maintained the original structure, with high walls enclosing the gardens, in which you can stroll along pretty paths. The court-yard now makes a shaded terrace, where the mellow stone and terracotta downpipes can be seen to best advantage. Public rooms (with a mezzanine floor above the bar area) are furnished in traditional Sicilian style, as are the bedrooms; suites have Jacuzzi baths.

The restaurant at Baglio della Luna serves both classic Italian and traditional Sicilian dishes, and wine from the owner's private vineyard is on offer. Here, in the dining-room, is the hotel's best and most eye-catching feature: full length windows (which are opened in warm weather) through which there is a panoramic view of the Valley of the Temples.

Nearby Valley of the Temples, Agrigento

Contrada Maddalusa, 92100 Agrigento
Tel (0922) 511061
Fax (0922) 598802
Location 3 km south of Agrigento, in the Valley of the Temples, in own grounds; parking
Food & drink breakfast, lunch, dinner
Prices rooms LLL with breakfast; meals LL
Rooms 21 double, 3 suites, all with bath or shower; all rooms have central heating, phone, TV, air-conditioning, minibar
Facilities sitting room, dining room, bar, terrace, garden
Credit cards AE, MC, V
Children accepted
Disabled no special facilities
Pets accepted
Closed never
Proprietor Ignazio Altieri

Sicily

Moderno

Despite the tourists, Erice is an enchanting medieval town, encircled by walls, and makes an excellent base for a night or two, as does the Moderno, situated toward the top of the narrow main street (it's best to park in the public parking area near Porta Trapani, then walk through the arch and up the narrow main street to the hotel). As the name suggests, the hotel, in a 19thC building, is decorated in contemporary style – mixed with traditional Sicilian elements – which shows flair, with pictures, ornaments and plants everywhere. Public rooms are simply but effectively furnished, with several groups of sofas, chairs and tables at which to sit and relax, including a mezzanine floor. Bedrooms are generally spacious, some furnished in traditional style, some with modern pine furniture. Bathrooms are small, but spotless.

The restaurant, according to a recent reporter, offers 'a well-prepared, wide-ranging menu', and the roof terrace provides a wonderful view of the tiled roofs of Erice, and (for those who are prepared to look down) of the silver-grey stone-paved roads below.

Nearby Greek temple and theatre at Segasta.

Via Vittorio Emanuele 63, 91016 Erice (Trapani)
Tel (0923) 869300
Fax (0923) 869139
Location 15 km NE of Trapani, in town centre; no private parking
Prices rooms LLL with breakfast
Rooms 41, all with bath or shower; all rooms have phone, TV, minibar
Facilities sitting areas, dining-room, bar, roof terrace

Credit cards AE, DC, MC, V
Children accepted
Disabled lift to bedrooms
Pets accepted
Closed never
Proprietor Giuseppe Catalano

Sicily

Country guesthouse, Gangi

Tenuta Gangivecchio

If you want peace and seclusion, then look no further than the converted 13thC Benedictine monastery of Tenuta Gangivecchio, reached after a long drive through the beautiful Madonie region south-east of Palermo. The home of the Tornabene family, the monastery lies at the bottom of a steep valley, hidden behind tall wooden doors that open to reveal a magnificent courtyard. First came a restaurant, whose reputation for marvellous Sunday lunches, prepared by Signora Wanda, soon spread far and wide, despite its remote location. More recently, the family have converted the stables into guest accommodation. In colder months there is a roaring fire in the reception area, while rooms are simple and stylish, with tiled floors, whitewashed walls and beamed ceilings. The guest wing has its own dining-room, with views on to the garden; here classic Sicilian dishes are served, using many ingredients from the property, including almonds, walnuts and herbs. There are also three springs to provide the water.

This is a silent and calming spot, where horse riding in the lovely countryside is also available for the experienced.
Nearby Gangi (6 km); Madonie region.

C da Gangivecchio, 90024 Gangi
Tel & fax (0921) 689191
Location 130 km SE of Palermo. Take exit 'Tre Monzelli' from A19; follow the SS120 to Gangi (41 km) Go through town, turn right to Gangivecchio; after 1 km, turn left at yellow sign indicating Tenuta Gangivecchio; after 5 km, the Tenuta is on right; in extensive grounds; ample parking
Prices rooms L with breakfast; DB&B LL; meals L-LL
Rooms 9 double/triple, with shower; 1 suite with bath; all rooms have central heating, phone, TV, hairdrier
Facilities 2 restaurants, sitting-rooms; swimming-pool, table-tennis, mountain bikes, horse riding **Credit cards** MC, V **Children** not suitable **Disabled** not suitable **Pets** not accepted
Closed 20th Jul to 1 Aug
Proprietor Paolo Tornaben

Sicily

Seaside hotel, Giardini-Naxos

Arathena Rocks

An attractive and well-priced alternative to staying in a hotel on the busy sands of Giardini-Naxos (not a peaceful resort), where you can swim in the sea from the rocks, as well as in the pool.

The Arathena Rocks is run by a friendly family (who speak English), and reception staff on hand in the airy lobby are welcoming. The sitting-room, which has a distinctly Baroque feel, is full of brightly coloured sofas. There is a blue tiled bar and salon, and tiles also feature in the dining-room (where simple dishes are served). There are other ceramics too, such as the Chinese dragons at the entrance, and the green shrubs which decorate the top floor balconies. All in all, the white-walled Mediterranean building, with its balconies and terraces, and its shady gardens with statues and palms, is a delight. Hewn from the rocks is a large (unheated) swimming-pool, where, in season, you can enjoy snacks at the poolside bar.

Bedrooms are cool, spacious and cheerfully decorated, each one different, but often containing painted furniture, many with views over the sea and Mount Etna. Try, if you can, for one of the top-floor balcony rooms.

Nearby Taormina, Mt Etna.

Via Calcide Eubea 55, 98035
Giardini-Naxos
Tel (0942) 51349
Fax (0942) 51690
Location at the end of the bay, down a private road; parking
Food & drink breakfast, lunch, dinner.
Prices rooms LL-LLL with breakfast; meals L
Rooms 45, all with bath or shower; all rooms have central heating, phone

Facilities sitting-room, dining-room, 2 bars, terrace, garden, swimming-pool, tennis court, minibus to Taormina
Credit cards MC, V
Children welcome
Disabled lift to bedrooms
Pets accepted
Closed Nov to Mar
Proprietor Natale Arcidiacono

Sicily

Eremo della Giubliana

If you are coming by car, this small, elegant hotel is well worth the journey. Alternatively, you can fly to the hotel's private airfield, from where you can also take sightseeing trips as far away as Malta or Tunisia.

Situated far away from major roads in a pastoral landscape of rolling farmland cut by white lanes, the hotel has been the home of the Nifosì family since the 18thC. It was built as a fortified convent in the 15thC, and was later used by the Knights of the Order of St John on their way to Malta. In converting the central core of the convent, Signor Nifosì, an architect, has spared no effort to ensure that it is displayed to its best advantage, retaining the original structure and the pitch and limestone floors, and transforming the monks' cells into comfortable bedrooms, with elegant, modern bathrooms.

Food is important at the Eremo, and the owners personally supervise the cooking, using local produce, of traditional Sicilian highland dishes. It was disappointing, therefore, to hear recently from a German reader disappointed by the food. The best Sicilian wines – some of them full of character – are available from the well-stocked medieval cellar. **Nearby** Ragusa (7 km).

Aziende Agricole Nifosi, Contrada Giubiliana, S.P. per Marina di Ragusa
Tel (0932) 669119
Fax (0932) 623891
Location signposted off the road from Ragusa to Marina di Ragusa; ample parking
Food & drink breakfast, lunch, dinner
Prices rooms LL-LLL with breakfast; meals L-LL
Rooms 10 double, 2 suites, all with bath; all rooms have central heating, phone, TV, hairdrier
Facilities sitting-room, dining-room, terrace, meeting room
Credit cards AE, MC, V
Children welcome
Disabled 3 rooms on ground floor
Pets small animals accepted
Closed never
Proprietors Nifosì family

Sicily

Luxury hotel, Siracusa

Grand Hotel

Situated in the old part of Siracusa on the island of Ortigia, the Grand Hotel is a splendid example of a luxurious Mediterranean hotel. Restructured and modernized in 1995, its smart exterior stands out from the old and time-worn buildings around it. The hotel's heyday was during the first 15 or so years of the century when it was a fashionable venue for rich tourists and local aristocracy, who would meet for musical soirées and showings of early films.

Today's visitor is first greeted by a cool and elegant reception area with circular marble stairs and bronze sculpture. Other public rooms are clad in marble, stained glass, and crystal, mixing modern art and furnishings with antiques, which enhance the original Art Deco elements of the decorations. Bedrooms, which all have sea views, are luxurious and thoughtfully equipped. There is a bar in the old pale stone-walled cistern and a sophisticated roof-garden restaurant, with magnificent views of the Grand Harbour and sea front. Here you can choose between Sicilian dishes or 'international'. For those for whom expense is not a drawback, this is the best hotel in town.

Nearby Greek theatre, Paradise Quarry.

Viale Mazzini 12, 96100 Siracusa
Tel ((0931) 464600
Fax (0931) 464611
Location on the Ortigia seafront; parking
Food & drink breakfast, lunch, dinner
Prices rooms LLL-LLLL with breakfast; dinner LLL
Rooms 9 single, 30 double, 19 suites, all with bath; all rooms have phone, TV, radio, air-conditioning, minibar,
hairdrier
Facilities sitting-room, dining-room, bar, conference room, private beach (free shuttle)
Credit cards AE, DC, MC, V
Children accepted
Disabled specially adapted rooms
Pets accepted
Closed never
Manager Signor Caladrucceo

Sicily

Country villa, Siracusa

Villa Lucia

The owner of this elegant, if faded, patrician villa, Marquise Maria Luisa Palermo, receives her guests with an old world charm and her family home is just that, a 'private residence, not a hotel' filled with personal effects – books, pictures, *objets d'art*, idiosyncratic antiques. Peacefully situated in its own Mediterranean park within easy reach of the sea, Villa Lucia has the air of a fading, somewhat impecunious, yet still proud grande dame, and what it lacks in modern comforts it makes up for in atmosphere.

A striking tiled floor stretches through the principal reception room and into the airy dining room (although there is no restaurant, guests can reserve dinner in advance). A wooden staircase leads to the bedrooms, many of which have sloping, beamed ceilings. Each room is, of course, different, simply decorated with family possessions. The plain bathrooms are larger than average. Try for a room in the villa, rather than the annexe. During our most recent visit, two more rooms were being added on the ground floor. There are also plans for a swimming-pool, and some much-needed replanting of the garden.

Nearby Greek theatre, Paradise Quarry, harbour.

Contrada Isola, 96100 Siracusa
Tel (0336) 888537
Fax (0931) 61817
Location Plemmurio, on headland opposite Ortigia island, close to town centre, garden, parking
Meals breakfast, dinner on request
Prices rooms LL-LLL with breakfast
Rooms 14, 5 in villa, 9 in annexe, all with bath or shower; rooms in villa have central heating, phone, TV, minibar; rooms in annexe have minibar
Facilities sitting-room, dining-room, conservatory
Credit cards AE, DC, MC, V
Children accepted
Disabled no special facilities
Pets small pets accepted (daily charge)
Closed never
Proprietor Dott. Maria Luisa Palermo

Sicily

Seaside villa, Taormina

Villa Belvedere

The Belvedere is a simple but stylish hotel which has been in the same family since 1902, with each generation making its changes without altering the inherent charm of the place. Currently in charge is Frenchman Claude Pécaut and his Italian wife, both of them friendly and helpful. One of the villa's great assets is its location. It is close to the middle of Taormina, commanding a spectacular panorama of the bay and the slopes of Etna to the south. Flowery gardens lead down to a small pool where the setting and poolside bar (light meals and Sicilian regional dishes) tempt guests to linger all day and postpone the more serious business of sight-seeing. Arrangements can also be made to take guest to and from local beaches.

There is no proper dining room, but plenty of choice amongst restaurants in Taormina. And the hotel does have two prettily furnished sitting-rooms, and a sunny breakfast room. All in all a sound choice for a reasonably priced family hotel, warmly endorsed by a recent reporter who also mentioned the 'expert valet parking (parking is at a premium in the town)' and the 'clean bright bedrooms with stunning views from the balconies'.
Nearby Greek theatre, Corso Umberto, public gardens.

Via Bagnoli Croce 79,
Taormina 98039 Messina
Tel (0942) 23791
Fax (0942) 625830
Location close to public gardens and old town, with garden and parking for 15 cars
Food & drink breakfast, light meals
Prices rooms LL-LLL with breakfast
Rooms 50 , all with bath or shower; all have central heating, phone; 26 have air-conditioning
Facilities 2 sitting areas, 2 bars, breakfast room, TV room; swimming-pool
Credit cards MC, V
Children accepted
Disabled no special facilities
Pets welcome if well-behaved
Closed mid-Nov to 20 Dec, mid-Jan to Mar
Proprietor Claude and Silvia Pécaut

Sicily

Hilltop hotel, Taormina

Villa Ducale

It's hard to fault Villa Ducale. Originally a coaching inn, it was converted into a patrician home at the turn of the century by the great-grandfather of the present owner, Andrea Quartucci. In 1993, he and his wife opened the house to guests and their new venture was an instant success. Why? Because of the wonderful terrace, the feel of a family home, the unexpected, special touches and the friendliness of the staff.

No two rooms are alike (try for one with a private terrace), but they all have fine linen on the beds, billowing curtains and terrazzo floors, painted furniture and pretty bedheads; in one junior suite is the painted bed, inlaid with mother-of-pearl, of Andrea's grandparents. Many walls are decorated with *trompe l'oeil* or with fruit, a symbol of richness in Sicilian culture.

Perhaps the real quality of Villa Ducale comes through best at breakfast, served until 11.30. You won't easily forget sitting on the broad balcony, the table before you laden with fruit, local cheeses, specially baked bread and Sicilian iced cakes, with its amazing view across the town, the bay and Mount Etna. Sipping a drink there at sunset is pretty romantic, too.

Nearby Greek theatre, Corso Umberto; excursions to Etna.

Via Leonardo da Vinci 60, Taormina 98039 Messina
Tel (0942) 28153
Fax (0942) 28710
Location above Taormina, on road to Castelmola; limited parking
Food & drink breakfast, light snacks
Prices rooms LLL-LLLL with breakfast
Rooms 9 double, 2 single, 2 junior suites, all with bath; all rooms have central heating, phone, TV, air-conditioning, minibar, hairdrier
Facilities sitting room, library, bar, breakfast room, terrace, free minibus to beaches
Credit cards AE, DC, MC, V
Children welcome
Disabled access difficult
Pets small animals accepted
Closed Nov 20 to Dec 20
Proprietors Dr Andrea and Rosaria Quartucci

Sicily

Seaside hotel, Taormina

Villa Paradiso

Next to the public gardens and close to the heart of historic Taormina, the Villa Paradiso also has the advantage of a glorious panorama along the coast and across to the hazy cone of Etna. The only drawback to the location is that it is on a main road, which means some noise for back rooms and major problems with parking in high season.

The hotel is a well-maintained white building, and the public rooms have all the style and atmosphere of a private villa: white arches, patterned carpets on tiled floors, stylish sofas and an imaginative collection of prints, paintings and watercolours. The restaurant makes the most of the views, and the food is distinctly above average. Every bedroom has a balcony, and inevitably the most sought-after are those at the front with sea views. The majority are larger than you would expect from a *pensione;* some have attractive painted furniture. You can reach the beaches by cable-car or – more conveniently – the hotel minibus, which takes you to the Paradise Beach Club in Letojanni (free facilities for guests from the beginning of June).

Nearby Greek theatre, Corso Umberto and public gardens; excursions to Etna.

Via Roma 2, Taormina 98039 Messina
Tel (0942) 23922
Fax (0942) 625800
Location on SE edge of town; small public car park next door, paying garage nearby
Food & drink breakfast, dinner
Prices rooms L-LLL with breakfast
Rooms 35 double, 21 with bath, 2 with shower; 3 single, all with shower; 11 suites, all with bath; all rooms have central heating, air-conditioning, phone, satellite TV, radio, hairdrier **Facilities** 2 sitting-rooms, bar, dining-room, terrace **Credit cards** AE, DC, MC, V **Children** welcome; special meals and baby-sitting on request **Disabled** access possible **Pets** small cats and dogs only accepted
Closed never
Proprietor Salvatore Martorana

Sicily

Country villa, Taormina

Villa Sirina

Just a kilometre below the town centre, in a valley in the Taormina foothills, Villa Sirina sits in its own grounds filled with citrus and oleander. Rooms in the pink-washed house have views either to the sea (500 m away), or the mountains.

First impressions are favourable. The entrance hall, with its antique pieces of furniture mixed with modern, and unframed montage of bright splashy paintings on the walls, has great style, and there is a warm welcome from the kind host, Salvatore Cacopardo. Bedrooms are simply furnished, white walled, clear and bright, enlivened by the jolly views through the French windows. These lead, in every case, to a terrace or a balcony. Bathrooms are neat and white.

The same lime green paint which decorates some of the bedheads and mirrors in the bedrooms has found its way into the informal dining room, covering the rush-seated chairs and creating a colourful contrast with the bright yellow tablecloths. Here breakfast is served, and in the evening, traditional Sicilian dishes. A large picture window overlooks the pool and terrace with its bar and seaward views.

Nearby Greek theatre, Corso Umberto and public gardens.

Contrada Sirina, Taormina 98039 Messsina
Tel (0942) 51776
Fax (0942) 51671
Location 1.5 km south of town centre; in own garden; parking
Food & drink breakfast, dinner
Prices rooms LL-LLL with breakfast; DB&B LL; meals LL
Rooms 15 double, all with bath or shower; all rooms have central heating, phone, TV, hairdrier
Facilities restaurant, 2 sitting-rooms, reading room; terraces, sun room, swimming-pool
Credit cards AE, DC, MC, V
Children accepted, if well behaved
Disabled no special facilities
Pets not accepted
Closed Nov to 1 Mar
Proprietor Salvatore Cacopardo

Sicily

Country hotel, Valderice

Baglio Santacroce

Located in the Erice foothills, on the outskirts of Valderice, this is a family owned and run hotel set in a predominantly stone farmhouse dating back to 1636. With its central courtyard, thick bare stone walls, (in both bedrooms and bathrooms), terracotta tiled floors and beamed ceilings, the hotel has a rustic, countrified feel enhanced by the simple furnishings such as handwoven rugs, old, carved wood or wrought-iron bedsteads and chairs made from olive wood.

Modernity makes a somewhat unwelcome appearance in the restaurant (which serves Sicilian dishes with an emphasis on fish), situated below the main building, built around the rock which protrudes into the bar. In the summer months there is also a conservatory restaurant which has splendid views over the pretty terraced gardens and the Gulf of Cornino and Mount Cofano.

There is a small, inviting swimming-pool to one side of the building, and the gardens are very peaceful, with roses, cacti and ivy-clad dry stone walls. The nearest town of Valderice has little allure, but the charming medieval town of Erice is not far away.
Nearby Erice, Trapani.

91019 Valderice (Trapani)
Tel (0923) 891111
Fax (0923) 891192
Location 1 km E of Valderice off S187 Valderice - Castallamare road, in own grounds; parking
Food & drink breakfast, lunch, dinner
Prices rooms LL with breakfast; meals LL
Rooms 25, all with shower; all rooms have central heating, phone, TV

Facilities sitting-room, dinin-room, bar, terrace, garden, swimming-pool
Credit cards AE, DC, MC, V
Children accepted
Disabled no special facilities
Pets accepted
Closed never
Proprietor Cusenza family

Sicily

Country villa, Agrigento

Villa Athena

Agrigento's Valley of the Temples is one of Europe's most compelling ancient sites, and Villa Athena is set right in the midst (rooms 205 and 206 have the best views). Sadly, a recent reporter felt that the hotel had little else to recommend it, being both tired (peeling exterior paint, broken light) and a staging post for coachloads of tourists.

Via dei Templi 33, 92100 Agrigento (Trapani) **Tel** (0922) 596288 **Fax** (0922) 402180 **Meals** breakfast, lunch, dinner **Prices** rooms LL-LLL with breakfast; DB&B LL **Rooms** 34 double, 6 single, all with shower, central heating, air-conditioning, TV, phone **Credit cards** AE, MC, V **Closed** never

Town hotel, Erice

Elimo

An excellent alternative to the Moderno, in the same street. A recent reporter described it as a happy mixture of traditional and modern, with attractive public rooms, individual bedrooms, a rooftop terrace and a pretty courtyard.

■ Via Vittorio Emanuele 75, 91016 Erice (Trapani) **Tel** (0923) 869377 **Fax** (0923) 869252 **Meals** breakfast, lunch, dinner **Prices** rooms LL-LLL with breakfast **Rooms** 21, all with bath or shower, central heating, phone, TV, minibar **Credit cards** AE, DC, V **Closed** never

Town hotel, Siracusa

Domus Mariae

'Haven of peace and gentleness' and 'best friend in Sicily' are typical visitors' book comments at this former convent still owned and run by Ursuline nuns. Modern furnishings, ornate chapel, peaceful atmosphere. In a quiet, faded part of medieval Siracusa.

■ Via Vittorio Veneto 76, 96100 Siracusa **Tel** (0931) 24858/ 24854 **Fax** (0931) 24858/24854 **Meals** breakfast, lunch, dinner **Prices** rooms LL-LLL with breakfast; dinner L **Rooms** 9 double, 3 single, all with bath or shower, phone, TV **Credit cards** AE, DC, MC, V **Closed** never; restaurant only, Nov

Seaside hotel, Taormina

Villa Fiorita

A small, clean bed-and-breakfast built into the rock high on a mountain terrace, with a grand panorama. Rooms are basic, but there is a pretty terrace for summer breakfasts, and a wood-burning stove in the lobby for the winter months. Small swimming-pool, but the funicular down to the beach is nearby.

■ Via L Pirandello 39, 98039 Taormina (Messina) **Tel** (0942) 24122 **Fax** (0942) 625967 **Meals** breakfast **Prices** rooms LL with breakfast; suites LLL **Rooms** 24, all with bath or shower, air-conditioning, phone, colour TV, radio, minibar **Credit cards** AE, MC, V **Closed** never

Index of hotel names

In this index, hotels are arranged in order of the first distinctive part of their names. Very common prefixes such as 'Hotel', 'Albergo', 'Il', 'La', 'Dei' and 'Delle' are omitted. More descriptive words such as 'Casa', 'Castello', 'Locanda' and 'Villa' are included.

Index of hotel names

Index of hotel names

Index of hotel names

Index of hotel locations

In this index, hotels are arranged in order of the names of the cities, towns or villages they are in or near. Hotels located in a very small village may be indexed under a larger place nearby. An index by hotel name precedes this one.

Index of hotel locations

Index of hotel locations

Index of hotel locations